THOMSON PREPARATION COURSE FOR THE TOEIC® TEST 2

Roberta Steinberg

Thomson Asia Pte Ltd

Singapore • Albany • Belmont • Bonn • Cincinnati • Detroit • Johannesburg
London • Madrid • Melbourne • Mexico City • New York • Paris • Tokyo • Toronto

First published 1999 by:
International Thomson Asia ELT
60 Albert Street
#15-01 Albert Complex
Singapore 189969

© 1999 Thomson Asia Pte Ltd

All rights reserved. No part of this publication covered by the copyright hereon may be reproduced or used in any means — graphics, electronic, or mechanical, including photocopying, recording, taping, or information storage and retrieval systems — without prior permission in writing from the publisher.

The publication of ***Thomson Preparation Course for the TOEIC® Test 2*** was directed by the International Thomson Asia ELT Team:
- Karen Chiang, *ELT Director*
- Christopher Wenger, *Senior Development Editor*
- Joan Quick, *Development Editor*
- Teri Tan, *Production Editor*
- Connie Wai, *Production Co-ordinator*
- Agnes Malinis, *Copy Editor*

- Additional editorial support provided by David Bohlke and Jody Stern

Cover design by Raketshop Design Studio, Philippines

Printed by Chong Moh Offset Printing Pte Ltd, Singapore

1 2 3 4 5   03 02 01 00 99
ISBN 0-534-83522-8

CONTENTS

Acknowledgements

Preface 1

Score Conversion Chart 3

Test One 5
Tapescript 43
Answers & Explanations 48

Test Two 59
Tapescript 97
Answers & Explanations 102

Test Three 111
Tapescript 150
Answers & Explanations 155

Test One – Answer Sheet 165

Test Two – Answer Sheet 167

Test Three – Answer Sheet 169

Author's Acknowledgements

I'd like to thank several people who helped conceptualize and actualize *Thomson Preparation Course for the TOEIC® Test*. First, thanks to Karen Chiang whose idea they were. Second, many thanks to my editor Chris Wenger who also served as photoscourer and project optimist. Third, I'm deeply indebted to my copy editor extraordinaire, Jody Stern. Finally, thanks to my husband, Avishai Shafrir, who patiently helped with math problems, suggested topics, and role-played dialogues, as well as to Patty Brickett, who enthusiastically brainstormed "office conversations" while sitting through swim meets. These books are lovingly dedicated to my parents Melvyn and Jeannette Ostroff Steinberg.

To the Test-taker...

The goal of the *Thomson Preparation Course for the TOEIC® Test* is to familiarize you with the format, directions, difficulty level, and substance of actual TOEIC® tests. After taking the three sample tests and reviewing the answers and explanations, you should know what is to be expected on the TOEIC® test. The point is not for you to memorize any of the questions and answers on the sample tests, as none of these questions will appear in the actual test. Rather, these tests will indicate your general strengths in English as well as the weaknesses you need to overcome before taking an actual TOEIC® test. The value of this book can be measured by comparing the score of your first practice test with subsequent tests.

Test-taking Tips

Before taking a sample test...

1. Increase your general knowledge of English. The purpose of the TOEIC® test is to measure your general English ability. Improving your ability in English takes time and should include work in all four skills: listening, speaking, reading, and writing, as well as specific work in grammar and vocabulary.

2. Prepare yourself by carefully studying the directions for each part of the TOEIC® test. The directions are **always** the same on each test. Make sure you are familiar with the structure of each part and what is expected of you. This will allow you simply to glance at the directions when you take the test, saving you valuable time.

While taking a sample test...

1. Try to create as authentic a test-taking environment as possible by doing the following:
   - time yourself strictly as instructed
   - do an entire test in one sitting
   - do not eat, drink, or leave the room

   Following these suggestions will help give you an idea of how to manage your time most effectively during the test.

2. **Always** guess. There is no penalty for a wrong answer on the TOEIC® test, so never leave an answer blank. If you run out of time, fill in one answer [either (A), (B), (C), or (D)] for every blank number on your answer sheet. There is no letter which is a better choice. Statistically you have a better chance of getting more answers correct if you choose the same letter.

After taking a sample test...

1. Correct your exam.

2. Carefully review the **Answers and Explanations** section. If there is a question or answer you still don't understand, ask a native English speaker or fluent colleague for clarification, or consult appropriate reference materials.

3. Analyze your strengths and weaknesses. If you had difficulty with Parts I–IV, try to find time every day to listen to English programs on the radio, or watch television programs or videos featuring native English speakers. If you had difficulty with Part V, focus on word forms. Be familiar with noun, verb, adjective, and adverb endings. If you had mistakes in Part VI, find a grammar text that can help you review the grammar items that were problematic. If you had difficulty with Part VII, read English newspapers and magazines that feature a variety of international and business-related readings and advertisements.

4. Do not take the next test immediately. If you carefully review the Answers and Explanations section and begin a program to improve your areas of weakness, you will see an improvement on your next test.

I hope these sample tests have been helpful and instructive. I look forward to developing additional materials for you. Good luck!

Roberta Steinberg

SCORE CONVERSION CHART

Raw Scores	Converted Scores: Listening	Converted Scores: Reading	Raw Scores	Converted Scores: Listening	Converted Scores: Reading
98-100	495	470	56	260	215
97	495	465	55	255	210
96	495	460	54	250	205
95	495	455	53	245	200
94	490	450	52	235	190
93	490	445	51	230	185
92	485	435	50	225	180
91	480	430	49	220	175
90	475	425	48	215	165
89	470	415	47	205	160
88	465	410	46	200	155
87	460	400	45	195	150
86	455	39	44	185	140
85	450	390	43	180	135
84	445	385	42	175	130
83	435	380	41	165	125
82	430	370	40	160	120
81	425	365	39	155	115
80	420	360	38	145	105
79	410	350	37	140	100
78	400	345	36	135	95
77	390	340	35	130	90
76	385	335	34	120	85
75	380	330	33	115	80
74	375	320	32	110	75
73	365	315	31	105	65
72	360	310	30	100	60
71	350	305	29	90	55
70	345	300	28	85	50
69	340	295	27	80	40
68	335	285	26	70	35
67	330	280	25	65	30
66	325	275	24	60	25
65	320	270	23	50	20
64	310	265	22	45	15
63	305	255	21	40	10
62	300	250	20	35	10
61	290	245	19	30	10
60	285	240	18	25	5
59	275	230	17	20	5
58	270	225	16	15	5
57	265	220	0-15	5	5

TEST
one

TEST OF ENGLISH FOR INTERNATIONAL COMMUNICATION

General Directions

This is a test of your ability to use the English language. The total time for the test is approximately two and a half hours. It is divided into seven parts. Each part of the test begins with a set of specific directions. Be sure you understand what you are to do before you begin to work on a part.

You will find that some of the questions are harder than others, but you should try to answer every one. There is no penalty for guessing. Do not be concerned if you cannot answer all of the questions.

Do not mark your answers in this test book. **You must put all of your answers on the separate answer sheet** that you have been given. When putting your answer to a question on your answer sheet, be sure to fill in the answer space corresponding to the letter of your choice. Fill in the space so that the letter inside the oval cannot be seen, as shown in the example below.

EXAMPLE

Mr. Palmer _____ with the president last month.
(A) meet
(B) meeting
(C) met
(D) to meet

Sample Answer: (A)   (B)   ●   (D)

The sentence should read, "Mr. Palmer met with the president last month." Therefore, you should choose answer (C). Notice how this has been done in the example given.

Mark only **ONE** answer for each question. If you change your mind about an answer after you have marked it on your answer sheet, completely erase your old answer and then mark your new answer. You must mark the answer sheet carefully so that your score can be recorded accurately.

LISTENING COMPREHENSION

In this section of the test, you will have the chance to show how well you understand spoken English. There are four parts to this section, with special directions for each part.

Directions

For each question, you will see a picture in your test book and you will hear four short statements. The statements will be spoken just one time. They will not be written in your test book; therefore, you must listen carefully in order to understand what the speaker says.

When you hear the four statements, look at the picture in your test book and choose the statement that best describes what you see in the picture. Then, on your answer sheet, find the number of the question and mark your answer. Look at the sample picture.

EXAMPLE

Now listen to the four statements.

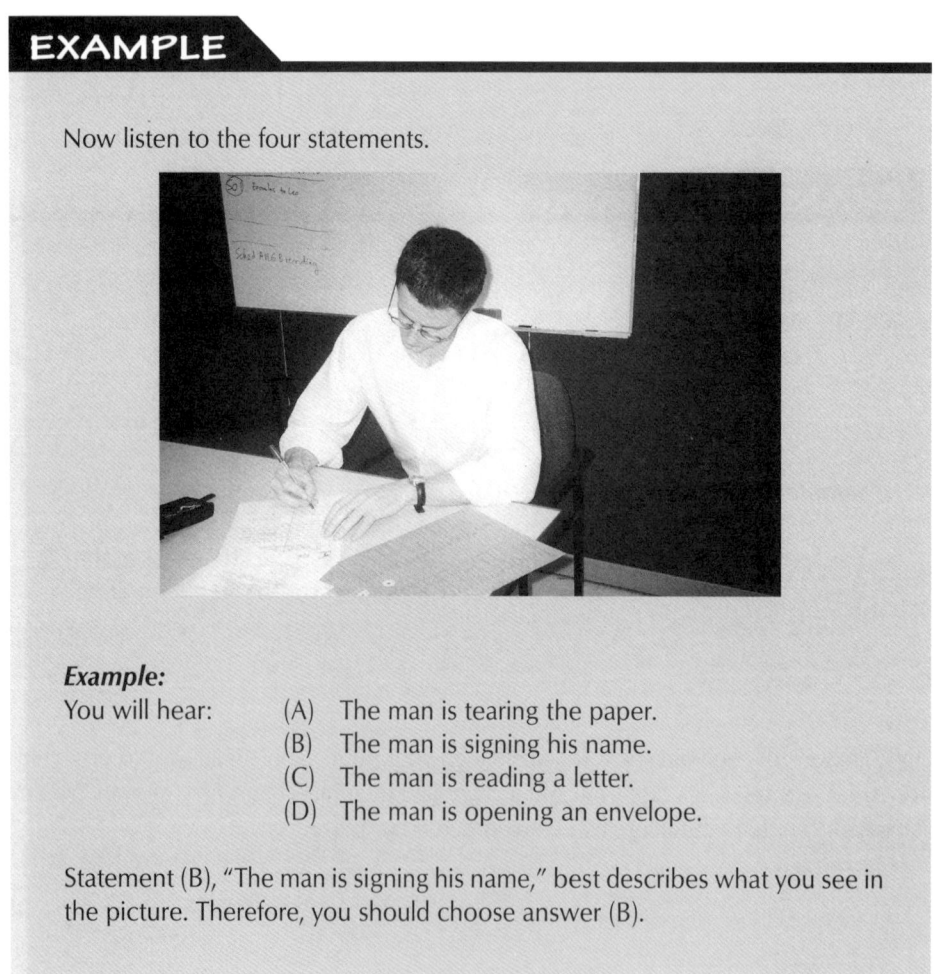

Example:

You will hear:
- (A) The man is tearing the paper.
- (B) The man is signing his name.
- (C) The man is reading a letter.
- (D) The man is opening an envelope.

Statement (B), "The man is signing his name," best describes what you see in the picture. Therefore, you should choose answer (B).

TEST ONE

10

11

12

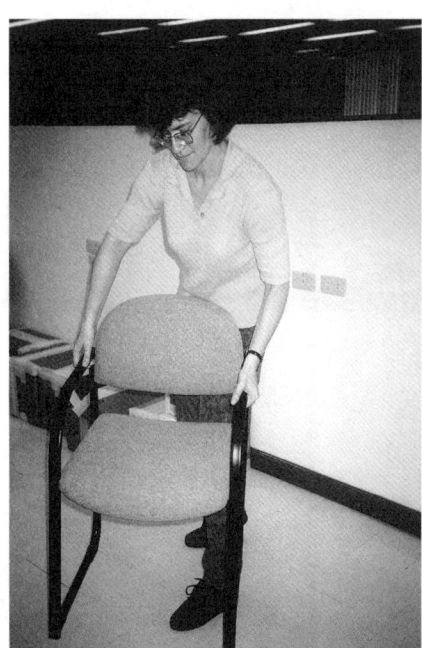

18

19

20

GO ON TO THE NEXT PAGE

Part II

Directions

In this part of the test, you will hear a question spoken in English, followed by three responses, also spoken in English. The question and the responses will be spoken just one time. They will not be written out for you; therefore, you must listen carefully to understand. You are to choose the best response to each question.

EXAMPLE

Now listen to a sample question.

You will hear: Good morning, John. How are you?

You will also hear: (A) I am fine, thank you.
                     (B) I am in the living room.
                     (C) My name is John.

The best response to the question "How are you?" is choice (A), "I am fine, thank you." Therefore, you should choose answer (A).

21. Mark your answer on your answer sheet.
22. Mark your answer on your answer sheet.
23. Mark your answer on your answer sheet.
24. Mark your answer on your answer sheet.
25. Mark your answer on your answer sheet.
26. Mark your answer on your answer sheet.
27. Mark your answer on your answer sheet.
28. Mark your answer on your answer sheet.
29. Mark your answer on your answer sheet.
30. Mark your answer on your answer sheet.
31. Mark your answer on your answer sheet.
32. Mark your answer on your answer sheet.
33. Mark your answer on your answer sheet.
34. Mark your answer on your answer sheet.
35. Mark your answer on your answer sheet.
36. Mark your answer on your answer sheet.
37. Mark your answer on your answer sheet.
38. Mark your answer on your answer sheet.
39. Mark your answer on your answer sheet.
40. Mark your answer on your answer sheet.
41. Mark your answer on your answer sheet.
42. Mark your answer on your answer sheet.
43. Mark your answer on your answer sheet.
44. Mark your answer on your answer sheet.
45. Mark your answer on your answer sheet.
46. Mark your answer on your answer sheet.
47. Mark your answer on your answer sheet.
48. Mark your answer on your answer sheet.
49. Mark your answer on your answer sheet.
50. Mark your answer on your answer sheet.

Directions

In this part of the test, you will hear short conversations between two people. The conversations will not be written in your test book. You will hear the conversations only once; therefore, you must listen carefully.

In your test book, you will read a short question about each conversation. The question will be followed by four short answers. You are to choose the best answer to each question and mark it on your answer sheet.

51. What did David Wong think?
    (A) That his interview was at 11:30
    (B) That he should have called first
    (C) That he had come on time
    (D) That Ms. Chang would call him

52. What's the man's problem?
    (A) His disk is stuck in the computer.
    (B) The computer will not turn on.
    (C) No one showed up to help him.
    (D) He cannot find his files.

53. What will the man probably do?
    (A) Fly to Hong Kong
    (B) Find the cheapest rate
    (C) Go to the post office
    (D) Use the basic rate

54. What does the man agree to do?
    (A) Paint her office
    (B) Store some items overnight
    (C) Get her some help
    (D) Move her things back

55. Where does this conversation take place?
    (A) In an ambulance
    (B) In a car
    (C) At a hospital
    (D) At the police station

56. What does the man want to do?
    (A) Create radio commercials
    (B) Go over budget
    (C) Advertise on television
    (D) Develop a new product line

57. What does the man suggest?
    (A) That she give him some lessons
    (B) That she compete in some tournaments
    (C) That she show him some golf courses
    (D) That she become professional

58. What will determine their action?
    (A) The negotiation team's decision
    (B) The number of rocks on their property
    (C) The rent increases
    (D) The terms of the lease

59. What is said about dinner?
    (A) It will start at ten.
    (B) The sitter will join them.
    (C) There will be only hors d'oeuvres.
    (D) It has not started yet.

60. Where does this conversation take place?
    (A) At a department store
    (B) At a photo store
    (C) At a bank
    (D) At an airport

GO ON TO THE NEXT PAGE

61. What did the woman learn?
(A) That the meeting location had been changed
(B) That arrangements need to be made
(C) That Al needs some chairs brought to his office
(D) That the midmanagement meeting had been canceled

62. Why did John Williams call?
(A) His co-worker told him to call Miss Jason.
(B) Miss Jason had called him.
(C) His message light wouldn't go off.
(D) He needs to tell his co-worker something.

63. What do we learn about Linda Rivera?
(A) She took a trip.
(B) She started her own company.
(C) She has been out sick.
(D) She was fired.

64. How often is the magazine now published?
(A) Once a week
(B) Once a month
(C) Three times a year
(D) Four times a year

65. What's the problem?
(A) Some workers are on vacation.
(B) There's a delay in production.
(C) Some people are sick.
(D) Orders have been lost.

66. What does she want to do?
(A) Call the repair service
(B) Wait until the machine on her floor is fixed
(C) Check each floor's machine
(D) Use another copy machine

67. What is the woman being asked to do?
(A) Rent an Italian restaurant
(B) Make a list of retirees
(C) Invite some guests
(D) Call Gloria

68. What is said about developing the film?
(A) It will take an hour.
(B) It will be developed in the store.
(C) Only Photo One develops black and white film.
(D) It will be sent out.

69. What does the man NOT want to do?
(A) Hire a mover
(B) Give his sister his couch
(C) Borrow a truck
(D) Move furniture on the weekend

70. What are they discussing?
(A) Organizing a conference
(B) Taking a class together
(C) Changing e-mail addresses
(D) Signing up for graduate school

71. Where does this conversation take place?
(A) At a circus
(B) At a supermarket
(C) At a movie theater
(D) At a magazine counter

72. What is Karen's problem?
(A) She overslept.
(B) She forgot her appointment.
(C) Her truck was towed.
(D) Her car broke down.

73. What are they discussing?
(A) New hirings
(B) The possibility of layoffs
(C) A fire at the office
(D) Going downtown

74. What does the woman suggest the man do?
    (A) Travel abroad soon
    (B) Exchange some money
    (C) Wait for the local currency to go up
    (D) Keep track of the stock market

75. When will they meet for lunch?
    (A) On Wednesday
    (B) On Thursday
    (C) On Friday
    (D) Any day next week

76. What will Janet probably do?
    (A) Wear her coat one more winter
    (B) Look for a cheap coat
    (C) Ask lots of people where to buy a coat
    (D) Buy a coat like Steve's

77. Why is the woman waiting to order her cards?
    (A) She can't decide which color to choose.
    (B) Her company is moving to a new address.
    (C) She will be getting a new phone number.
    (D) She does not know how many to order.

78. What does the woman say?
    (A) Everyone will get a new computer immediately.
    (B) She's glad he likes his computer.
    (C) Department heads will get new computers in June.
    (D) She's not getting a new computer right now.

79. What is said about the company where the people work?
    (A) It is selling its goods to discount stores.
    (B) It is going out of business.
    (C) It is going to sell bottom-of-the-line goods.
    (D) Its profits are on the decline.

80. What will the man probably do?
    (A) Buy something from the vending machine
    (B) Go to the store
    (C) Have some water
    (D) Drink some apple juice

Part IV

Directions

In this part of the test, you will hear several short talks. Each will be spoken just one time. They will not be written out for you; therefore, you will have to listen carefully in order to understand and remember what is said.

In your test book, you will read two or more questions about each short talk. The questions will be followed by four answers. You are to choose the best answer to each question and mark it on your answer sheet.

81. Who is reporting?
    (A) The First Night director
    (B) A Boston police officer
    (C) A meteorologist
    (D) Snow shovelers

82. What is the good news?
    (A) Boston is hosting a celebration.
    (B) There will be less wind than last year.
    (C) It will not snow.
    (D) It will be ten degrees warmer than predicted.

83. What are people advised to do?
    (A) Leave early
    (B) Cover their heads
    (C) Bake layered cakes
    (D) Shovel the snow

84. Where is the announcement being made?
    (A) In a performance
    (B) In a classroom
    (C) In a studio
    (D) In a record store

85. What can be bought?
    (A) Recording devices
    (B) Tickets
    (C) Film
    (D) Cassettes

86. Why is Jason Wah not playing?
    (A) He missed the bus.
    (B) He has a broken arm.
    (C) He is substituting for Miss Brown.
    (D) He moved to Iceland.

87. What has the woman just done?
    (A) Watched the news at 6
    (B) Answered a few questions
    (C) Exited the voting booth
    (D) Interpreted results

88. Where is the man from?
    (A) A polling firm
    (B) The governor's office
    (C) A television station
    (D) Election headquarters

89. Why does the man approach the woman?
    (A) To film her for the evening news
    (B) To ask her opinion of the governor
    (C) To learn her name
    (D) To find out how she voted

90. What is the purpose of the form?
    (A) To publicize technology upgrades
    (B) To request future purchases
    (C) To outline the budget
    (D) To describe available furniture

91. What are the employees asked to do?
    (A) Replace the existing technology
    (B) Return the forms by mid-June
    (C) Reupholster their furniture
    (D) Transfer files from cabinets to computers

92. What is the average age of the employees?
    (A) 35
    (B) 65
    (C) 70
    (D) 73

93. What does the company produce?
    (A) Invoices
    (B) Keys
    (C) Typewriters
    (D) Pins

94. What is one of the benefits of working at Vera?
    (A) The keyless entry
    (B) Flexible work hours
    (C) The art collection
    (D) The new equipment

95. Why are people asked to give up their seats?
    (A) The plane is delayed.
    (B) The later flight has fewer passengers.
    (C) Too many people booked seats.
    (D) Ticket agents wish to fly.

96. What will someone who gives up a seat get?
    (A) A seat in business class
    (B) A round-trip ticket to another destination
    (C) A free ticket to Seoul
    (D) Three tickets to Honolulu

97. At what time will someone who gives up a seat leave?
    (A) 1:00
    (B) 2:00
    (C) 5:00
    (D) 7:00

98. Where does this announcement take place?
    (A) At a company retreat
    (B) On a bus tour
    (C) On the beach
    (D) At a tennis tournament

99. What time will the buses leave?
    (A) 10:00
    (B) Noon
    (C) 3:00
    (D) 4:00

100. What does the speaker advise?
    (A) To meet the buses at the lake
    (B) To use sunscreen
    (C) To get tickets for lunch
    (D) To remember the basketball game

This is the end of the Listening Comprehension portion of the test. Turn to Part V in your test book.

GO ON TO THE NEXT PAGE

YOU WILL HAVE ONE HOUR AND FIFTEEN MINUTES TO COMPLETE PARTS V, VI, AND VII OF THE TEST.

READING

In this section of the test, you will have the chance to show how well you understand written English. There are three parts to this section, with special directions for each part.

Directions
This part of the test has incomplete sentences. Four words or phrases, marked (A), (B), (C), (D), are given beneath each sentence. You are to choose the **ONE** word or phrase that best completes the sentence. Then, on your answer sheet, find the number of the question and mark your answer.

EXAMPLE

Because the equipment is very delicate, it must be handled with _____ .
(A) caring
(B) careful
(C) care
(D) carefully

The sentence should read, "Because the equipment is very delicate, it must be handled with care." Therefore, you should choose answer (C).

Now begin work on the questions.

101. Please include your address and day and evening telephone numbers with all _____.
(A) discussion
(B) connection
(C) correspondence
(D) persuasion

102. Maintaining a good working relationship _____ management and labor is a challenge.
(A) among
(B) between
(C) into
(D) beside

103. Ms. Shon's _____ will explain the new payroll procedures this Friday at noon in Room 211.
(A) accessory
(B) supplementary
(C) addendum
(D) assistant

104. Perfume prices are dramatically _____ this year than they were in the previous five years.
(A) lower
(B) fewer
(C) poorer
(D) needier

105. Although the renovated office has a window, it is too small for both my bookshelf _____ the file cabinet.
(A) or
(B) and
(C) nor
(D) also

106. The president _____ a new logo for the company products and materials.
(A) select
(B) is being selected
(C) selected
(D) selecting

107. Everyone was surprised that the renovations were completed _____ quickly.
(A) than
(B) such
(C) too
(D) so

108. Rarely _____ five inches in one day.
(A) does it rain
(B) rains
(C) it rains
(D) it does rain

109. The personnel director is _____ ordering business cards.
(A) responsible to
(B) in charge of
(C) assigned by
(D) delegated for

110. Attendance at amusement parks has nearly _____ in the last decade.
(A) increased
(B) twice
(C) doubled
(D) duplicated

111. If your subscription to *The New York Times* lapses, you may renew _____ by phone.
(A) your
(B) him
(C) them
(D) it

112. The two leading hotels announced plans for a joint _____.
(A) cooperation
(B) venture
(C) proportion
(D) consequence

113. The hotel _____ for the conference featured a nine-hole golf course.
(A) that he selected
(B) selected it
(C) that he selected it
(D) it that he selected

114. By _____ large, stocks continued to rebound after last week's sell-off.
(A) in
(B) at
(C) and
(D) for

115. The airline must _____ a hundred new flight attendants before March 1.
(A) to hire
(B) be hired
(C) will hire
(D) hire

116. _____ the first computers, today's models are portable and multifunctional.
(A) Alike
(B) Unlike
(C) Dislike
(D) Likely

GO ON TO THE NEXT PAGE

117. The winning contractor _____ all the other competitors.
    (A) understudied
    (B) underwent
    (C) underbid
    (D) undertow

118. The sender's signature was _____ on the airbill.
    (A) illegible
    (B) illiterate
    (C) illegitimate
    (D) illogical

119. Infomercials are program-length TV commercials that are devoted _____ to one product.
    (A) unique
    (B) alone
    (C) lonely
    (D) solely

120. Many previous all-male occupations _____ to women in the 1960's and 1970's.
    (A) have opened
    (B) were opened
    (C) have been opening
    (D) are opened

121. The handouts for the presentation are _____ the magazines on the top shelf.
    (A) about face
    (B) besides
    (C) underneath
    (D) overall

122. Long-distance phone calls _____ from office telephones.
    (A) cannot be made
    (B) will not be admitted
    (C) have no permission
    (D) have no authority

123. Choosing a location for a new business is _____ to its success.
    (A) dependent
    (B) programmatic
    (C) important
    (D) critical

124. An *at sight* letter of credit means that payment is made _____ upon presentation of documents.
    (A) as soon as
    (B) once
    (C) direct
    (D) immediately

125. Members of the committee agreed that they found the presentation _____.
    (A) convinced
    (B) convincingly
    (C) convincing
    (D) with conviction

126. The appetizers in the kitchen are yours _____.
    (A) tasting
    (B) to taste
    (C) taste
    (D) are tasted

127. _____ Mr. Tanaka to replace Ms. Wong, his salary would be doubled.
    (A) Were
    (B) Should
    (C) Despite
    (D) Especially

128. Direct deposit is a convenient way to _____ expenses.
    (A) induce
    (B) deduce
    (C) reduce
    (D) produce

129. So far, those who have sampled the new product are _____ about it.
(A) exciting
(B) excitement
(C) excited by
(D) excited

130. Readers _____ to the magazine pay less per issue than those buying it at a newsstand.
(A) subscribe
(B) subscribing
(C) subscribed
(D) are subscribing

131. Although not all the items you ordered are in stock, a _____ shipment will be made next week.
(A) partial
(B) part
(C) partially
(D) parted

132. The index rates thousands of stocks, one against _____, as overvalued or undervalued.
(A) other
(B) all other
(C) the other
(D) others

133. Many financial firms in the region have recently _____ on staff.
(A) looked out
(B) dropped down
(C) fired off
(D) cut back

134. _____ consumer demand, cereals will now be packaged in wax bags instead of cardboard cartons.
(A) Whereas
(B) In response to
(C) Due to the fact that
(D) Along with

135. Finding an accountant _____ specialty and interests match your needs is critically important.
(A) who
(B) which
(C) whose
(D) that

136. Last year the average American worker worked 123 days to _____ all tax obligations for the year.
(A) satisfy
(B) mediate
(C) overdraw
(D) bypass

137. Lucia Hostalet has been _____ to the mayor's task force.
(A) dealt
(B) contacted
(C) appointed
(D) considered

138. _____ possible, Mr. Loffreda personally signs all correspondence.
(A) However
(B) Depending
(C) Seemingly
(D) Whenever

139. Polyester sleeping bags, sold by mail order, come with a 5-year replacement _____.
(A) guaranties
(B) guarantee
(C) guarantor
(D) guardian

140. All donations _____ by the trustees of the foundation.
(A) will be acknowledged
(B) will acknowledge
(C) acknowledged
(D) acknowledging

GO ON TO THE NEXT PAGE

Directions

In this part of the test, each sentence has four words or phrases underlined. The four underlined parts of the sentence are marked (A), (B), (C), (D). You are to identify the **ONE** underlined word or phrase that should be corrected or rewritten. Then, on your answer sheet, find the number of the question and mark your answer.

EXAMPLE

All <u>employee</u> are required <u>to wear</u> their <u>identification</u> badges <u>while</u> at work.
    A   B   C   D

Choice (A), the underlined word "employee," is not correct in this sentence. The sentence should read, "All employees are required to wear their identification badges while at work." Therefore, you should choose answer (A).

Now begin work on the questions.

141. Every country has <u>its</u> own access number
                              A
<u>which</u> makes calling home or <u>another</u>
 B   C
countries really <u>simple</u>.
                 D

142. <u>As</u> enrollment for the upcoming seminar
    A
"Principles and Practice of Fundraising" will
be <u>limit</u>, please submit <u>the</u> registration form
   B   C
<u>by</u> May 16.
 D

143. Factories in <u>and</u> around Paris <u>turn out</u> a wide
          A   B
<u>various</u> of products, <u>including</u> most of
  C   D
France's automobiles.

144. <u>Most</u> the country has a warm, <u>tropical</u> climate
  A   B
that <u>varies</u> <u>little</u> from season to season.
     C   D

145. The museum of science and technology <u>it</u>
                                   A
features exhibits <u>on</u> communication, <u>nuclear</u>
             B   C
energy, and <u>space travel</u>.
          D

146. Nancy Wong, the <u>newly</u> appointed Director
                  A
of Purchasing, <u>has decided</u> that all
              B
<u>purchase requests</u> <u>to be</u> submitted in writing.
    C   D

147. Airline regulations <u>allow</u> only one piece of
             A
<u>suitcase</u> <u>to be carried</u> <u>on board</u> the flight.
  B   C   D

148. Employees are <u>automatically</u> enrolled in the
                    A
company's <u>retirement</u> plan <u>after completing</u>
              B   C
two <u>year</u> of service.
      D

149. Items <u>may be exchanged</u> for <u>merchandise</u>
                  A   B
<u>only</u> without <u>receipt</u>.
  C   D

150. Management's <u>popularest</u> decision this year
                          A
is the establishment of an <u>on-site</u> daycare
                                  B
center <u>which</u> <u>opened</u> last month.
              C   D

151. <u>In addition</u> <u>creating</u> programs for his own
          A   B
company, our president advises <u>start-up</u>
                                          C
firms in the fields of finance <u>and</u> technology.
                                      D

152. Although each office has <u>state-of-the-art</u>
                                        A
computers, Mrs. Ramirez <u>insists on</u> using
                                  B
a manual typewriter for all of

<u>his</u> <u>correspondence</u>.
  C   D

153. All <u>municipal</u> buildings stopped <u>to allow</u>
              A   B
smoking <u>in</u> lobbies and elevators <u>as of</u> the
              C   D
first of the year.

154. By <u>using</u> a calling card <u>when</u> making calls
              A   B
from country <u>to</u> country, travelers can <u>saved</u>
                    C   D
money.

155. Please <u>contact</u> the personnel director
                    A
<u>to discuss</u> <u>company</u> benefits and policies
    B   C
once you have read and <u>sign</u> the contract.
                              D

156. <u>Due to</u> <u>increased</u> profits, <u>end-of-the-year</u>
          A   B   C
bonuses will appear <u>in December paycheck</u>.
                              D

157. Buses with <u>handicapping</u> access <u>will allow</u>
                        A   B
passengers in wheelchairs <u>to use</u> public
                                  C
transportation in the <u>downtown area</u>.
                              D

158. <u>Franchises</u> are becoming <u>increasing</u> popular
          A   B
with the <u>aspiring</u> <u>small</u> business owner.
              C   D

159. Our red and blue van, which <u>leaves</u> from
                                          A
Parking Lot A, <u>will take</u> you to the airport
                    B
<u>in time to</u> your five o'clock <u>flight</u>.
    C   D

160. By <u>subscription</u> to our magazine for two
          A
years, you <u>will save</u> twenty-seven percent
              B
<u>over</u> a one-year <u>renewal</u>.
  C   D

GO ON TO THE NEXT PAGE

Directions

The questions in this part of the test are based on a variety of reading material, such as notices, letters, newspaper and magazine articles, and advertisements. You are to choose the **ONE** best answer, (A), (B), (C), or (D), to each question. Then, on your answer sheet, find the number of the question and mark your answer. Answer all questions following a passage on the basis of what is **stated** or **implied** in that passage.

EXAMPLE

Read the following example.

> The Museum of Technology is designed for people to experience science at work. Visitors are encouraged to use, test, and handle the objects on display. Special demonstrations are scheduled for the first and second Wednesdays of each month at 1:30 p.m. Open Tuesday-Friday, 2:30-4:30 p.m., Saturday 11:00 a.m.-4:30 p.m., and Sunday 1:00-4:30 p.m.

When during the month can visitors see special demonstrations?
(A) Every weekend
(B) The first two Wednesdays
(C) One afternoon a week
(D) Every other Wednesday

The passage says that the demonstrations are scheduled on the first and second Wednesdays of the month. Therefore, you should choose answer (B).

Now begin work on the questions.

Questions 161-162 refer to the following advertisement.

FARM FOR SALE in TURKEY...

3,000 hectares, arable
Suited for: poultry, cattle, sheep,
variety of crops.
Includes mature orchard of 200 hectares.

Contact Ted Dickson at 44 1573 892002

161. Which type of animal is NOT mentioned as suitable?
 (A) Cows
 (B) Chickens
 (C) Lambs
 (D) Pigs

162. Where would this advertisement most likely appear?
 (A) On television
 (B) In a newspaper
 (C) In a journal
 (D) In a yearbook

Questions 163-165 refer to the following report.

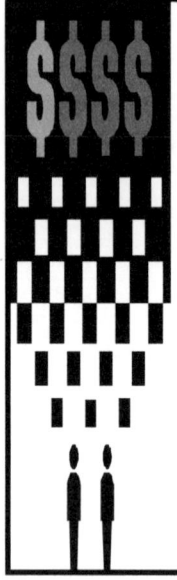

YOU CAN'T PUT A PRICE ON EVERYTHING PENNSYLVANIA HAS DONE FOR BUSINESS

But it's somewhere around $3 billion. The governor's strategy of tax cuts and workers' compensation reforms has helped reduce the cost of doing business in Pennsylvania by $3 billion since 1995. Fifteen million dollars is available to relocate companies to Pennsylvania. Funding has doubled for customized job training. Companies are now eligible for research and development tax credits. To learn more about all the positive changes we're making for business in Pennsylvania, simply call or fax us.

You can also visit us at our Internet site at:
www.pennsylvania.com.

---

163. Who would respond to the announcement?
 (A) The governor
 (B) Tax collectors
 (C) Business owners
 (D) Fundraisers

164. What has helped lower the cost of doing business in Pennsylvania?
 (A) Customized job training
 (B) Tax increases
 (C) Changes in workers' compensation
 (D) Funding for research

165. What should interested readers do?
 (A) Call a specific number
 (B) Visit Pennsylvania
 (C) Create a Pennsylvania website
 (D) Buy a fax machine

Questions 166-167 refer to the following form.

INTERNATIONAL CUSTOMS AIRBILL

1 FROM
Date _____ Sender's Account Number _____
Sender's Company Name _____
Address _____
_____
_____
_____ Phone _____

2 TO
Recipient's Name _____
Address _____
_____
_____
_____ Phone _____

3 SERVICE (Check ONE)
☐ International First   ☐ International Priority   ☐ International Economy

4 TRANSPORTATION CHARGES PAID BY (Check ONE)
☐ Sender   ☐ Recipient   ☐ Third Party   ☐ Credit Card   ☐ Cash

5 REQUIRED SIGNATURE OF SENDER
_____

---

166. Which of the following is NOT requested?
 (A) The method of payment
 (B) The signature of the recipient
 (C) The type of service
 (D) The sender's company name

167. How can transportation charges be paid?
 (A) By check
 (B) By money order
 (C) By C.O.D.
 (D) By credit card

Questions 168-170 refer to the following advertisement.

SOME PEOPLE SEEK RELAXATION ON TROPICAL ISLANDS.
OTHERS FIND IT IN THEIR BACKYARDS.

While a week in a tropical paradise is nice, you can enjoy the ultimate relaxation experience all year long with a *Hot Tubs 'R' Us* spa.
The water is always hot, clean, and ready to soothe you with state-of-the-art hydrotherapy.
Hot Tubs 'R' Us spas are easy to set up, too. You can order your spa today and relax in it tomorrow. The only travel involved is stepping out your back door.
To find out how you can start relaxing in a *Hot Tubs 'R' Us* portable spa, the world's most luxurious model, call 800-554-8228 for a free brochure and the address of the dealer nearest you.

168. What information does the advertisement give you?
(A) The dimensions of the spa
(B) Directions for installing a spa
(C) How to get a brochure
(D) The addresses of spa retailers

169. Where would someone install a spa?
(A) On a tropical island
(B) Inside a home
(C) Wherever one is vacationing
(D) In one's back yard

170. Where would one most likely purchase this spa?
(A) At a department store
(B) From a dealer
(C) From a travel agent
(D) In a tropical paradise

Questions 171-173 refer to the following news report.

$$$$$$$$$$$$$$$$$$$$$$$$$$$$$$$$

A group of bankers scheduled a meeting with the Bank of England in March of 1998 to discuss technical preparations for the introduction of Europe's single currency, expecting about 20 experts to attend. They scrambled for chairs when 95 showed up.

Across Europe and around the world, bankers and corporate executives are quickly waking up to the realization that the economic and monetary union is barely one year away and that the launch of the "euro," as the single currency will be called, will demand costly and far-reaching changes in the way everyone does business.

In 2002, countries across Europe are to abandon their national currencies. Until then, banks and companies will have to modify everything, including computer systems as well as billing and payroll forms, to accept the euro.

$$$$$$$$$$$$$$$$$$$$$$$$$$$$$$$$

171. What is the most appropriate title for this news report?
 (A) Scrambling for Chairs at the Bank of England
 (B) Banking Opportunities in 2002
 (C) Europe Tackles the Big Shift to a Single Currency
 (D) Payroll Forms, Scheduling Meetings, and Corporate Executives

172. What is the euro?
 (A) The name of Europe's new single currency
 (B) The organization of European corporate executives
 (C) The computer system used in Europe
 (D) Europe's banking and monetary union

173. When will countries using the euro abandon their national currencies?
 (A) In 1998
 (B) In 2000
 (C) In 2001
 (D) In 2002

Questions 174-176 refer to the following notice.

Established U.S. importer seeks capital to expand distribution of antique French furniture to interior designers in the USA. Has established sizable markets in New York, L.A., Boston, and Atlanta. Additional demand exists in Dallas, Miami, and Chicago but can't currently finance the $150,000 needed for expansion. Contact me for a detailed description of market projections.

Mr. Root/Fax: (617) 323-7022

174. What does Mr. Root seek?
 (A) Furniture distributors
 (B) Capital for expansion
 (C) Market researchers
 (D) Interior designers

175. What does Mr. Root import?
 (A) Designer clothing
 (B) Trade shows
 (C) Antiques
 (D) French wine

176. Where does Mr. Root currently do business?
 (A) Dallas
 (B) Miami
 (C) Chicago
 (D) Atlanta

Questions 177-179 refer to the following advertisement.

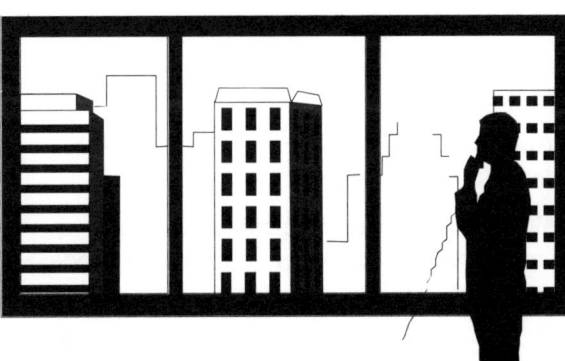

177. What can one do at GRS Office Centers?
    (A) Rent office space
    (B) Purchase office equipment
    (C) Speak to image consultants
    (D) Find tailoring services

178. For whom is this advertisement specifically intended?
    (A) Conference organizers looking for sites
    (B) Systems analysts seeking customers
    (C) Companies wishing to share expenses
    (D) Office workers seeking employment

179. Which of the following aspects of the centers does the advertisement emphasize?
    (A) Its casualness
    (B) Its efficiency
    (C) Its international locations
    (D) Its congeniality

Questions 180-183 refer to the following notice.

ORDER INFORMATION

1. Upon receipt, please examine your merchandise for any defects or shipping inaccuracies. We will replace defective merchandise within 15 days of the invoice date.

2. Returned goods must be unused and in their original condition. Be sure to try everything on to ensure proper fit. Once items have been worn, altered, personalized, or laundered, they cannot be returned.

3. Items returned for exchange or refund must be returned within 30 days of receipt or they will not be accepted.

4. There will be additional shipping expenses charged for exchanges.

5. All returns are the responsibility of the customer. Protect yourself from loss by sending the package by insured mail.

6. Shipping rates are for packing, insurance, and delivery. These charges are not reimbursable.

7. Please allow up to 2 billing cycles for return credit to appear on your credit card statement.

180. Which of the following is true about an item returned for exchange?
 (A) It can be washed first.
 (B) It can be returned within a year.
 (C) It can be tried on.
 (D) Its shipping charges are free.

181. Who must pay the shipping for returned items?
 (A) The customer
 (B) The company
 (C) The credit card company
 (D) The laundry

182. How should the returned items be sent?
 (A) By special delivery
 (B) By ship
 (C) By credit card
 (D) By insured mail

183. Which of the following is not a part of the shipping charge?
 (A) Packaging costs
 (B) Insurance fees
 (C) Delivery charges
 (D) Costs for alterations

Questions 184-186 refer to the following news article.

Australian gold production is expected to rise 5.9% to 316.7 metric tons by June 30th, despite a sharp drop in the world price, according to the Australian Bureau of Agricultural and Resource Economics. Last year's output was 299.1 tons.

In its quarterly projection statement, the government's forecasting and analytical agency said the expected increase will come from newly commissioned mines and major expansions of existing operations. However, it also said the decreasing cost of gold has prompted the industry to defer projects and restructure high-cost operations.

184. What can be said about the forecast of Australian gold production for the year ending June 30?
 (A) A sharp drop is predicted.
 (B) More gold will be mined this year.
 (C) The amount of gold to be mined is 299.1 tons.
 (D) It is linked to the world price.

185. What does the Australian Bureau of Agricultural and Resource Economics do?
 (A) It commissions mines.
 (B) It expands existing operations.
 (C) It predicts gold production.
 (D) It mines precious metals.

186. What can be said about the production of Australian gold?
 (A) Its expensive operations have been altered.
 (B) It is not impacted by the price of gold.
 (C) The number of mines has been decreasing.
 (D) As production increases, so does the price.

Questions 187-190 refer to the following letter.

International Recruitment Associates

albert street ◆ singapore

February 5

Mr. Tatsuhiko Seo
Director, Personnel Department
Software Success
Namiki 2-8-136-101
Tokyo, Japan

Dear Mr. Seo,

International Recruitment Associates (IRA) is pleased to announce the opening of our newest branch in Tokyo. With headquarters in Singapore, IRA is located in eight countries, including the United States and Germany. Companies such as yours turn to us to find the best candidate for openings in the fields of software development, technology, and engineering. With our worldwide base of operations, we have thousands of potential applicants at our fingertips.

We are enclosing our brochure, and testimonials from satisfied clients around the world. Please contact me by phone, or fax if you have any questions. Our local representative will contact you within the next two weeks to set up a meeting at your convenience.

Sincerely,

Tony Tan
Director of Marketing

TT:as
Enclosure

187. What is the purpose of this letter?
 (A) To invite Software Success to the branch inauguration
 (B) To recruit Mr. Seo to work for IRA
 (C) To interview software job seekers
 (D) To inform Software Success of a branch opening

188. How many branches does IRA have?
 (A) 2
 (B) 8
 (C) 100
 (D) Thousands

189. For which job opening would someone contact IRA?
 (A) Market researcher
 (B) Travel agent
 (C) Personnel director
 (D) Software designer

190. How should Mr. Seo contact Mr. Tan?
 (A) In person
 (B) By e-mail
 (C) By phone
 (D) In a letter

Questions 191-192 refer to the following advertisement.

Call Monday, Tuesday, or Wednesday from 8:00 a.m.–4:30 p.m.

If you have a puppy for sale, an extra refrigerator you don't need, or one too many television sets, advertise in the MARKET BASKET, a column which appears daily in the Northeast's largest newspaper.

All classifieds must be prepaid unless you are a monthly account customer. Restrictions may apply. We accept cash, check, or credit card. To become a monthly customer please call 617-929-0345 to request a credit application. Check the paper for the appropriate heading for your classified ad as we have a limited number of available sections.

191. What might be advertised in the "Market Basket" section?
 (A) A Siamese kitten
 (B) Fruits and vegetables
 (C) A job opening
 (D) Credit cards

192. Which of the following statements is true?
 (A) Customers may request their own heading.
 (B) Advertisements may be placed any day before 4:30 p.m.
 (C) Monthly customers need not pay in advance.
 (D) "Market Basket" appears in newspapers throughout the country.

Questions 193-194 refer to the following offer.

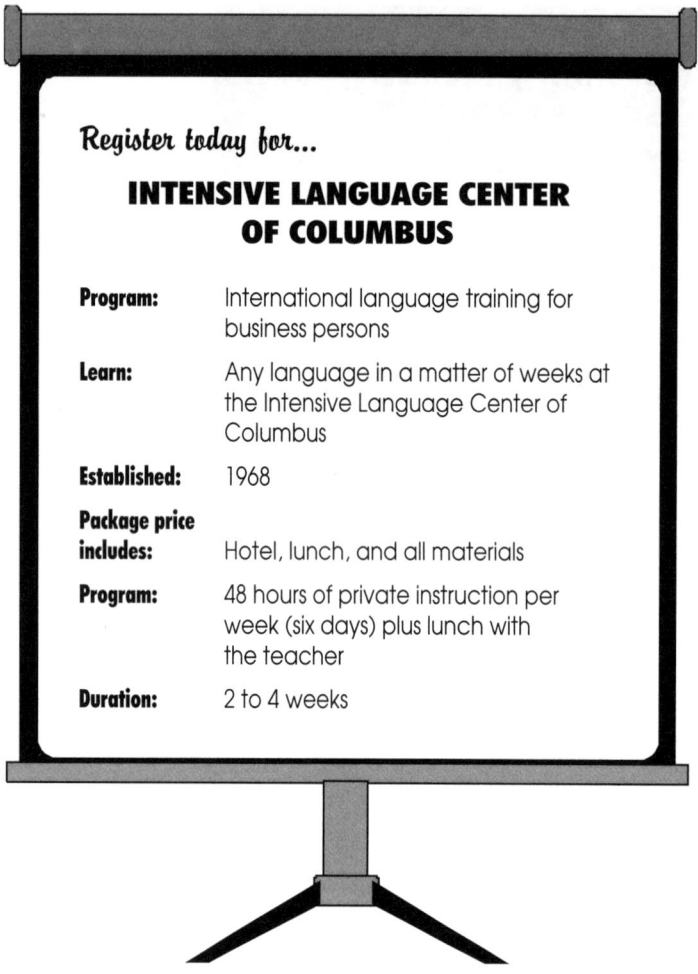

193. How many hours of instruction per day are included?
     (A) 2
     (B) 4
     (C) 6
     (D) 8

194. What does the program fee include?
     (A) Lodging with families
     (B) All instructional materials
     (C) Airfare to Columbus
     (D) Three meals a day

Questions 195-197 refer to the following article.

Nobody's quite sure who came up with the first paper clip, but it's a good thing somebody did. Imagine having to tie papers together with a ribbon threaded through a series of holes, or being forced to fasten documents with rust-prone steel pins. These became forgotten annoyances around the turn of the century with the introduction of the modern, bent-wire paper clip. A Norwegian named Johan Vaaler may be the man responsible. He put together a few clip designs, including one that looks similar to the now standard design, in 1899 and patented them in America in 1901. However by that time, a few other paper-clip patents were on the market. When all is said and done, any attempt to sort out the origins and the patent history of the paper clip may be impossible. The paper clip was such a good idea that many people thought of it at once.

195. How were papers fastened before the invention of the paper clip?
(A) With glue
(B) With steel pins
(C) With staples
(D) With rubber bands

196. What can be said about Johan Vaaler?
(A) He was the first to patent the paper clip.
(B) He received a lot of money for his invention.
(C) He was a naturalized American citizen.
(D) He tried out several paper clip designs.

197. What is known about the original paper clip?
(A) It differs greatly from the paper clip of today.
(B) It is a twentieth-century invention.
(C) It is unclear who first invented it.
(D) It was an immediate success.

Questions 198-200 refer to the following invitation.

The Museum of Science annual donor appreciation dinner will be held in the museum's cafeteria on May 21 at 7:00 p.m. In addition to the Board of Trustees and Overseers, all donors who have contributed $1,000 or more this year will be mailed two complimentary tickets.
In attendance will be the governor and local celebrities.

PROGRAM

7:00 - 7:30 p.m. — Reception

7:30 p.m. — Dinner

8:30 - 9:30 p.m. — Video presentation of museum's expansion plans, theater proposal, and fundraising efforts.

198. Where will the dinner be held?
    (A) In the museum theater
    (B) In the cafeteria
    (C) In the expanded wing
    (D) In the governor's mansion

199. Who is the dinner intended for?
    (A) Theater designers
    (B) The Governor of Michigan
    (C) Local celebrities
    (D) Donors who gave a minimum amount

200. How long will the dinner last?
    (A) An hour
    (B) An hour and a half
    (C) Two hours
    (D) Two and a half hours

Stop! This is the end of the test. If you finish before time is called, you can go back to Parts V, VI, and VII and check your work.

TAPESCRIPT

Sample Item
M: (A) The man is tearing the paper.
(B) The man is signing his name.
(C) The man is reading a letter.
(D) The man is opening an envelope.

1. M2: (A) The message appears on the side of a building.
(B) The sign warns motorists not to throw anything away.
(C) The announcement encourages customers to use the bank.
(D) The traffic signal stands out along a busy highway.

2. W: (A) The man has a flat tire.
(B) The man is unloading the spare tire from the trunk.
(C) The man is checking the tire's air pressure.
(D) The man is too tired to drive his vehicle.

3. M1: (A) He's leaning back in his chair.
(B) He's dialing a customer's number.
(C) He's rearranging his desk.
(D) He's looking up a phone number.

4. M1: (A) Two men are paddling in the same kayak.
(B) The river is filled with many kayakers.
(C) The men are dropping their paddles into the river.
(D) The men in the kayaks are rowing closer to one another.

5. M2: (A) They're getting back on the tour bus.
(B) They're standing at a spot for sightseeing.
(C) They're looking through the telescope.
(D) They're having their picture taken in front of the wall.

6. W: (A) The woman is setting the computer on top of the desk.
(B) The man and woman are sitting in front of the computer.
(C) The woman is typing something on the computer.
(D) The man is looking at the woman's computer screen.

7. M2: (A) The file cabinet is open.
(B) The man is filing his papers in the drawer.
(C) The man is glancing at an open file.
(D) The man's glasses are on the desk.

8. M1: (A) The man is leaning on his elbow as he reads.
(B) People are eating their meals outside.
(C) The man is taking a nap.
(D) The man is putting down some newspapers to sit on.

9. W: (A) The audience is applauding the singers.
(B) Both men are holding microphones in front of them.
(C) The orchestra is accompanying the singers.
(D) The duet is being performed for the first time.

10. M2: (A) Many pedestrians are in the crosswalk.
(B) The woman has begun to cross the street.
(C) The woman is waiting on the sidewalk.
(D) The woman is signaling the pedestrians to cross.

11. M1: (A) The waiter is taking the order.
(B) The dishes need to be cleared.
(C) The customer is cutting the salad with a knife.
(D) The customer's order has arrived.

12. W: (A) Each person is holding a copy of the report.
(B) The four people are standing around the table.
(C) The woman is turning the pages as she gives her presentation.
(D) All four people are focusing their attention on the report.

13. M1: (A) The woman is digging a hole in the sand.
(B) The sand castle is being washed away.
(C) The woman is sanding the board to make it smooth.
(D) The woman is looking for a resort on the beach.

14. M2: (A) The woman is folding the chair for storage.
(B) The woman is moving the furniture.
(C) There are no empty seats available in the office.
(D) The woman is measuring the table.

15. W: (A) The musicians are all playing instruments.
(B) The members have left their instruments out on the sidewalk.
(C) The band is performing music.
(D) All of the performers are wearing sunglasses.

16. M1: (A) The woman is stirring her beverage.
(B) The woman is taking a bite of food.
(C) The woman is waiting in line for a cup of coffee.
(D) The woman is serving dessert to her guests.

17. M2: (A) The woman is wrapping a gift.
(B) The man is purchasing a gift for the woman.
(C) The woman has put the present on the table.
(D) The man is looking at the object in the woman's hands.

18. W: (A) The woman is using a pencil to write a report.
(B) The woman is sharpening a pencil.
(C) The knife is too sharp for the woman to touch.
(D) The woman is shredding some documents.

TEST ONE

19. M2: (A) The woman is showing some home movies of her trip.
    (B) Everyone is wearing glasses in order to see the pages.
    (C) The woman in the middle is holding a photo album on her lap.
    (D) The woman is taking pictures to put into her album.

20. W: (A) The couple is looking at the display through the shop window.
    (B) The couple is going into the store through the glass door.
    (C) The couple is sampling the store's merchandise.
    (D) The owner is handing out samples for the couple to try.

Sample Question
W: Good morning, John. How are you?
M: (A) I am fine, thank you.
M: (B) I am in the living room.
M: (C) My name is John.

21. W: What time are you leaving?
    M: (A) Every afternoon.
    M: (B) At six.
    M: (C) In Room 212.

22. M: Should we reserve the conference room?
    W: (A) It's company policy.
    W: (B) I reserved a seat on the train.
    W: (C) At the elevator.

23. W: Where did you buy your furniture?
    M: (A) It's a cheap way to travel.
    M: (B) When I met you.
    M: (C) From a catalogue.

24. M: Why didn't you sign up for the computer training?
    W: (A) Because my typewriter is broken.
    W: (B) I was too late.
    W: (C) At Room 219.

25. W: Whose idea was it to get paid weekly?
    M: (A) My check is deposited directly into my account.
    M: (B) The new personnel director's.
    M: (C) No thanks, I don't need it.

26. M: Which flight is she taking?
    W: (A) As soon as you're finished.
    W: (B) I think the 2:15.
    W: (C) The desk lamp is brightest.

27. M: Can you tell me where the closest dry cleaner is?
    W: (A) There's one on the corner of 31st and Broadway.
    W: (B) It's closed.
    W: (C) My office is cleaned on Tuesdays.

28. W: Are only bilingual applicants being considered?
    M: (A) Either one is fine.
    M: (B) I speak French.
    M: (C) They get preference.

29. M: Should I wait for the new model to come out?
    W: (A) It's cold outside.
    W: (B) I would if I were you.
    W: (C) Fifteen minutes ago.

30. W: Do you want to carpool to work?
    M: (A) Sure, then we can take the express lane.
    M: (B) I prefer to swim outdoors.
    M: (C) There's no traffic on weekends.

31. M: Do you prefer watching the news on TV or listening to it on the radio?
    W: (A) The TV — I enjoy seeing the pictures.
    W: (B) With headphones.
    W: (C) The radio is in the kitchen.

32. W: How about trying the new restaurant at the mall?
    M: (A) I'm a very good cook.
    M: (B) OK. I heard it was great.
    M: (C) I've been to the mall.

33. M: Was it too hot at the seashore in July?
    W: (A) My vacation was one week, not two.
    W: (B) I'm sure I'll be back in time.
    W: (C) No, we didn't mind the heat.

34. M: Have all the applicants finished the questionnaire?
    W: (A) Just about.
    W: (B) Not more than ten minutes each.
    W: (C) Sixteen questions in all.

35. W: What do you think of the lobby renovations?
    M: (A) Next spring.
    M: (B) They must have cost a fortune.
    M: (C) I thought it was in the basement.

36. M: Can I bring you back anything to drink?
    W: (A) No, I didn't like the movie.
    W: (B) Yes, I do.
    W: (C) Something cold would be great.

37. M: You just got back from Jakarta, didn't you?
    W: (A) Mr. Carter is waiting.
    W: (B) About two thousand miles.
    W: (C) Yes, I'm still feeling a little jet-lagged.

38. W: Have you seen the unemployment figures?
    M: (A) They're the lowest in twenty years.
    M: (B) I know those people.
    M: (C) No, I don't.

39. M: Did you know there's a fee if the rent payment is two days late?
    W: (A) You don't need to pay a security deposit.
    W: (B) That's why I always mail mine early.
    W: (C) I never pay by check.

TEST ONE

40. W: *Are they predicting rain for the coast?*
    M: (A) The queen's reign has lasted longer than anyone thought.
    M: (B) I thought I saw a ghost.
    M: (C) I hope not; I was planning a tennis game.

41. M: *When will they hire a replacement for Claire?*
    W: (A) Once she officially resigns.
    W: (B) Without my glasses, I can't see clearly.
    W: (C) A little higher would be better.

42. W: *When will the new phone system be installed?*
    M: (A) This is the operator.
    M: (B) Before the first of the year.
    M: (C) Sometime last month.

43. M: *Should I insure this package?*
    W: (A) Thank you; it's definite.
    W: (B) Yes, I'm sure it's a package.
    W: (C) Yes, it's easier to track it that way.

44. W: *Are the banks open on Saturday in the Far East?*
    M: (A) Each country is different.
    M: (B) Every Thursday afternoon.
    M: (C) No, it's too far from here.

45. M: *Is the reserved train more expensive?*
    W: (A) 15,000, but more have been ordered.
    W: (B) I think it is, but it's worth it.
    W: (C) The training equipment is pretty cheap.

46. W: *Were you able to get an appointment for anytime soon?*
    M: (A) No, I won't.
    M: (B) I don't see the point.
    M: (C) I'm lucky; she had a 2:30 cancellation.

47. M: *Have you tried the coffee from the vending machine?*
    W: (A) I don't take sugar.
    W: (B) No, Michael told me it was horrible.
    W: (C) I lent it to someone.

48. W: *How do I retrieve my messages?*
    M: (A) Dial your extension and then your personal code.
    M: (B) Yes, you have some messages.
    M: (C) No, it's a mess.

49. M: *How can I get reimbursed for the decorations I bought for Joe's party?*
    W: (A) No, you can't.
    W: (B) Everything looks beautiful.
    W: (C) Submit your receipts to Margie Carroll.

50. W: *Is your supervisor's name Jean or Joan?*
    M: (A) No, she's the accountant.
    M: (B) Neither. It's Joanne.
    M: (C) Yes, we can wear jeans on Friday.

51. M: I'm David Wong. I have a 10:30 interview with Ms. Chang.
    W: David Wong? I have you down for 11:30.
    M: 11:30? Do you have a telephone I could use?

52. M: Can you help me with this disk?
    W: What's the problem?
    M: I transferred some files to it, and now they don't show up.

53. M: Which company has the cheapest overnight rate to Hong Kong?
    W: I'm not sure, Mark. I think they're all basically the same.
    M: Then I'll just run this over to the post office.

54. W: Can I put some of my things in your office overnight?
    M: Sure, do you need some help?
    W: That would be great. They're coming to paint this afternoon.

55. W: Did you just hear the traffic update?
    M: Did they say there was an accident on the Expressway?
    W: We better get off at the next exit.

56. M: I think we should run some television ads for the new product line.
    W: That's a great idea, but won't that put us over budget?
    M: Let's get a proposal together and show it to the boss.

57. M: Jane, how do you know so much about golf courses?
    W: Oh, my parents were semi-professional and competed around the world.
    M: So maybe you could give me a few lessons.

58. W: Now it's a great time to renegotiate our lease.
    M: No kidding. Rents are falling like a rock.
    W: We'll have to see what our lease agreement says.

59. M: Do you remember what time dinner was supposed to start?
    W: It had better be soon. I've eaten so many hors d'oeuvres I'm almost full now.
    M: It's already eight, and I told the sitter I'd be home by ten.

60. W: You'll need identification with a picture to cash a check.
    M: Let's see. I know my license is in my wallet. Here it is.
    W: That's fine. Do you want large bills or small ones?

61. M: Did you hear? The midmanagement meeting has been moved to Al's office.
    W: Should we get some chairs?
    M: I heard Al is taking care of the arrangements.

62. M: Miss Jason? This is John Williams returning your call.
    W: Oh, I couldn't get my message light to go off, but Diane Brenner told me what to do.
    M: Let me know if it happens again. Several people have been having the same problem.

63. M: I haven't seen Linda Rivera in a long time.
    W: Oh, you haven't heard. She started her own travel agency.
    M: Oh, too bad. She was so good at finding the best connections.

64. W: Do you still subscribe to *Asian Business Monthly*?
    M: Yeah, but now it's *Asian Business Weekly*.
    W: Would you mind bringing three or four to the office?

65. M: Two customers have called me today looking for their orders.
    W: Most of the shipping department is out with the flu.
    M: I'll tell them there will be a delay.

66. W: The copy machine on this floor isn't working.
    M: The repair service has already been called.
    W: Can I use the one on the fifth floor?

67. M: We rented that new Italian restaurant on Main Street for Gloria's retirement party.
    W: Let me know if I can do anything.
    M: Well, since you've asked. Could you contact this list of former employees?

68. M: Do you know any place that develops black and white film?
    W: Try Photo One in Town Center. But if they do, it won't be done in one hour.
    M: Yeah, most places take a week because they send it out.

69. M: Could I borrow your truck this weekend?
    W: Sure. What do you need it for?
    M: I'm giving my sister my old couch, but it's not worth paying someone to move it.

70. W: Are you going to sign up for one of the technology classes?
    M: I guess we have to if we want to get an e-mail account.
    W: Take the one on the twenty-third with me.

71. W: I'm going to buy some popcorn. What can I get for you?
    M: Any kind of candy, but hurry up, or you'll miss the previews.
    W: I'll be right back.

72. M: Karen, what's wrong? Didn't you have a nine o'clock appointment with Mr. Stanley?
    W: I did, but my car broke down, so I had to wait for a tow truck to come.
    M: I'm sure you can reschedule.

73. M: With all the talk about downsizing, I'm afraid I'll be out of a job soon.
    W: If it's last hired, first fired, I'll be gone too.
    M: Let's hope we both keep our jobs.

74. W: Do you think the dollar will keep going up against the local currency?
    M: I hope not, because I have to travel abroad soon.
    W: Maybe you should buy the dollars soon rather than wait.

75. W: Let's have lunch together sometime next week.
    M: The only day that's good for me is Wednesday.
    W: Let me see. I did have plans, but I think I can change that date to Thursday.

76. W: I'm looking for a new winter coat, Steve. I really like the one you're wearing.
    M: Do you want top of the line, Janet, or just one to get you through the winter?
    W: This year I'm going to splurge. Where did you get yours?

77. W: I really like your new business cards. The green border makes them really distinctive.
    M: I couldn't decide whether to go with green or blue, but since my company's color is green, that's what I chose.
    W: I have to wait until I move my office because I'll be getting a new extension.

78. M: I thought everyone was getting a new computer.
    W: No, only department heads. The rest of us have to wait until next June.
    M: That's OK. I'm happy with the model I have.

79. W: Have you looked at the sales figures? Those discount stores have started to decrease our profits.
    M: I knew it would happen one day. They're selling the same stuff, only cheaper.
    W: Well maybe our end-of-the-season sale will help our bottom line.

80. M: Do the vending machines have only soda? I'm in the mood for apple juice.
    W: You'll probably have to go to the store if you want a non-carbonated drink.
    M: It's hot outside. I'll just have some water.

TEST ONE

Questions 81–83 refer to the following report:
M2: Good evening, Boston. This is meteorologist Barry Burbank with the New Year's Eve forecast. We are predicting the last day of the year to also be the coldest. Be prepared if you're planning to come downtown to the First Night festivities. Dress warmly, in plenty of layers, and make sure your head and hands are covered. The wind will make the temperature feel ten degrees colder than it actually is. The only good news is no snow will greet the new year.

Questions 84–86 are based on the following announcement:
M1: Welcome to tonight's concert. Please do not take any flash pictures during the performance. Also no recording devices of any kind are allowed in the hall. During the twenty-minute intermission you will be able to buy cassette and CD recordings of tonight's performance. Due to a broken arm, first violinist Jason Wah will miss this season's performances. Charlotte Brown, visiting soloist from the Icelandic Orchestra, will substitute for Mr. Wah.

Questions 87–89 refer to the following speech:
M2: Excuse me, ma'am. I see you've just left the voting booth, and I hope you have just a few minutes to answer a few questions. I'm from Channel 7's First News at Six, and we're conducting an exit poll to help us interpret the election results. With your help we'll be able to predict the winner in the gubernatorial race. Your anonymous answers will help us greatly.

Questions 90–91 refer to the following talk:
W: Please look at this form I'm distributing to everyone in the department. It asks you to fill in your dream list for all purchases you would like me to consider including in this year's budget. Obviously we won't be able to buy everything you ask for, but I will carefully consider every request. The company is committed to upgrading our technology equipment, but if any of your office furniture, such as bookshelves or file cabinets are defective, write them down as well. I'll need all the forms back by June 15th. If you would like my opinion, stop by my office.

Questions 92–94 refer to the following notice:
M2: If you're over 65, we have the job for you! Here at Vera Needle Company, the average age of our cheerful and loyal work force is 73. The carefully maintained equipment may be seven decades old, but the sophisticated pins, tubes and wires Vera produces are state-of-the-art, bringing in $3.5 million a year in revenues. There are no computers or copy machines, and invoices are prepared one at a time on a typewriter. If you'd like to set your own hours and wouldn't mind having a key to the factory, call us or come by for an interview. Remember, no one is too old or inexperienced!

Questions 95–97 refer to the following announcement:
M1: Your attention, please. Flight 707, departing at two o'clock for Seoul is overbooked. If you have an assigned seat on this flight and would be willing to give up your seat and take the next flight, please see the ticket agent immediately. You will definitely have a seat on the five o'clock flight, and you will receive a free round-trip Tokyo-Honolulu ticket, good for one year.

Questions 98–100 refer to the following announcement:
W: I hope everyone is having a good time at the retreat. I have just a few announcements. One, the tennis tournament will begin at ten. Secondly, a buffet lunch will be served at noon by the lake. Third, buses will leave at four from the basketball court. Have a great day, and don't forget to use sunscreen!

ANSWERS & EXPLANATIONS

1. **(B)** *The sign warns motorists not to throw away anything.*
   Choice (A) is incorrect because the message is on a road sign, not a building. Choice (C) is incorrect because there is no mention of a bank. Choice (D) is incorrect because it is not a busy highway and there is no traffic signal.

2. **(C)** *The man is checking the tire's pressure.*
   Choice (A) is incorrect because the tire is not flat. Choice (B) is incorrect because the tire is inflated, not flat, and he is not unloading the spare tire. Choice (D) is incorrect because the man does not appear to be tired; he is checking something.

3. **(A)** *He's leaning back in his chair.*
   Choice (B) is incorrect because he is talking, not dialing. Choice (C) is incorrect because he is not rearranging his desk; one hand is holding the telephone receiver, and the other hand is resting on the desk. Choice (D) is incorrect because he is not looking up a phone number in a telephone book.

4. **(D)** *The men in the kayaks are rowing closer to one another.*
   Choice (A) is incorrect because the men are paddling in separate kayaks. Choice (B) is incorrect because there are only two kayakers in the picture. Choice (C) is incorrect because the men are not dropping their paddles into the river; they are rowing with them.

5. **(B)** *They're standing at a spot for sightseeing.*
   Choice (A) is incorrect because there is no bus in the picture. Choice (C) is incorrect because they are not using the telescope. Choice (D) is incorrect because they are looking over a wall, not having their picture taken.

6. **(D)** *The man is looking at the woman's computer screen.*
   Choice (A) is incorrect because the woman is sitting in front of the computer, not setting the computer on top of the desk. Choice (B) is incorrect because only the woman is sitting. Choice (C) is incorrect because the woman is not typing in the picture. Her fingers are not on the keyboard.

7. **(C)** *The man is glancing at an open file.*
   Choice (A) is incorrect because there is no file cabinet in the picture, only a file. Choice (B) is incorrect because the man is holding a file, not filing papers. Choice (D) is incorrect because the man is wearing his glasses; they are not on the desk.

8. **(A)** *The man is leaning on his elbow as he reads.*
   Choice (B) is incorrect because there is only one person in the picture. Choice (C) is incorrect because the man is not napping; he's looking at a newspaper. Choice (D) is incorrect because the newspaper is already on the ground; he is not putting it down.

9. **(B)** *Both men are holding microphones in front of them.*
   Choice (A) is incorrect because the audiences is not visible in the picture. Choice (C) is incorrect because the orchestra is not visible in the picture. Choice (D) is incorrect because it is not known if the duet is being performed for the first time.

10. **(C)** *The woman is waiting on the sidewalk.*
    Choice (A) is incorrect because there are no other pedestrians in the picture. Choice (B) is incorrect because the woman is waiting, not crossing the street. Choice (D) is incorrect because the woman is not signaling to anyone.

11. **(D)** *The customer's order has arrived.*
    Choice (A) is incorrect because there is no waiter in the picture. Choice (B) is incorrect because the dishes have just been served with the food. Choice (C) is incorrect because the knife is on the table; the customer is not using it to cut the salad.

12. **(D)** *All four people are focusing their attention on the report.*
    Choice (A) is incorrect because three of the people are not holding a copy of the report. Choice (B) is incorrect because only one person is standing. Choice (C) is incorrect because the woman is neither holding the report nor giving a presentation.

13. **(A)** *The woman is digging a hole in the sand.*
    Choice (B) is incorrect because there is neither a sand castle nor water in the picture. Choice (C) is incorrect because the woman is digging sand, not sanding a board. Choice (D) is incorrect because the woman is digging, not looking for a resort.

14. **(B)** *The woman is moving the furniture.*
    Choice (A) is incorrect because the woman is not folding the chair. Choice (C) is incorrect because it is not known whether or not there are empty seats available in the office. Choice (D) is incorrect because the woman is moving a chair, not measuring a table.

15. **(C)** *The band is performing music.*
    Choice (A) is incorrect because one man is holding a microphone, not an instrument. Choice (B) is incorrect because the members are holding their instruments; they have not left them on the sidewalk. Choice (D) is incorrect because only two of the four performers are wearing sunglasses.

16. **(A)** *The woman is stirring her beverage.*
    Choice (B) is incorrect because the woman is not eating in the picture. Choice (C) is incorrect because the woman is sitting, not waiting in line. Choice (D) is incorrect because the woman is stirring, not serving dessert.

17. **(D)** *The man is looking at the object in the woman's hands.*
    Choice (A) incorrect because the woman is holding an object, not wrapping a gift. Choice (B) is incorrect because the man is sitting next to the woman, not purchasing a gift for her. Choice (C) is incorrect because the woman is holding the present; she has not put it down.

18. (B) *The woman is sharpening a pencil.*
    Choice (A) is incorrect because the woman is sharpening a pencil, not using it to write a report. Choice (C) is incorrect because the woman is holding a pencil, not a knife. Choice (D) is incorrect because the woman is sharpening a pencil, not shredding documents.

19. (C) *The woman in the middle is holding a photo album on her lap.*
    Choice (A) is incorrect because the woman is showing pictures, not movies. Choice (B) is incorrect because the woman in the middle is not wearing glasses. Choice (D) is incorrect because no one is taking pictures.

20. (A) *The couple is looking at the display through the store window.*
    Choice (B) is incorrect because the couple is standing outside the store, not going in. Choice (C) is incorrect because the couple is only looking at the merchandise, not sampling it. Choice (D) is incorrect because the owner is not visible in the picture.

21. (B) *At six* answers *at what time* the man is leaving. Choice (A) answers a *how often* question. Choice (C) answers a *where* question.

22. (A) *It's company policy* means the company requires the conference room to be reserved when one wants to use it. Choice (B) confuses *reserve a room* with *reserve a seat*. Choice (C) answers a *where* question.

23. (C) *From a catalogue* tells where the furniture was bought. Choice (A) is not a response to a *where* question. Choice (B) is an illogical response to a *where* question.

24. (B) *I was too late* explains the reason why the woman didn't sign up for the computer training. Choice (A) is an illogical response. Choice (C) answers a *where* question.

25. (B) *The new personnel director's* explains whose idea it was. Choice (A) confuses *getting paid* with related words: *check* and *account*. Choice (C) answers a *would you like* question.

26. (B) *I think the 2:15* indicates which flight the woman thinks she's taking. Choice (A) answers a *when* question. Choice (C) confuses *flight* and *light*, a word related to *lamp*.

27. (A) *There's one on the corner of 31st and Broadway* tells where the closest dry cleaner is. Choice (B) confuses *closest* and *closed*. Choice (C) confuses *cleaner* and *cleaned*.

28. (C) *They get preference* means that bilingual applicants are desirable. Choice (A) answers the question *which one*. Choice (B) answers a *what language* question.

29. (B) *I would if I were you* indicates the woman recommends waiting for the new model. Choice (A) is an illogical response. Choice (C) answers a past tense *when* question.

30. (A) *Sure, then we can take the express lane* explains that by carpooling the man can drive in a special lane, reserved for one with a certain number of passengers. Choice (B) is an illogical response. Choice (C) confuses *carpool* with a related word: *traffic*.

31. (A) *The TV — I enjoy seeing the pictures* explains why the woman prefers watching the news on TV rather than hearing it on the radio. Choice (B) answers the question of *how* the person prefers getting the news. Choice (C) answers a *where* question.

32. (B) *I heard it was great* responds positively to the suggestion of trying the new restaurant. Choice (A) confuses *restaurant* with a related word: *cook*. Choice (C) answers the question *have you ever been to the mall*.

33. (C) *No, we didn't mind the heat* means that they didn't think it was too hot at the seashore. Choice (A) confuses *too hot* and *two weeks*. Choice (B) is an illogical response.

34. (A) *Just about* indicates that almost all of the applicants have finished. Choice (B) answers the question *how long*. Choice (C) answers the question *how many*.

35. (B) *They must have cost a fortune* means the man thinks the lobby renovations must have been very expensive. Choice (A) answers the question *when will the lobby restorations be complete*. Choice (C) is an illogical response and answers a *where* question.

36. (C) *Somthing cold would be great* indicates the woman would appreciate the man's bringing her something cold to drink. Choice (A) answers the question *did you like the movie*. Choice (B) answers a *yes/no* question and is an inappropriate response to the question.

37. (C) *Yes, I'm still feeling a little jet-lagged* means the woman just got back, and she's having trouble adjusting to the time difference. Choice (A) is an illogical response. Choice (B) answers a *how far* question.

38. (A) *They're the lowest in twenty years* indicates the man has seen the figures. Choice (B) confuses *figures*, meaning *numbers* with *persons*. Choice (C) answers a *yes/no* question in the present tense.

39. (B) *That's why I always mail mine early* means the woman knows there's a fee for lateness, which explains why she's always early for her payment. Choice (A) confuses *paying a fee for late rent* with *paying a security deposit* — a fee paid at the time one first moves in. Choice (C) answers a question about *how* one pays.

40. (C) *I hope not; I was planning a tennis game* indicates the man hasn't heard the weather forecast and hopes it's incorrect. Choice (A) confuses *rain* and *reign,* the time a king or queen rules a country. Choice (B) confuses *coast* and *ghost.*

41. (A) *Once she officially resigns* answers when a replacement will be hired. Choice (B) confuses *Claire* and *clearly.* Choice (C) confuses *hire* and *higher.*

42. (B) *Before the first of the year* tells when the system will be installed. Choice (A) confuses *phone system* with a related word: *operator.* Choice (C) answers a past tense question, not a future question.

43. (C) *Yes, it's easier to track it that way* explains why it's a good idea to insure the package, because it will be easier to follow. Choice (A) confuses *(in)sure* and *definite.* Choice (B) answers the question *are you sure.*

44. (A) *Each country is different* means that the Saturday work policy is not the same for every country. Choice (B) answers a *how often* or *when* question. Choice (C) is an illogical response.

45. (B) *I think it is, but it's worth it* means the reserved train costs more money, but it's money well spent. Choice (A) answers a *how many* question. Choice (C) confuses *the reserved train* and *training equipment.*

46. (C) *I'm lucky; she had a 2:30 cancellation* means the man was able to get an appointment. Choice (A) answers a *will you* question. Choice (B) confuses *appointment* and *point.*

47. (B) *No, Michael told me it was horrible* explains why the woman hasn't tried the coffee from the machine. Choice (A) answers the question *how do you take your coffee.* Choice (C) confuses the words *vending* and *lent.*

48. (A) *Dial your extension and then your personal code* explains the steps in order to retrieve messages. Choice (B) answers a *do I have* question. Choice (C) confuses *messages* and *mess.*

49. (C) *Submit your receipts to Margie Carroll* explains what the man must do to be reimbursed. Choice (A) answers a *can I* question asking for permission. Choice (B) is an illogical response.

50. (B) *Neither. It's Joanne* means that the supervisor's name is not Jean or Joan. Choice (A) is an illogical response to a choice about names. Choice (C) confuses *Jean* the name with *jeans* the clothing.

51. (C) David says *I have a 10:30 interview with Ms. Chang* so he thought he had come on time. Choice (A) is incorrect because it is the receptionist who says the appointment is at 11:30, not David. Choice (B) is contradicted by his saying *I have a 10:30 interview.* It is now that he wants to use the phone. Choice (D) is not mentioned.

52. (D) The woman says the files *don't show up,* meaning they have not appeared. Choices (A) and (B) are not mentioned. Choice (C) is incorrect because it confuses a *person* showing up with the *files* showing up.

53. (C) The man says *I'll just run this over to the post office,* meaning he won't use a private company at all, but rather will use the postal service. Choice (A) is incorrect because he wants to send something to Hong Kong, not go there. Choice (B) is incorrect because he's not going to check out prices; he's simply going to use the post office because he is told the prices are basically the same. Choice (D) confuses *basically* with *basic rate.*

54. (B) The man says *sure,* meaning she can put some of her things in his office; he'll give her some space. Choice (A) is incorrect because the office is being painted by some people; he's not doing it. Choice (C) is incorrect because he offers her *some help;* he doesn't say he'll get her some. Choice (D) is not mentioned.

55. (B) The conversation takes place in a car because they are discussing *traffic, the expressway,* and the *next exit.* Choice (A) is incorrect because if they were in an ambulance they would not avoid the accident. Choices (C) and (D) are illogical because it cannot be inferred that they're in a building.

56. (C) The man says *I think we should run some television ads.* Choice (A) is incorrect because it is television ads they want to develop, not radio ads. Choice (B) is incorrect because the man does not want to go over budget although that may result. Choice (D) is incorrect because the product line is already developed.

57. (A) The man says to the woman *maybe you could give me a few lessons.* Choice (B) is incorrect because the woman's parents, not the woman, competed in tournaments. Choice (C) is incorrect because he suggests she give him golf lessons, not show him golf courses. Choice (D) says the woman's parents were semi-professional, but does not suggest that the woman herself become professional.

58. (D) The woman says *we'll have to see what our lease agreement says,* which means to check what the terms of the lease are. Choice (A) confuses *negotiate our lease* with *negotiation team.* Choice (B) confuses *falling like a rock* with *rocks on their property.* Choice (C) is incorrect because *rents are falling,* not increasing.

59. **(D)** The man asks when *dinner was supposed to start,* meaning it has not started yet. Choice (A) is incorrect; ten is the time the man told his baby sitter he'd be home. Choice (B) is not mentioned; the sitter is not at the dinner but at the parents' home. Choice (C) is incorrect because there is supposed to be a dinner after the hors d'oeuvres. Hors d'oeuvres are served before a dinner.

60. **(C)** The conversation takes place in a bank because the man wants to *cash a check* and the woman asks if he wants *large or small bills.* Choices (A), (B) and (D) are incorrect because while someone may indeed pay for something by writing a check in these places, enough change would not be given requiring the asking *Do you want large bills or small ones?* Only a bank would offer these services.

61. **(A)** The man tells the woman that the meeting has been moved to *Al's office*. Choices (B) and (C) are incorrect because *Al is taking care of the arrangements.* Choice (D) is incorrect because the meeting has not been canceled; it's merely been relocated.

62. **(B)** John Williams tells Miss Jason that he is *returning her call,* meaning that she had previously called him. Choice (A) is not mentioned. Choice (C) is incorrect because it is Miss Jason's light that wouldn't go off, not Mr. Williams'. Choice (D) is not mentioned.

63. **(B)** The woman says that *Linda Rivera started her own travel agency,* meaning she started her own company. Choice (A) is not mentioned; she didn't travel. Choices (C) and (D) are incorrect because she has not been seen since she started a different company, not because she was sick or fired.

64. **(A)** The man tells the woman that *Asian Business Monthly* has changed to *Asian Business Weekly,* meaning it is now published once a week. Choice (B) was previously correct, but has changed from monthly to weekly. Choices (C) and (D) are incorrect because the woman asks only for *three or four* issues to be brought to the office — there is no mention of three or four times a year.

65. **(C)** The woman says that *Most of the shipping department is out with the flu* which explains why customers have not received their orders. Choice (A) is incorrect because orders are delayed due to some workers being ill, not on vacation. Choice (B) is incorrect because the delay is not in production but in shipping. Choice (D) is incorrect because orders are not lost — they are merely delayed.

66. **(D)** The woman asks if she can use a copy machine *on the fifth floor.* Choice (A) is incorrect; the man says *a repair service has already been called.* Choice (B) is not mentioned. Choice (C) is not mentioned; the woman mentions only *the fifth floor.*

67. **(C)** The man asks the woman if she could *contact this list of former employees.* We can infer that this means she will invite them as guests to the party after contacting them. Choice (A) is incorrect because the restaurant has already been rented. Choice (B) is incorrect because the list already exists. Choice (D) is not mentioned. The party is *for* Gloria so we can assume she would not be on the list of former employees to be invited.

68. **(D)** The man says that developing black and white film will probably *take a week because they* (most places) *send it out.* Choice (A) is incorrect because the woman says *it won't be done in an hour.* Choice (B) is incorrect because the man says the film is sent out. Choice (C) is incorrect. Although the woman suggests *Photo One,* she doesn't say it's the only place that develops black and white film.

69. **(A)** The man is giving her sister his old couch, but he says *it's not worth paying someone to move it.* In other words, he doesn't want to hire a mover. Choice (B) is incorrect because he says he is giving his sister his old couch. Choice (C) is incorrect because he does want to *borrow* her truck for the weekend. Choice (D) is incorrect because he wants to move the couch over the weekend.

70. **(B)** The woman encourages the man to *take the one* (the technology class) *on the twenty-third* with her. In other words they want to take the class together. Choice (A) is incorrect because there is no mention of a conference. Choice (C) is incorrect because they do not have email accounts yet. They are taking the class in order to get them. Choice (D) is not mentioned. It is implied that the class is offered to company employees so it would not be part of a graduate school program.

71. **(C)** They are discussing refreshments (popcorn and candy) and *the previews,* which are short clips for upcoming movies at that theater, so the conversation undoubtedly takes place in a movie theater. Choices (A), (B), and (D) are therefore incorrect.

72. **(D)** Karen says *her car broke down,* and *she had to wait for a tow truck* (a truck that pulls other vehicles which need to be repaired). She therefore missed her appointment. Choice (A) is incorrect because there is no mention of her oversleeping. Choice (B) is incorrect because she didn't forget her appointment — she was unable to get to it. Choice (C) is incorrect because it wasn't her truck — it was her car which was towed by a truck.

73. **(B)** They use the words *downsizing, out of a job, hirings, firings, be gone,* and *keep our jobs,* so they are discussing the possibility of layoffs. *To lay off someone* is another way of saying *to fire someone.* Choice (A) is incorrect because *Last hired, first fired* means that the last people who were hired for the job would be the first to be fired. No mention is made of *new hirings.* Choice (C) confuses being *fired,* or losing one's job, with *a fire.* Choice (D) confuses *downtown* with *downsizing.*

74. (B) The woman says *Maybe you should buy the dollars soon*, meaning he should exchange some money. Choice (A) is incorrect because the man says he has to travel abroad — the woman does not suggest traveling soon. Choice (C) is incorrect because the woman mentions that the dollar is going up against the local currency; she does not suggest he wait for the local currency to go up. Instead she suggests he buy dollars soon. Choice (D) is not mentioned.

75. (A) The man says *the only day that's good for him is Wednesday*. The woman adds that although she had plans for Wednesday, she thinks she can change them. Choice (B) is incorrect because Thursday is the day which the woman will change her previous Wednesday plan to. Choice (C) is incorrect because the woman says she wants to have lunch *sometime before Friday,* not *on* Friday. Choice (D) confuses *sometime* next week with *anytime* next week, and is merely a suggestion. They agree to meet on Wednesday.

76. (D) Janet says *this year she's going to splurge,* meaning spend a lot of money on a coat, and she asks Steve where he bought his, meaning she wants one like it. Choice (A) is incorrect because she will not wear her coat one more winter, but rather buy a new one. Choice (B) is incorrect because she will splurge, not buy a cheap coat. Choice (C) is not mentioned — she only seems interested in Steve's coat and doesn't indicate that she will ask other people.

77. (C) The woman says she can't order business cards now *because she'll be getting a new extension,* meaning a new phone number. Choice (A) is not mentioned by the woman. It is the man who couldn't decide the color but eventually chose green. Choice (B) is incorrect because the woman is moving her office location; the company is not moving so the address will stay the same. Choice (D) is not mentioned.

78. (D) The woman says *the rest of us have to wait until next June to get a new computer,* so it won't happen now. Choice (A) is contradicted by her saying that *the rest of us have to wait until next June to get a new computer.* Choice (B) is not mentioned although he says he's *happy* with the model he has. Choice (C) is incorrect; the department heads are getting new computers now and everyone else has to wait until June.

79. (D) The woman says that *discount stores have started to decrease our profits,* meaning the store's profits are *on the decline/declining.* Choice (A) is incorrect because they are not selling their goods to discount stores; they are competing with discount stores selling the same goods. Choice (B) is not mentioned and there is no indication it will happen. Choice (C) confuses *the bottom line* (the line on a company's accounting statement showing profit or loss) with *bottom-of-the-line goods* (goods of poor quality).

80. (C) The man says he'll *just have some water.* Choice (A) is incorrect because the man will have water, not soda from the vending machines. Because the woman tells the man he'll *probably have to go to the store for a non-carbonated drink,* he decides to *just have some water,* making Choice (B) incorrect. Choice (D) is incorrect because although the man *is in the mood for apple juice,* he is unwilling to go to the store to get it because it is too hot.

81. (C) The report is a weather forecast that begins *This is meteorologist Barry Burbank.* Choices (A), (B), and (D) are contradicted by this statement.

82. (C) The report concludes *The only good news is no snow will greet the new year.* Choice (A) may or may not be true but is incorrect because the report explicitly states what the good news is. Choice (B) is not mentioned. Choice (D) is contradicted by the news that *the wind will make the temperature feel ten degrees colder than it actually is.*

83. (B) People are advised to *make sure their heads and hands are covered.* Choice (A) is not stated or implied. Choice (C) is not mentioned and *layered cakes* is confused with the suggestion to wear *plenty of layers* (of clothes). Choice (D) is contradicted because no snow is expected.

84. (A) The announcement begins *Welcome to tonight's concert* and *during the performance* and *in the hall* all point to this being made in a performance. Choice (B) is a distracter for *in the hall.* Choice (C) is a distracter for *recording devices,* as in cassette players or video cameras. Choice (D) is a distracter for *CD recordings.*

85. (D) *During the intermission you will be able to buy cassette recordings.* Choice (A) is incorrect because *no recording devices are allowed in the hall.* Choice (B) is not mentioned. It is likely that those listening to the announcement have already bought tickets. Choice (C) is incorrect because concert goers are told not to *take any flash pictures during the performance,* so they won't need film.

86. (B) *Due to a broken arm, first violinist Jason Wah will miss the season's performances.* Choice (A) is not mentioned. Choice (C) is incorrect because Miss Brown is substituting for Mr. Wah. Choice (D) confuses Miss Brown's visiting from the Icelandic Orchestra with his moving to Iceland.

87. (C) The reporter tells the woman *I see you've just left the voting booth.* Choice (A) confuses the reporter's being *from First News at Six,* with someone watching the news report at six. Choice (B) is incorrect because the reporter hopes the woman will answer some questions. Choice (D) is what the reporter hopes to do after he interviews her and the other people.

88. (C) The man says *I'm from Channel 7's First News at Six,* which means it's a TV station. Choice (A) is incorrect because he wants to conduct an exit poll but does not say he is from a polling firm. Choice (B) is incorrect though he says he is interested in the *gubernatorial* (governor's) race. He is interested in election results but is not from election headquarters, so Choice (D) is incorrect.

89. (D) *With your help we'll be able to predict the winner in the gubernatorial race* means the reporter wants to know who she voted for. Choice (A) is not mentioned. Choice (B) is not mentioned because it is implied that he will ask who she voted for between two or more people, not simply ask her opinion on the current governor. Choice (C) is incorrect — he wants her to answer *anonymously,* without giving her name.

90. (B) The form asks for employees *to fill in your dream list for all purchases you would like me to consider.* Technology upgrades are mentioned but publicizing them isn't the purpose of the form, so Choice (A) is incorrect. Choice (C) is incorrect — she is asking for input concerning the budget, but is not outlining it. Choice (D) is incorrect because employees are asked to write down defective furniture; they're not asked to described available furniture.

91. (B) Employees are told that the speaker *will need all the forms back by June 15th,* or mid-June. Choice (A) is incorrect — the company may replace some equipment but the employees aren't asked to. Choice (C) is incorrect — only furniture such as file cabinets are mentioned. Choice (D) confuses *files from cabinets* with *file cabinets.*

92. (D) *The average age of the work force is 73.* Choice (A) confuses the age 35 with the number 3.5 million dollars in revenues. Choice (B) mentions age 65 in the opening line *if you're over 65, we have the job for you!* but it is not the average age. Choice (C) confuses *seven decades old* in describing the equipment with the age 70.

93. (D) The company produces *sophisticated pins, tubes, and wires.* Choice (A) confuses the fact that invoices are used at the company, but doesn't produce them. Choice (B) confuses the fact the employees are given a *key to the factory* with what is produced. Choice (C) confuses the fact that typewriters are used with what the company produces.

94. (B) The notice states *if you'd like to set your own hours, come by for an interview,* meaning that the work schedule is flexible. Choice (A) mentions using a *key to the factory,* so this is untrue. Choice (C) confuses *art* with *state-of-the-art,* meaning latest and most advanced. Choice (D) is contradicted by the fact that *the equipment may be seven decades old.*

95. (C) Passengers are told *Flight 707 is overbooked,* meaning too many people booked flights. Choice (A) is not mentioned. Choice (B) may or may not be true but it is not the reason people are being asked to give up their seats. Choice (D) is not mentioned.

96. (B) Anyone willing to give up a seat on this flight *will receive a free round-trip Tokyo-Honolulu ticket.* Choice (A) is not mentioned. Choice (C) confuses the destination of Flight 707 (Seoul) with the destination of the free ticket. Choice (D) confuses *free* with *three.*

97. (C) Those giving up a seat on Flight 707 *will have a seat on the five o'clock flight.* Choice (A) confuses the time one o'clock with the fact that the free ticket is good for one year. Choice (B) confuses the time of Flight 707 with the time of the later flight. Choice (D) confuses the time 7:00 with the number of this flight, 707.

98. (A) The announcement begins *I hope everyone is having a good time at the retreat,* a special relaxing place for people to get together. Choice (B) is not possible because the retreat has already begun. Choice (C) is incorrect because they are not at the beach; some may go to the lake later. Choice (D) is incorrect because the announcement states the tennis tournament will be held later.

99. (D) Participants are told *the buses will leave at four.* Choice (A) confuses the time of the tennis tournament with the departure time. Choice (B) confuses the time of the buffet lunch with the departure time. Choice (C) is not mentioned and confuses *third* and *three.*

100. (B) The speaker concludes by saying *Have a great day, and don't forget to use sunscreen.* Choice (A) is incorrect; the participants are told to meet the buses *at the basketball court,* not the lake. Choice (C) is incorrect; the speaker only states it is a buffet lunch. Choice (D) confuses leaving from the basketball court with a basketball game.

101. (C) *Correspondence,* meaning written communication such as letters or email, is the only appropriate noun in this context. Choice (A) means *serious talk* but is not logical. Choice (B) means *a joining together,* and Choice (D) means *act of convincing.*

102. (B) *Between* is the preposition used with two things. Choice (A) is the preposition used with more than two things. Choice (C) indicates movement *to the inside.* Choice (D) indicates location *at the side of.*

103. (D) Only a person, such as an *assistant,* meaning *associate,* can *explain the new payroll procedure.* Choice (A) is a noun thing. Choice (B) is an adjective. Choice (C) is a noun thing.

104. (A) *Prices are lower this year.* Choice (B) is illogical. Choices (C) and (D) are not logical. Prices cannot be *poor* or *needy.*

105. (B) *Both... and* is a paired conjunction; *both my bookshelf and the file cabinet.* Choices (A), (C), and (D) cannot be used with *both.*

106. (C) The simple past form of the verb, *The president selected a new logo,* is needed in this sentence. Choice (A), is not the third person singular form of the verb. Choice (B) is the passive form. Choice (D) is the present participle and not a full verb form.

107. (D) The adverb *so* is used before the adverb *quickly.* Choice (A) which can be either a conjunction or a preposition is not followed by an adverb. Choice (B) cannot precede an adverb. Choice (C) is not logical in this context; the use of *too* implies a negative result but there is no indication that the speaker feels negatively, only *surprised.*

108. (A) The correct word order following a negative adverb like *rarely* is helping verb, *does,* subject, *it,* base form, *rain.* In Choices (B), (C), and (D), the necessary word order is not followed.

109. (B) *The personnel director is in charge of ordering business cards;* it is that person's job. Choice (A) is incorrect; *for,* not *to,* should follow responsible. Choice (C) is a passive verb. Choice (D) is incorrect; *for,* not *to,* should follow *delegated.*

110. (C) The present perfect form of the verb completes this sentence; *Attendance at amusement parks has nearly doubled in the last decade.* Choice (A), although the past participle, is illogical because attendance would not *nearly* increase in a decade. Choice (B) is an adverb. Choice (D), although the past participle, is illogical because *duplicated* means *made an exact copy.*

111. (D) It is the third-person singular object pronoun used for things, referring to the singular *New York Times. Times* is singular because it is the name of a publication. Choice (A) is the second-person object pronoun. Choice (B) is the third-person singular object pronoun used for men. Choice (C) is the third-person plural object pronoun.

112. (B) *Venture* means *a business enterprise involving some risk in expectation of gain.* Choice (A) is redundant with the adjective *joint,* meaning *cooperative.* Choice (C) means *a part considered in relation to the whole.* Choice (D) means *something that logically follows from an action or a condition.*

113. (A) The correct word order for a relative clause is *that,* relative pronoun, *he,* subject of the relative clause, *selected,* verb in the clause. Choices (B), (C), and (D) are in the wrong order.

114. (C) *By and large* is an idiom which means in general. Choices (A), (B), and (D) are not logical.

115. (D) The base form, *hire,* must follow the modal, *must.* Choices (A) and (C) cannot follow *must.* Choice (B) can follow *must* but a passive construction is illogical.

116. (B) *Unlike,* a preposition followed by the noun *computers,* indicates that a contrast follows. Choice (A) is either an adjective or an adverb which is used to show similarity. Choice (C) is a verb. Choice (D) is an adjective meaning *probable.*

117. (C) *Underbid* means *offer an amount lower than a competitor's,* and is the only logical choice. Choice (A) means *learned someone else's role so as to be able to replace the regular performer.* Choice (B) means *experienced.* Choice (D) is a noun which means *the seaweed pull of receding waves after they break on the shore.*

118. (A) *Illegible* means unable to be read, and is the only logical choice. Choice (B) means *unable to read or write.* Choice (C) means *illegal or born without married parents.* Choice (D) means *senseless.*

119. (D) An adverb is required. *Solely* is an adverb meaning *exclusively.* Choice (A) *unique* is an adjective meaning *one of a kind.* Choice (B) *alone* means *by oneself/by itself* and is illogical. Choice (C) *lonely* is an adjective meaning *feeling sad and alone.*

120. (B) *In the 1960s and 1970s* indicates that the past tense is needed. In addition, the passive mood is needed; *occupations were opened* (by others). Choice (A) is the present perfect tense. Choice (C) is the present perfect progressive tense. Choice (D) is the present tense passive mood.

121. (C) The preposition, *underneath,* means *below.* Choice (A) *about face* is a noun thing meaning *a complete change.* Choice (B) *besides* can either be an adverb or a preposition meaning *in addition to.* Choice (D) *overall* is either an adjective or an adverb meaning *in general.*

122. (A) In this context, a passive construction is needed. *Cannot be made* is the only passive verb that is logical. Choice (B) is passive but illogical. *A call* cannot be *admitted*. Choices (C) and (D) are illogical and require a noun person subject.

123. (D) *Is critical to* means *is essential for*. Choice (A) is not used with *to*. Choice (B) is illogical. Choice (C) is used with *for*.

124. (D) The adverb *immediately* follows the action verb *made*. Choice (A) is an idiom, usually followed by the word *possible*. When Choice (B) is followed by *upon*, it usually introduces a fairy tale as in *Once upon a time...* Choice (C) is an adjective, not an adverb.

125. (C) The adjective form *convincing* modifies *presentation*. Choice (A) is the past participle. Choice (B) is an adverb. Choice (D) is a preposition and a noun.

126. (B) The infinitive is needed; *The appetizers are yours to taste*. Choice (A) is a gerund. Choice (C) is a noun. Choice (D) is the present tense, passive mood.

127. (A) When *were*, meaning *if*, is used to introduce a conditional sentence, the infinitive is used in the dependent clause. Choice (B) cannot be used with the infinitive, only the base form. Choice (C) is a preposition. Choice (D) is an adverb.

128. (C) *To reduce expenses* means *to lower them*. Choice (A) means *persuade*. Choice (B) means *infer*. Choice (D) means *make*.

129. (D) The past participle adjective form, *excited*, is necessary because the people are excited by the product. Choice (A) is the active participle adjective. Choice (B) is a noun. Choice (C) includes an unnecessary preposition.

130. (B) *Readers subscribing* is the active participle from a reduced adjective clause, *who are subscribing*. Choices (A), (C), and (D), all verbs, are illogical because there is already a verb, *pay*, in the clause.

131. (A) An adjective, *partial*, follows the article, *a*, and precedes the noun, *shipment*. Choice (B) is a noun. Choice (C) is an adverb. Choice (D), although an adjective, means *separated*, and is illogical in this sentence.

132. (C) A noun is needed after the preposition *against*; *One against the other* means *comparing each one with every other one*. Choice (A) is an adjective. Choice (B) is an adverb and an adjective. Choice (D) is a noun but is not used in this expression.

133. (D) *Cut back* means *reduced*. Choice (A) means *surveyed*. Choices (B) and (C) are illogical verb and preposition combinations.

134. (B) *Consumer demand*, a (compound) noun, can be preceded by the prepositional phrase *in response to*. Choice (A) is a conjunction or a noun. Choice (C) precedes a clause. Choice (D), a preposition meaning *together with*, is illogical in this sentence.

135. (C) The possessive relative pronoun, *whose*, must precede a noun. Choices (A), (B), and (D) are all relative pronouns which precede a verb (*the man who is...*) or a subject and a verb (*the man who he saw...*).

136. (A) *To satisfy* means *to fulfill*. Choice (B) means *help two sides reach agreement*. Choice (C) means *take more money from the bank than is in the account*. Choice (D) means *avoid*.

137. (C) In this passive construction only *appointed*, meaning *chosen*, is the appropriate verb. Choice (A) is illogical. Choices (B) and (D) require *by*, not *to*.

138. (D) *Whenever possible* is an expression meaning *if possible*. Choices (A) and (C) are not logical. Choice (B) cannot precede *possible*.

139. (B) *Guarantee* is the correct singular noun thing meaning *written* promise of satisfaction of a product. Choice (A) is the incorrect plural form. Choices (C) and (D) are person nouns.

140. (A) The passive form, *will be acknowledged*, is needed in this sentence. Choice (B) is the active future tense. Choice (C) is the past participle or an adjective. Choice (D) is the present participle or an adjective.

141. (C) Use the adjective form, *other*, before the plural noun *countries*.

142. (B) The participle form of the verb is needed to make a correct passive form — *limited*.

143. (C) A noun is needed; *variety* should be used.

144. (A) The preposition *of* is needed after *Most*.

145. (A) *It* is not necessary because the sentence already has a subject: *museum*.

146. (D) Use *must* before *be* to make the passive form of the verb.

147. (B) The error is one of word choice; use *luggage*, the non-count noun following *one piece of*.

148. (D) The plural form of year should be used — *two years of service*.

149. (D) The count noun *receipt* must be preceded by an article, *a*.

150. (A) The correct superlative form is *most popular*.

151. (A) The preposition *to* is needed following *in addition*.

152. (C) *Mrs. Ramirez*, a woman, takes the feminine possessive adjective: *her*.

153. (B) When *stop* means *quit*, it must be followed by the gerund: *allowing*. When *stop* is followed by the infinitive form, it means *stop in order to do something*.

154. (D) The base form, *save*, follows the modal, *can*.

155. (D) The past participle form, *signed*, is needed following the ellipted helping verb *have*.

156. (D) Use the plural form of the noun — *paychecks*.

157. (A) The past participial should be used — *handicapped*.

158. (B) Before an adjective, an adverb should be used — *increasingly popular*.

159. (C) The correct preposition should be *for; in time for*.

160. (A) Following a preposition, use a gerund — *By subscribing*.

161. (D) The farm is *suited for: poultry* (chickens), *cattle* (cows), *and sheep* (lambs); pigs are not mentioned. Choices (A), (B), and (C) are explicitly mentioned.

162. (B) This advertisement is typical of those found in the classified sections in newspapers; therefore, Choices (A), (C), and (D) are incorrect.

163. (C) *Fifteen million dollars is available to relocate companies to Pennsylvania*; business owners can take advantage of this offer. Choice (A) is incorrect because this plan is the *governor's strategy;* he already resides in Pennsylvania. Choice (B) confuses *tax cuts* with *tax collectors*, Choice (D) confuses *funding* with *fund-raisers*.

164. (C) *The governor's strategy of worker's compensation reforms have helped reduce the cost of doing business in Pennsylvania*. Choice (A) is incorrect; increased funding for customized job training is a result of the governor's strategy. Choice (B) confuses *tax cuts* with *tax increases*. Choice (D) is incorrect; it confuses *funding for research* with *the research tax credits* which companies are now eligible for.

165. (A) Readers can *call*. Choice (B) is not mentioned. Choice (C) confuses *visiting a website* and *creating a website*. Choice (D) confuses *contacting them by fax* and *buying a fax machine*.

166. (B) Although the *signature of sender* is requested, the *signature of the recipient* is not. Choices (A), (C), and (D) are clearly requested.

167. (D) Transportation charges can be paid by *credit card*. Choices (A), (B), and (C) are not mentioned.

168. (C) *Call 800-554-8228 for a free brochure*. Choices (A), (B), and (D) are not mentioned.

169. (D) *Hot Tubs "R" Us spas are easy to set up. The only travel involved is stepping out your back door,* to one's backyard. Choice (A) confuses *a week in a tropical paradise* with *installing a spa on a tropical island*. Choices (B) and (C) are not mentioned.

170. (B) *Call for a free brochure and the address of the dealer nearest you* implies one buys a spa from a dealer. Choices (A), (C), and (D) are contradicted by *Call for a free brochure and the address of the dealer nearest you*.

171. (C) In all three paragraphs, the move to a single currency in Europe is mentioned, making *Europe Tackles the Big Shift to a Single Currency* the best title. Choice (A) is an insignificant detail in the first paragraph. Choice (B) is not mentioned. Although *payroll forms, scheduling meetings, and corporate executives* [(Choice (D)] are each mentioned once, these items are not the main idea of this report.

172. (A) *The euro, as the single currency will be called*. Choices (B), (C), and (D) are contradicted by *The euro, as the single currency will be called*.

173. (D) *In 2002, countries across Europe are to abandon their national currencies*. Choices (A), (B), and (C) are contradicted by *In 2002, countries across Europe are to abandon their national currencies*

174. (B) *Seeks capital to expand distribution*. The advertiser is a *furniture distributor*. He is not seeking distributors but rather the money to *expand distribution*, so Choice (A) is incorrect. Choice (C) is incorrect because he has already done the *market research*. Choice (D) is incorrect; he currently distributes to *interior designers* but no mention is made of seeking more.

175. (C) *Established U.S. importer... of antique French furniture;* Mr. Root imports *antiques*. Choice (A) confuses *interior designers* with *designer clothing*. Choice (B) is not mentioned. Choice (D) confuses *French furniture* with *French wine*.

176. (D) *Has established markets in Atlanta*. Although additional demand exists in Choices (A), (B), and (C), there have been no markets established in those cities yet.

177. (A) *Discover how you can rent your own office suite*. Choice (B) is incorrect because only *shared equipment with other firms* is mentioned. Choice (C) is not mentioned. Choice (D) confuses *tailored office plans* with *tailoring services*.

178. (C) *Discover how you can rent your own office suite while sharing... with other firms.* This is for those *looking for an efficient and economical solution to office needs* by sharing expenses. Choices (A), (B), and (D) are not mentioned.

179. (B) The advertisement begins *If you are looking for an efficient... solution*; emphasizing the centers' efficiency. Choice (A) is not mentioned. Although international firms benefit, Choice (C) is incorrect because the locations are coast-to-coast, meaning in the United States. Choice (D), *congeniality*, meaning friendliness, is not mentioned.

180. (C) *Be sure to try everything on to ensure proper fit.* Choice (A) is incorrect because *once items have been laundered, (washed) they cannot be returned.* Choice (B) is incorrect because *items must be returned within 30 days.* Choice (D) is incorrect *there will be additional shipping charges for exchanges.*

181. (A) *All returns are the responsibility of the customer.* The notice also *states shipping rates... are not reimbursable*, meaning the company will not pay the customer back for the cost of shipping. Choices (B), (C), and (D) are contradicted by this information.

182. (D) *Protect yourself from loss by sending the package by insured mail.* Choice (A) is not mentioned. Choice (B) confuses *shipping rates* with *ship*. Choice (C) is only a way of paying for the shipment, not sending.

183. (D) *Shipping rates are for packing, insurance, and delivery costs.* Choice (D) *costs for alterations* is not mentioned.

184. (B) *Gold production is expected to rise*, meaning more gold will be mined. Choice (A) is incorrect because the price has decreased, not production. Choice (C) is the amount mined last year. Choice (D) is contradicted by the statement *Gold production is expected to rise... despite a sharp drop in world price.*

185. (C) The Bureau is *the government's forecasting and analytical agency*; meaning that it predicts production. Choices (A) and (B) are incorrect because the Bureau does not *commission mines* or *expand existing operations*; they predict rather that this is where *expected increases (in production) will come from*. Choice (D) is incorrect because they are not involved in mining but forecasting.

186. (A) *The decreasing cost of gold has prompted the industry to... restructure high-cost operations.* Choices (B) and (D) are not supported by the text. Choice (C) confuses the *decreasing cost of gold* to *the number of mines (that) has been decreasing.*

187. (D) *IRA is pleased to announce the opening of our newest branch.* Choice (A) is not mentioned. IRA is a recruitment company, placing candidates with companies; they are not recruiting Mr. Seo [(Choice (B)] but rather wish to inform him of their services. Choice (C) is not mentioned.

188. (B) *IRA is located in eight countries.* Choice (A) confuses two branches with the two examples (The United States and Germany) given. Choice (C) is not mentioned. Choice (D) confuses the number of branches with *thousands of potential applicants.*

189. (D) *Companies... turn to us to find the best candidate for openings in the fields of software development.* Choices (A), (B), and (C) are not mentioned.

190. (C) Tony Tan tells Mr. Seo *please contact me by phone, or fax.* Choices (A), (B), and (D) are contradicted by this.

191. (A) The advertisement begins *If you have a puppy for sale*; presumably kittens could be advertised as well. Although refrigerators are mentioned, fruits and vegetables [(Choice (B)], are not and may be confused with the name *Market Basket*. Choice (C) is not mentioned. Choice (D) is mentioned only as a form of payment, not as something being advertised.

192. (C) *All classifieds must be prepaid unless you are a monthly account customer.* Choice (A) is contradicted by *we have a limited number of available sections*. Choice (B) is contradicted by *call Monday, Tuesday, or Wednesday*. Choice (D) is contradicted by *the Northeast's largest newspaper*.

193. (D) *48 hours of private instruction per week (six days)* equals 8 hours of instruction per day. Choices (A) and (B) confuse the duration of the program with the hours of instruction. Choice (C) confuses the number of days with the number of hours of instruction.

194. (B) *Package price includes: Hotel, lunch, and all materials.* Choice (A) is contradicted by the fact that the fee includes a hotel. Choice (C) is not mentioned. Choice (D) is contradicted by the mention of only *lunch* as being included in the price.

195. (B) *Imagine having to fasten documents with rust-prone steel pins* which is what people had to do before the invention of paper clips. Choices (A), (C), and (D) are not mentioned.

196. (D) Johan Vaaler *put together a few clip designs.* Choice (A) is contradicted by the fact that when Vaaler patented his design *a few other paper-clip patents were on the market.* Choices (B) and (C) are not mentioned.

197. (C) *Nobody's quite sure who came up with the first paper clip* and *many people thought of it at once*. Choice (A) is contradicted by *it looks similar to the now standard design*. Choice (B) is contradicted by the fact that the paper clip was patented *in 1899*, the nineteenth century. Choice (D) is not mentioned and cannot be inferred.

198. (B) The *dinner will be held in the museum's cafeteria*. Choices (A), (C), and (D) are contradicted by The *dinner will be held in the museum's cafeteria*.

199. (D) *All donors who have contributed $1,000 or more this year will be mailed two complimentary tickets*. Choice (A) is not mentioned. Choices (B) and (C) are incorrect because the dinner is *the annual donor appreciation dinner* even though *the governor and local celebrities will be attending*.

200. (A) The *dinner* begins at 7:30 and the *video presentation* begins at 8:30, making the dinner an hour. This fact contradicts Choices (B), (C), and (D).

TEST
two

TEST OF ENGLISH FOR INTERNATIONAL COMMUNICATION

General Directions

This is a test of your ability to use the English language. The total time for the test is approximately two and a half hours. It is divided into seven parts. Each part of the test begins with a set of specific directions. Be sure you understand what you are to do before you begin to work on a part.

You will find that some of the questions are harder than others, but you should try to answer every one. There is no penalty for guessing. Do not be concerned if you cannot answer all of the questions.

Do not mark your answers in this test book. **You must put all of your answers on the separate answer sheet** that you have been given. When putting your answer to a question on your answer sheet, be sure to fill in the answer space corresponding to the letter of your choice. Fill in the space so that the letter inside the oval cannot be seen, as shown in the example below.

EXAMPLE

Mr. Palmer _____ with the president last month.
(A) meet
(B) meeting
(C) met
(D) to meet

Sample Answer: (A)   (B)   ●   (D)

The sentence should read, "Mr. Palmer met with the president last month." Therefore, you should choose answer (C). Notice how this has been done in the example given.

Mark only **ONE** answer for each question. If you change your mind about an answer after you have marked it on your answer sheet, completely erase your old answer and then mark your new answer. You must mark the answer sheet carefully so that your score can be recorded accurately.

LISTENING COMPREHENSION

In this section of the test, you will have the chance to show how well you understand spoken English. There are four parts to this section, with special directions for each part.

Directions

For each question, you will see a picture in your test book and you will hear four short statements. The statements will be spoken just one time. They will not be written in your test book; therefore, you must listen carefully in order to understand what the speaker says.

When you hear the four statements, look at the picture in your test book and choose the statement that best describes what you see in the picture. Then, on your answer sheet, find the number of the question and mark your answer. Look at the sample picture.

EXAMPLE

Now listen to the four statements.

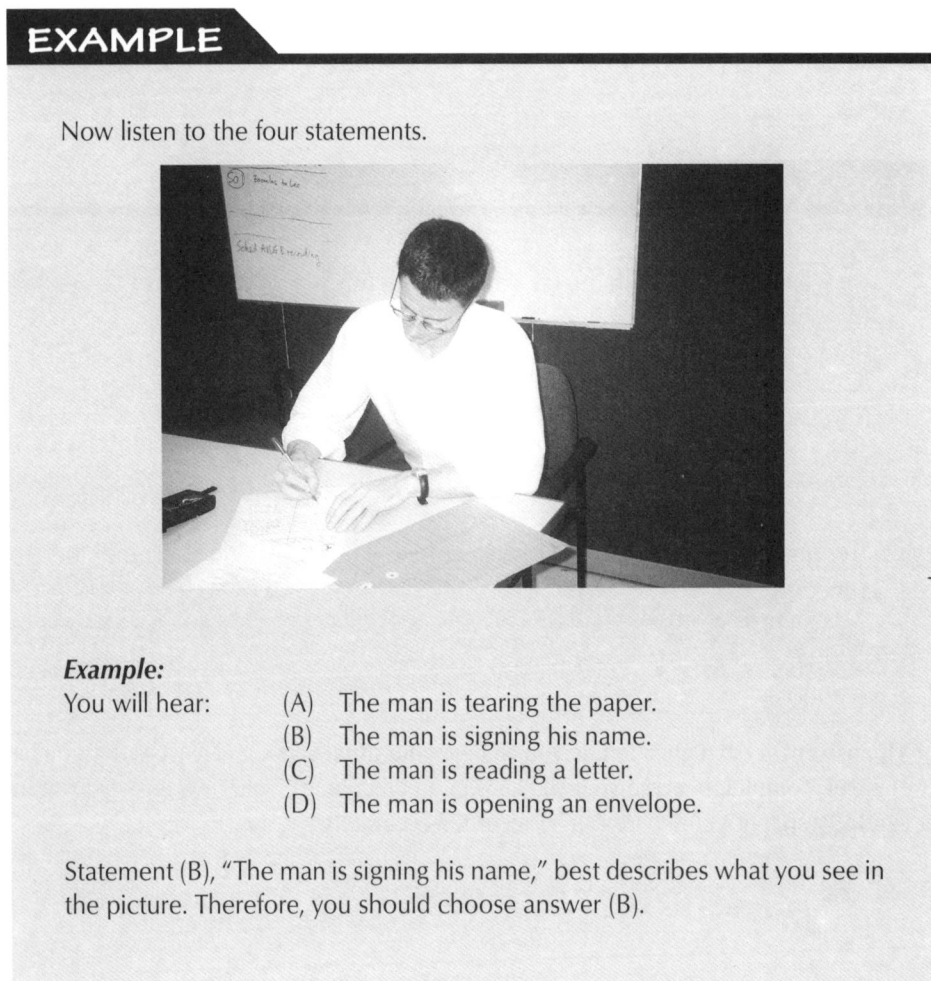

Example:
You will hear: (A) The man is tearing the paper.
 (B) The man is signing his name.
 (C) The man is reading a letter.
 (D) The man is opening an envelope.

Statement (B), "The man is signing his name," best describes what you see in the picture. Therefore, you should choose answer (B).

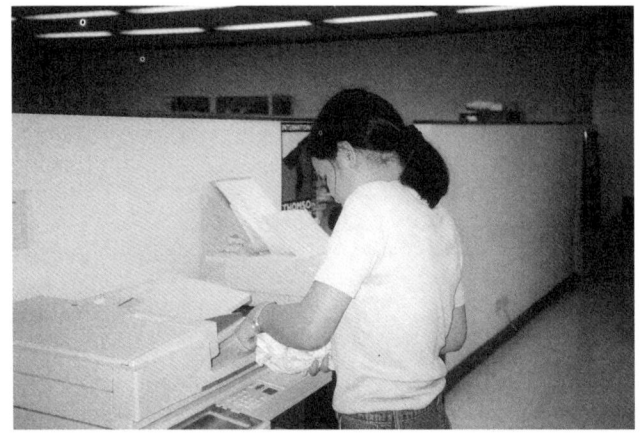

GO ON TO THE NEXT PAGE

9

10

11

12

13

14

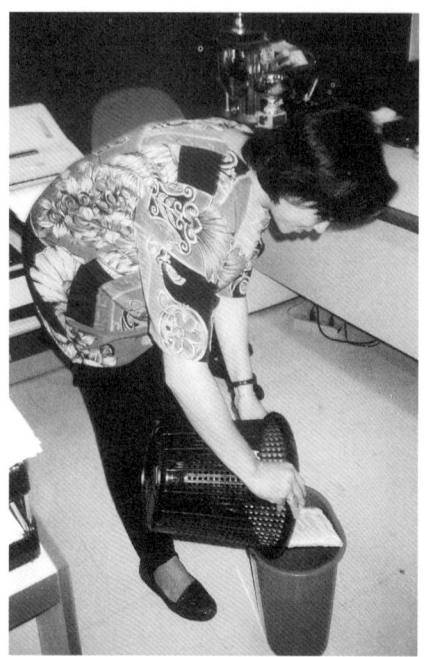

Part ii

Directions

In this part of the test, you will hear a question spoken in English, followed by three responses, also spoken in English. The question and the responses will be spoken just one time. They will not be written out for you; therefore, you must listen carefully to understand. You are to choose the best response to each question.

EXAMPLE

Now listen to a sample question.

You will hear: Good morning, John. How are you?

You will also hear: (A) I am fine, thank you.
 (B) I am in the living room.
 (C) My name is John.

The best response to the question "How are you?" is choice (A), "I am fine, thank you." Therefore, you should choose answer (A).

21. Mark your answer on your answer sheet.
22. Mark your answer on your answer sheet.
23. Mark your answer on your answer sheet.
24. Mark your answer on your answer sheet.
25. Mark your answer on your answer sheet.
26. Mark your answer on your answer sheet.
27. Mark your answer on your answer sheet.
28. Mark your answer on your answer sheet.
29. Mark your answer on your answer sheet.
30. Mark your answer on your answer sheet.
31. Mark your answer on your answer sheet.
32. Mark your answer on your answer sheet.
33. Mark your answer on your answer sheet.
34. Mark your answer on your answer sheet.
35. Mark your answer on your answer sheet.
36. Mark your answer on your answer sheet.
37. Mark your answer on your answer sheet.
38. Mark your answer on your answer sheet.
39. Mark your answer on your answer sheet.
40. Mark your answer on your answer sheet.
41. Mark your answer on your answer sheet.
42. Mark your answer on your answer sheet.
43. Mark your answer on your answer sheet.
44. Mark your answer on your answer sheet.
45. Mark your answer on your answer sheet.
46. Mark your answer on your answer sheet.
47. Mark your answer on your answer sheet.
48. Mark your answer on your answer sheet.
49. Mark your answer on your answer sheet.
50. Mark your answer on your answer sheet.

Directions

In this part of the test, you will hear short conversations between two people. The conversations will not be written in your test book. You will hear the conversations only once; therefore, you must listen carefully.

In your test book, you will read a short question about each conversation. The question will be followed by four short answers. You are to choose the best answer to each question and mark it on your answer sheet.

51. What does the man say?
    (A) The meeting was canceled.
    (B) He has a lot of work to do.
    (C) The meeting was supposed to start at ten.
    (D) He will check with the secretary.

52. Where are they?
    (A) In an office
    (B) In a clothing store
    (C) At a travel agency
    (D) At a bank

53. What is said about Susan?
    (A) She worked all alone.
    (B) She is the new office manager.
    (C) She was fired.
    (D) She submitted purchase orders.

54. Where does this conversation take place?
    (A) At a restaurant
    (B) At a supermarket
    (C) On a boat
    (D) On the telephone

55. When did Mr. Kennedy's accident happen?
    (A) While he was horseback riding
    (B) While he was working
    (C) While he was walking his dog
    (D) While he was on a trip

56. Where are the papers now?
    (A) With John
    (B) With Ms. Wilson
    (C) With the negotiators
    (D) With a delivery service

57. How are people in the export department currently paid?
    (A) According to merit
    (B) On a straight salary
    (C) By commission
    (D) By salary plus commission

58. What are they discussing?
    (A) A funny joke
    (B) Where to vacation
    (C) Which airlines to fly
    (D) Expiring frequent-flyer miles

59. When are concert tickets cheaper?
    (A) Wednesday afternoon
    (B) Friday evening
    (C) Saturday afternoon
    (D) Sunday evening

60. How will the budget be trimmed?
    (A) By not hiring temporary workers
    (B) By decreasing sales
    (C) By having employees take the same vacation weeks
    (D) By laying off workers

GO ON TO THE NEXT PAGE

61. What are they going to do?
(A) Play nine holes of golf
(B) Visit a new store
(C) Practice their putting outdoors
(D) Enjoy the springtime weather

62. Why is the Learning Store out of dinosaur toys?
(A) They forgot to order them.
(B) They already sold ten thousand.
(C) The manufacturer didn't make enough.
(D) The delivery service is on strike.

63. What are they discussing?
(A) What time it is
(B) A telephone number
(C) A bus stop
(D) How to get someplace

64. Why hasn't the woman gotten a flu shot yet?
(A) She does not know the clinic's address.
(B) She has not had a free evening.
(C) She is not at high risk.
(D) She did not know how much it costs.

65. Where does the conversation take place?
(A) At a repair shop
(B) On the stairs
(C) At a gym
(D) In an elevator

66. What is the woman's problem?
(A) She wants a different computer.
(B) Her room is too small.
(C) She has to change floors.
(D) She needs a larger desk.

67. What will they probably do?
(A) Go to Market Street
(B) Investigate billboard costs
(C) Redo the budget
(D) Hire new designers

68. Who is responsible for the delay?
(A) The designers
(B) The contractors
(C) The building commissioner
(D) The traffic engineer

69. What do they want to do?
(A) Wait in line
(B) Take their bags
(C) Go to lunch
(D) Attend the convention

70. What are they discussing?
(A) Meal allotments
(B) Travel arrangements
(C) Expense reimbursements
(D) Check cashing

71. What do we learn?
(A) The woman doesn't have children.
(B) The woman dislikes amusement parks.
(C) Children have never attended company picnics.
(D) The annual picnic is always at the same site.

72. Why can't he get the *Tribune*?
(A) That newsstand does not sell it.
(B) It is sold out.
(C) The weekend edition has not arrived.
(D) It is not very popular.

73. What will the company pay for?
(A) Fifty percent of the initiation fee
(B) All charges
(C) Half the initiation fee and all monthly costs
(D) A portion of the monthly cost

74. What does the man offer?
    (A) To do her mother's shopping
    (B) To take her to the hospital
    (C) To drive her home
    (D) To pick up her car

75. Which color had the man wanted his office to be painted?
    (A) Green
    (B) White
    (C) Yellow
    (D) Apricot

76. Why is the woman probably not going to refinance her condominium now?
    (A) She is moving to Australia.
    (B) She is not sure how long she'll be living in it.
    (C) She is waiting for the rates to go down.
    (D) She will do it in four years.

77. What kind of book is the woman looking for?
    (A) One that is easy to carry
    (B) One that will make her cry
    (C) One that has imaginary characters
    (D) One that is not too serious

78. What are they discussing?
    (A) How to get refunds
    (B) A humorous sales clerk
    (C) Decreases in computer prices
    (D) Where to shop for electronic products

79. What does the woman ask the man?
    (A) Whether she should apply for a different job
    (B) Whether she should speak to the personnel director
    (C) Whether she should advertise the position
    (D) Whether she should wait three weeks

80. What did the woman say?
    (A) She had her interview already.
    (B) She spent two hours with the consultant.
    (C) She gave the consultant lots of suggestions.
    (D) She hopes the consultant will institute changes.

GO ON TO THE NEXT PAGE

Directions

In this part of the test, you will hear several short talks. Each will be spoken just one time. They will not be written out for you; therefore, you will have to listen carefully in order to understand and remember what is said.

In your test book, you will read two or more questions about each short talk. The questions will be followed by four answers. You are to choose the best answer to each question and mark it on your answer sheet.

81. What is the smart card?
    (A) A word processor
    (B) A computerized card
    (C) A big credit card
    (D) A travel agent

82. What transforms the smart card?
    (A) The touch of a hand
    (B) The plastic rectangle
    (C) A mini-computer
    (D) A micro-processor

83. Which of the following can the smart card hold?
    (A) Travel directions
    (B) Package routing
    (C) Hotel reservations
    (D) Electric gadgets

84. Who asked that the vacation policy be examined?
    (A) Some workers
    (B) Part-time employees
    (C) Policy makers
    (D) Bonnie Carter

85. How many weeks of vacation can an employee who has worked for six years take?
    (A) 1
    (B) 2
    (C) 3
    (D) 4

86. What is true about the current policy?
    (A) There is a request policy for vacation weeks.
    (B) A newly hired worker has no vacation time.
    (C) Two weeks of vacation can be taken together.
    (D) Workers can take unpaid vacation time.

87. Until when will Quebec be an official disaster area?
    (A) Tuesday
    (B) Wednesday
    (C) Friday
    (D) Saturday

88. What information is included in the bulletin?
    (A) The weather forecast for the week
    (B) Specific locations of shelters
    (C) Which vehicles are allowed on the roads
    (D) When electricity will be restored

89. What feature of the shelters is not mentioned?
    (A) The heat
    (B) The security
    (C) The crowdedness
    (D) The noise

TEST TWO

90. When will the railroad strike begin unless demands are met?
    (A) Monday
    (B) Tuesday
    (C) Wednesday
    (D) Thursday

91. Which of the following may be striking this week?
    (A) Ferry workers
    (B) Airline pilots
    (C) Bus drivers
    (D) Union organizers

92. What is the key word to describe this year's perfume collection?
    (A) Expense
    (B) Taste
    (C) Spice
    (D) Label

93. Where are the men's perfumes being sold?
    (A) At lumber mills
    (B) At supermarkets
    (C) In restaurants
    (D) At department stores

94. Which of the following was NOT mentioned as an ingredient in this year's perfumes for men?
    (A) Black pepper
    (B) Coffee
    (C) Nutmeg
    (D) Amber

95. Where is this announcement being made?
    (A) On a cruise ship
    (B) In the terminal
    (C) On an airplane
    (D) In an auditorium

96. Where is the emergency card found?
    (A) Near the emergency exit
    (B) In the attendant's pocket
    (C) Near the overhead compartment
    (D) In the seat pocket

97. What is the seatbelt recommendation?
    (A) Obey the lighted signs
    (B) Keep it fastened
    (C) Do what the attendant does
    (D) Undo the belt for comfort

98. Where does this talk take place?
    (A) At a meeting
    (B) In a university classroom
    (C) In Don Stevens' office
    (D) At a luncheon

99. What did Don Stevens do before he accepted his new position?
    (A) He developed software.
    (B) He was a university president.
    (C) He was a lecturer.
    (D) He sold computer systems.

100. What is the procedure for notifying Don of a problem?
    (A) Stop him in the hall
    (B) Call him on the phone
    (C) Send him an e-mail
    (D) Fill out a form

This is the end of the Listening Comprehension portion of the test. Turn to Part V in your test book.

GO ON TO THE NEXT PAGE

YOU WILL HAVE ONE HOUR AND FIFTEEN MINUTES TO COMPLETE PARTS V, VI, AND VII OF THE TEST.

READING

In this section of the test, you will have the chance to show how well you understand written English. There are three parts to this section, with special directions for each part.

Directions

This part of the test has incomplete sentences. Four words or phrases, marked (A), (B), (C), (D), are given beneath each sentence. You are to choose the **ONE** word or phrase that best completes the sentence. Then, on your answer sheet, find the number of the question and mark your answer.

EXAMPLE

Because the equipment is very delicate, it must be handled with _____ .
(A) caring
(B) careful
(C) care
(D) carefully

The sentence should read, "Because the equipment is very delicate, it must be handled with care." Therefore, you should choose answer (C).

Now begin work on the questions.

101. _____ I have notified everyone of tomorrow's presentation, I'm not sure who will attend.
 (A) Because
 (B) Either
 (C) Consequently
 (D) Although

102. _____ early retirement is becoming a popular option.
 (A) Doing
 (B) Making
 (C) Taking
 (D) Deciding

103. In most countries bicycles _____ automobiles.
 (A) enumerate
 (B) outnumber
 (C) innovate
 (D) denominate

104. Boston is one of the United States' _____ and most historic cities.
 (A) oldest
 (B) elderly
 (C) ancient
 (D) older

76 TEST TWO

105. Mr. Sasaki is now in charge of _____ control.
    (A) invasion
    (B) invention
    (C) inventory
    (D) investigation

106. The travel industry has been at the _____ of technology for a long time.
    (A) forecast
    (B) foregone
    (C) forerunner
    (D) forefront

107. The tables list the most actively traded stocks based _____ daily volume.
    (A) on
    (B) by
    (C) at
    (D) in

108. Thanks to a last-minute shopping _____, retailers posted their best December sales in five years.
    (A) toss
    (B) surge
    (C) currency
    (D) battery

109. The company _____ by a nationally-known research firm.
    (A) the surveyed market had
    (B) had the surveyed market
    (C) had the market surveyed
    (D) the market had surveyed

110. The secretary complained of feeling _____ working by herself.
    (A) only
    (B) loner
    (C) exclusively
    (D) lonely

111. More and more doctors are finding that natural treatments relieve pain _____ drugs, but without the serious occasional side effects.
    (A) as well as
    (B) better
    (C) quickly than
    (D) as good as

112. The seminar was held in such a warm room that many of the participants _____.
    (A) fell sleepy
    (B) dozed off
    (C) dropped off
    (D) slept it off

113. Applicants are _____ interviewed over the phone before coming to the office.
    (A) ever
    (B) usual
    (C) often
    (D) uncommonly

114. Catalogue shopping represents an _____ percentage of retail sales.
    (A) increase
    (B) increasingly
    (C) increaser
    (D) increasing

115. Trainees meet with Dr. Park every Friday to discuss _____ adjustment.
    (A) its
    (B) our
    (C) him
    (D) their

116. People who have money in a checking account can _____ bills simply by writing a check.
    (A) to pay
    (B) pay
    (C) paid
    (D) be paid

GO ON TO THE NEXT PAGE

117. The true _____ of the new products will be measured by their popularity among teenagers.
(A) test
(B) examination
(C) hypothesis
(D) score

118. _____ times, the accounting firm has hired temporary workers to keep up with the additional workload.
(A) In
(B) Over
(C) At
(D) Through

119. Mr. Shafrir patiently spells his name for his clients who frequently _____ it.
(A) misdemeanor
(B) misdirect
(C) misapply
(D) mispronounce

120. The Consumer Price Index is a _____ economic indicator.
(A) lead
(B) leading
(C) leaded
(D) leader

121. The items you purchased are on back _____ and should be shipped by the end of the month.
(A) supply
(B) burner
(C) order
(D) refill

122. The downtown bed and breakfast agency has _____.
(A) a two-night minimum reservation policy
(B) a policy two-night minimum reservation
(C) a reservation two-night policy minimum
(D) a minimum policy two-night reservation

123. Due to increasing numbers of women working outside the home, the demand for daycare _____.
(A) that they rise
(B) that rise
(C) is risen
(D) has risen

124. The blue parking permits are no longer _____.
(A) just
(B) valid
(C) correct
(D) convincing

125. We prefer to hire a candidate with a degree in the field, but work experience may be _____.
(A) justified
(B) replaced
(C) substituted
(D) succeeded

126. Neither this year's software version _____ last year's is compatible with the five-year-old computer.
(A) and
(B) not
(C) or
(D) nor

127. Mr. Sow's office is _____ the copy machine on the tenth floor.
(A) beside
(B) under
(C) against
(D) beneath

128. _____ jobless rates inching up last month, the lowest unemployment figures in forty years were recorded this year.
(A) Even though
(B) Despite
(C) But
(D) However

129. Paper money and coins were originally used as the only _____ of exchange.
    (A) technique
    (B) position
    (C) medium
    (D) amount

130. The national phone company announced that its plan to _____ rates on long-distance calls is too expensive.
    (A) slant
    (B) slit
    (C) sweep
    (D) slash

131. Members of the design team were not surprised that Ms. Sanchez created the company logo by _____.
    (A) itself
    (B) herself
    (C) themselves
    (D) oneself

132. Complaints can provide rich _____ that can help an organization improve its operation.
    (A) feedback
    (B) return
    (C) appraisal
    (D) calculation

133. Calls will be answered in the _____ in which they were received.
    (A) sequencing
    (B) line
    (C) order
    (D) direction

134. A good deal of your accountant's time can be saved by preparing information _____.
    (A) advanced
    (B) forward
    (C) formerly
    (D) beforehand

135. In today's high-tech office, designers strive to create a space where workers have a _____ privacy.
    (A) sense
    (B) sense to
    (C) sense of
    (D) sensed

136. Reducing stress in the workplace takes committed management and possibly _____ investment.
    (A) finance
    (B) financial
    (C) financing
    (D) finances

137. _____ airline companies require twenty-four hour advance notice for a special meal request.
    (A) Most
    (B) Almost
    (C) Most of
    (D) Mostly

138. All recruits for international assignments _____ a background check.
    (A) underrate
    (B) undercover
    (C) undergo
    (D) understudy

139. The payroll manager, to _____ the letter was addressed, forwarded the inquiry to the vice president.
    (A) where
    (B) which
    (C) him
    (D) whom

140. Businesses that show either a history of growth or growth potential _____ investors.
    (A) appeal
    (B) attract
    (C) adhere
    (D) attribute

GO ON TO THE NEXT PAGE

Directions

In this part of the test, each sentence has four words or phrases underlined. The four underlined parts of the sentence are marked (A), (B), (C), (D). You are to identify the **ONE** underlined word or phrase that should be corrected or rewritten. Then, on your answer sheet, find the number of the question and mark your answer.

EXAMPLE

All <u>employee</u> are required <u>to wear</u> their <u>identification</u> badges <u>while</u> at work.
    A   B   C   D

Choice (A), the underlined word "employee," is not correct in this sentence. The sentence should read, "All employees are required to wear their identification badges while at work." Therefore, you should choose answer (A).

Now begin work on the questions.

141. The interest <u>paid</u> on bonds <u>depend</u> <u>on</u> the
                      A   B   C
<u>amount</u> of risk assumed by the buyer.
  D

142. Nineteen states <u>they</u> have <u>only</u> one telephone
                     A   B
area code <u>for</u> the <u>entire</u> state.
          C   D

143. <u>The company</u> added <u>her</u> food production line
      A   B
<u>approximately</u> five <u>years ago</u>.
    C   D

144. All employees <u>must sign</u> up for <u>one of the</u>
               A   B
e-mail information sessions, but <u>an</u> additional
                            C
session may be <u>add</u>.
       D

145. <u>Scheduled</u> interviews <u>will take place</u> <u>at</u> nine
     A   B   C
to five in the recently <u>renovated</u> Chamber of
                      D
Commerce building.

146. It is <u>no</u> <u>longer</u> necessary to <u>take</u> a reservation
      A B   C
on the <u>hourly</u> New York-Washington, D.C.
      D
express train.

147. An <u>additional</u> vacation week will be available
      A
to <u>most of</u> workers <u>due to</u> the plant <u>closure</u>.
    B   C   D

148. Each country sets <u>its</u> own policy on
                  A
<u>whether or not</u> dual <u>citizenship</u> is <u>permitting</u>.
    B   C   D

149. As a matter of courtesy, it <u>best</u> to carry
                                 A
    business cards <u>printed</u> <u>both</u> in English and in
                      B   C
    the language of the country <u>being visited</u>.
                                       D

150. <u>During</u> a power <u>failure</u>, batteries provide an
        A   B
    <u>emergency</u> supply of electricity for telephones,
        C
    hospitals, and <u>others</u> essential buildings.
                       D

151. The annual meeting of the <u>stockholders</u> this
                                   A
    June will be a <u>two-days</u> program <u>dealing</u>
                      B   C
    solely with the takeover <u>proposal</u>.
                                  D

152. <u>The newest</u> real estate firm in town is using
        A
    <u>coloring</u> refrigerator magnets <u>displaying</u> the
        B   C
    company logo as a <u>marketing</u> tool.
                          D

153. Customers <u>were delighted</u> to learn that there
                    A
    is an <u>additional</u> ten percent discount <u>on top</u>
              B   C
    the twenty percent <u>end-of-season</u> markdown.
                            D

154. Fruit <u>and</u> vegetable prices <u>hardly rarely</u>
              A   B
    <u>fall</u> in winter months <u>in contrast to</u> summer
        C   D
    months.

155. Jen Ostroff <u>appointed</u> vice president for
                     A
    <u>corporate</u> <u>communications</u> effective
        B   C
    <u>immediately</u>.
        D

156. <u>More and more companies</u> are offering
            A
    employees a cafeteria plan of benefits,
    <u>providing</u> <u>a variety of</u> <u>optional</u>.
        B   C   D

157. Please submit <u>in writing</u> any requests for
                       A
    <u>additional</u> computer <u>equipments</u> to
        B   C
    Ms. Takahashi <u>before the end</u> of the week.
                       D

158. <u>Not</u> surprisingly, <u>no</u> two business firms
        A   B
    <u>operate</u> <u>with</u> exactly the same manner.
        C   D

159. Brussels, Belgium's <u>fifth largest</u> city, is
                              A
    <u>the center of</u> the country's banking, <u>insuring</u>,
        B   C
    and transportation <u>industries</u>.
                            D

160. The governments of Australia, Canada, and
    New Zealand <u>provide</u> <u>great</u> <u>finance</u> support
                    A   B   C
    for the <u>study of</u> ballet.
                D

Directions

The questions in this part of the test are based on a variety of reading material, such as notices, letters, newspaper and magazine articles, and advertisements. You are to choose the **ONE** best answer, (A), (B), (C), or (D), to each question. Then, on your answer sheet, find the number of the question and mark your answer. Answer all questions following a passage on the basis of what is **stated** or **implied** in that passage.

EXAMPLE

Read the following example.

> The Museum of Technology is designed for people to experience science at work. Visitors are encouraged to use, test, and handle the objects on display. Special demonstrations are scheduled for the first and second Wednesdays of each month at 1:30 p.m. Open Tuesday-Friday, 2:30-4:30 p.m., Saturday 11:00 a.m. -4:30 p.m., and Sunday 1:00-4:30 p.m.

When during the month can visitors see special demonstrations?
(A) Every weekend
(B) The first two Wednesdays
(C) One afternoon a week
(D) Every other Wednesday

The passage says that the demonstrations are scheduled on the first and second Wednesdays of the month. Therefore, you should choose answer (B).

Now begin work on the questions.

Questions 161-163 refer to the following announcement.

A visit to Boston wouldn't be complete without a stop at Copley Place, the city's newest and most elegant shopping center.
Easily accessible by the city's subway, there is also an underground parking garage.
The mall includes two floors of shopping, featuring the most exclusive retail shops in the country.
On the first floor is a ten-screen movie theater.
After a movie or shopping, stop at one of the eight restaurants located on
the mall's second floor food court.

The mall is open Monday through Saturday from 9 A.M. to 10 P.M. and Sundays from noon to 6 P.M.

161. What is Copley Place?
 (A) A mall
 (B) A subway stop
 (C) A supermarket
 (D) A movie rental store

162. How many movies are showing at one time?
 (A) 6
 (B) 8
 (C) 9
 (D) 10

163. On which day does Copley Place close early?
 (A) Monday
 (B) Wednesday
 (C) Saturday
 (D) Sunday

Questions 164-167 refer to the following advertisement.

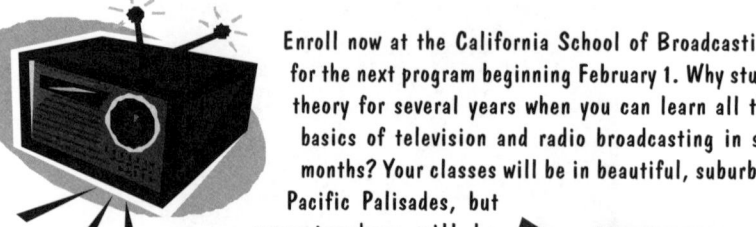

164. What is the California School of Broadcasting?
    (A) A television station
    (B) A movie studio
    (C) A training site
    (D) A theoretical institute

165. How long is the program?
    (A) One month
    (B) Five months
    (C) Six months
    (D) Several years

166. What would students like to work as?
    (A) Actors and actresses
    (B) Astrologers
    (C) Broadcast announcers
    (D) Cinematographers

167. What feature of the program is NOT discussed?
    (A) The length
    (B) The cost
    (C) The location
    (D) The facilities

Questions 168-170 are based on the following document.

CREDIT CARD INFORMATION

Payments

Your monthly statement is payable in full upon receipt. The mailing address for payments is shown to the right. Using the enclosed envelope, mail the bottom portion of the first page of this statement with your check drawn on a bank located in the U.S. Do not send cash. Payments received after 12:00 noon or on weekends or holidays may not be credited until the next business day. Please do not send post-dated checks.

Lost or Stolen Cards

If your card is lost or stolen in the United States, call us immediately at 1-800-928-4657. Outside the U.S., contact our nearest office or call us collect. You are fully protected against any fraudulent use of the card when you notify us immediately. Your maximum liability is $50 should you fail to report loss or theft.

168. What is printed to the right?
 (A) A telephone number
 (B) An address
 (C) The credit card number
 (D) Locations abroad

169. Which payment will be credited on the same business day?
 (A) A payment made on the weekend
 (B) A payment made on a holiday
 (C) A payment made at 9:00 a.m.
 (D) A payment made at 3:00 p.m.

170. Why would someone be charged $50?
 (A) For failing to report a stolen card
 (B) For fraudulently using the card
 (C) For paying the bill late
 (D) For sending a post-dated check

Questions 171-172 refer to the following news item.

Working Women Inc., a leader in the retailing of classic apparel for business women, has announced a steep quarterly loss because of poor holiday and post-holiday sales. The London-based company said sales at stores open at least a year fell 10.9 percent for the five weeks ending January 3, largely because of a weak response to the semiannual holiday sale that began on December 26. **Working Women** and other apparel makers have experienced poor holiday sales due to shoppers buying electronics, jewelry, and basic items instead of clothes.

171. What is the company's product?
  (A) Basic furniture
  (B) Women's clothing
  (C) Electronics
  (D) Jewelry

172. Why is Working Women reporting a steep quarterly loss?
  (A) Most stores have been open less than a year.
  (B) The holiday sale began late this year.
  (C) Shoppers bought other products this season.
  (D) Their prices were too high.

Questions 173-174 refer to the following advertisement.

Why live in just a home, when you could have so much more?

Boca East is everything a great home in Boca Raton should be...and more! It is the lifestyle that you have always promised yourself. At Boca East, everything that makes Boca Raton wonderful is at your fingertips.

You'll live adjacent to the golf course and tennis courts at the world famous Boca Raton Resort and Club. You'll be nearby fine dining, shopping in downtown Boca, and the beautiful Atlantic Ocean.

There is a spectacular on-site work-out facility with aerobics, yoga, circuit training, and the latest fitness rage, spinning. There are also private areas for personal training services, which can be arranged through your concierge. There is almost nothing else like it at any price. See our two- and three-bedroom condominium models.

173. What is Boca East?
    (A) A resort and club
    (B) A dining facility
    (C) A condominium complex
    (D) An ocean-view high-rise

174. Which facility is on the grounds?
    (A) A golf course
    (B) A shopping center
    (C) Tennis courts
    (D) A health club

Questions 175-178 refer to the following notice.

**Mondays
Wednesdays
Fridays
and Saturdays are
WORLDMARKET days.**

The *Sun Star's* WORLDMARKET regularly features two pages of classified advertising for the following categories:

MONDAY	Recruitment, Education, Secretarial, Internet Services
WEDNESDAY	Business Opportunities, Franchises, Commercial Real Estate, Telecommunications, Automotive, Entertainment
FRIDAY	Holidays, Travel, Residential Real Estate, Dining Out
SATURDAY	Arts, Friendships, International Meeting Point, Nannies & Domestics

A great deal happens at WORLDMARKET, the world's best daily. Call, fax, or e-mail Sarah Perry at 44 171 439 9860.

---

175. What is the *Sun Star*?
(A) A telephone directory
(B) A shopper's guide
(C) A newspaper
(D) A market

176. On which day would one place an advertisement to sell a car?
(A) Monday
(B) Wednesday
(C) Friday
(D) Saturday

177. On which day would someone look to find an apartment?
(A) Monday
(B) Wednesday
(C) Friday
(D) Saturday

178. Which of the following is NOT mentioned as a way to contact WORLDMARKET?
(A) By telephone
(B) By e-mail
(C) By fax
(D) By letter

Questions 179-182 refer to the following announcement.

EXPORTING

Great potential exists for businesses in the United States to become more active in exporting. Only 15% of U.S. exporters account for 85% of the value of U.S.-manufactured exports. One-half of all exporters sell in only one foreign market. 20% of exporters (3% of U.S. companies) export to more than five foreign markets.

Competing effectively abroad allows companies to keep the edge they need at home. However, due to the real costs and risks associated with exporting, it is up to each company to weigh the necessary commitment against the potential benefits. Below you will find suggestions and names of agencies which can assist you.

Recommendations for successful exporting:

1. Select overseas distributors carefully.
2. Treat international distributors on an equal basis with their domestic counterparts.
3. Continue to pursue export business even when the U.S. market is healthy.
4. Obtain qualified export counseling and develop a master plan before starting an export business.
5. Do not assume that a marketing technique that works in Japan will be equally successful in France or Portugal.
6. Be willing to adapt products to meet regulations and cultural preferences of other countries.
7. Print service, sale, and warranty messages in local languages.

179. What percentage of U.S. companies sell to more than five markets abroad?
  (A) 3%
  (B) 15%
  (C) 20%
  (D) 85%

180. What does the announcement suggest companies do when the U.S. market is doing well?
  (A) Concentrate on the U.S. market
  (B) Fire the export manager
  (C) Learn Japanese and Portuguese
  (D) Continue to export

181. What should potential exporters do with respect to their product?
  (A) Sell only to one distributor
  (B) Change products to meet local standards
  (C) Export to France
  (D) Select an American distributor

182. What probably follows the recommendations?
  (A) Names of successful exporters
  (B) Addresses of distributors
  (C) Locations of export counselors
  (D) A list of agencies

GO ON TO THE NEXT PAGE

Questions 183-184 are based on the following article.

Biolife Inc. of Oslo announced yesterday that it has started the process of finding a successor to Robert Sable, the company's president and chief executive. For a long time it has been Sable's desire to retire at 62, which is two years away. Once Sable turned 60 this past November, the organization began to plan for his successor. The search for a replacement could take up to two years. The vitamin company has begun a worldwide search but is focusing its recruitment efforts in Europe and Asia.

183. When will Robert Sable retire?
 (A) At 60
 (B) At 61
 (C) At 62
 (D) At 64

184. What does Biolife Inc. sell?
 (A) retirement advice
 (B) vitamins
 (C) recruitment services
 (D) biotechnology

Questions 185-187 are based on the following advertisement.

Recruitment

ADMINISTRATOR

Small, expanding law firm is seeking an administrator to work closely with one partner to manage and enlarge the five-lawyer firm. Responsibilities include accounting and budgeting.

The ideal candidate will have had experience in business planning. Legal experience not required. Please send salary requirements, a resume, and two letters of recommendation to:

Managing Partner
The Law Office of Linda Jason
Fisherman's Wharf, Bay 219
San Francisco, California, USA

---

185. What is the firm seeking?
(A) A secretary
(B) A lawyer
(C) A manager
(D) A billing clerk

186. What is true about the firm?
(A) It is growing.
(B) Its clients are fishermen.
(C) Linda Jason is its only lawyer.
(D) It is a large firm.

187. Which of the following is NOT required to be sent?
(A) Salary requirements
(B) Letters of recommendation
(C) A resume
(D) A cover letter

Questions 188-190 refer to the following news article.

YOUR BUSINESS NAME CAN BE ONE OF YOUR MOST EFFECTIVE AND LEAST EXPENSIVE MARKETING TOOLS.

Too often, however, we choose a name without giving thought to its marketing value. Some people opt for using their own names; others may create a clever but obscure name, or one that has sentimental value. As a result, the names might end up costing them business, instead of attracting it. A common mistake in choosing a name is selecting a misleading name; for example, calling a firm "Writing Services" while it actually produces medical equipment. Another mistake is choosing a name that is hard to spell or pronounce. It is also a mistake to select a name that is too general, such as ABC Company. Your main goal should be to choose a name which your customers can easily remember whenever they want your product or service.

188. According to the article, what can be an inexpensive marketing tool for a company?
 (A) Its service
 (B) Its location
 (C) Its logo
 (D) Its name

189. What is wrong with calling a firm that repairs cars "Kind Kar Kare"?
 (A) It is not creative.
 (B) It is hard to spell.
 (C) It is misleading.
 (D) It is too sentimental.

190. What makes a good choice?
 (A) Easy pronunciation
 (B) Inventive spelling
 (C) Overgeneralizing
 (D) Obscurity

Questions 191-193 refer to the following report.

SICK BUILDING SYNDROME

As more and more workers moved from manufacturing to white collar jobs in this century, it was believed they would toil in a vastly healthier work environment. While work conditions have improved in many ways, the modern office is not without problems. Climate-controlled office buildings, once seen as the ultimate symbol of urban modernity, have not been the trouble-free environment their proponents had anticipated. The first reports of "sick buildings," which cause some of their inhabitants to become ill, were greeted with disbelief. As more building owners have been forced to undertake expensive repairs, and as more workers have reported headaches, shortness of breath and dizziness, there has been wider recognition that contaminated buildings can pose serious health threats.

191. Why was it believed that the workplace would be healthier for workers?
(A) Because of better lighting
(B) Because of a shift to office jobs
(C) Because of modern buildings
(D) Because of air conditioning

192. What was the initial reaction to workers who got sick from their buildings?
(A) Employers sent them to doctors.
(B) Workers were told to take time off.
(C) Building owners were forced to renovate.
(D) People didn't believe them.

193. Which of the following is NOT an example of worker complaints?
(A) Shortness of breath
(B) Vomiting
(C) Headaches
(D) Dizziness

GO ON TO THE NEXT PAGE

Questions 194-196 refer to the following memo.

To: All Employees
From: Geoffrey Stevens, Vice President
Re: Illegal Software Copying

It has come to the attention of management that many employees are illegally making software diskettes of copyrighted material for personal use. As everyone should be aware, company policy forbids the duplication of commercial software. This practice not only deprives authors of royalties but also is against the law. According to one of our employees, Michael Lane, the author of a widely-used accounting program, four pirated versions are made for every one of his programs sold.

We are very serious in our commitment to eradicating piracy. Although other companies tolerate this illegal practice, we have decided that any employee who copies software will be immediately disciplined. A hearing will be held to determine whether or not to terminate employment.

194. Who is Michael Lane?
 (A) A software programmer
 (B) The vice president
 (C) The company accountant
 (D) A law enforcement official

195. For every 28 pirated versions of the accounting program, how many legitimate packages are sold?
 (A) 4
 (B) 7
 (C) 28
 (D) 112

196. What will happen to an employee who pirates software?
 (A) He will lose his job.
 (B) He will pay royalties.
 (C) He will be arrested.
 (D) He will be disciplined.

Questions 197-198 refer to the following report.

In the not-too-distant future, instead of spending a vacation by the sea, we may be able to relax in the ocean itself. Once there, we will routinely enter private underwater crafts and zoom off to take a close-up look at the sea's mysteries. A new creation, called a Deep Rover, is an acrylic, egg-shaped, underwater craft that is made in one- or two-person models. It can dive to more than half a mile beneath the surface of the sea. One can learn to operate the small sub in just a few hours. No special underwater suit is required. The vessel comes equipped with sensitive robotic arms that enable passengers to interact with the sea's environment. However, at a price of $600,000 they will probably be out of reach for most people.

197. Which of the following is NOT true about the Deep Rover?
    (A) Passengers can interact with the sea.
    (B) A special diving suit is required.
    (C) Its operation can be mastered in a few hours.
    (D) It is constructed of man-made materials.

198. Where did this report probably appear?
    (A) In a science fiction journal
    (B) In a movie scenario
    (C) In a magazine
    (D) In a medical journal

Questions 199-200 refer to the following article.

Movies have a short history in comparison to other art forms, such as music or painting. Movies originated in the late 1800s. By the early 1900s, filmmakers had developed specialized techniques and artistic theories. However, movies generated little scholarly attention until the 1960s. Today the motion picture is recognized as a principal art form. There are thousands of books about film, many universities and colleges offer individual film courses as well as advanced degrees in various aspects of filmmaking.

199. When did the making of motion pictures begin?
(A) In the late eighteenth century
(B) In the late 1800s
(C) In the early 1900s
(D) In the 1960s

200. Which of the following was NOT mentioned as an indication that film is a major art form?
(A) Thousands of film books are in print.
(B) Degrees are awarded to film students.
(C) Many colleges and universities offer film courses.
(D) Scholarly attention has focused on film throughout the century.

TAPESCRIPT

Sample Item
M: (A) The man is tearing the paper.
    (B) The man is signing his name.
    (C) The man is reading a letter.
    (D) The man is opening an envelope.

1. M2: (A) The man is taking something out of his bag.
    (B) The man is trying to find something on the computer.
    (C) The man is putting the backpack on the desk.
    (D) The man is cleaning out his locker.

2. M1: (A) The swimmer is diving into the water.
    (B) The swimming pool is empty.
    (C) The pool is being drained.
    (D) A person is swimming alongside the lane marker.

3. W: (A) The pie is being served to the guests.
    (B) The man is slicing the pie.
    (C) The baker is taking the pie from the oven.
    (D) The man is copying down a recipe for pie.

4. M2: (A) The woman is delivering the copies for inspection.
    (B) People are waiting in line to make copies.
    (C) The woman is cleaning the copy machine.
    (D) The copies the woman made are not clear.

5. M1: (A) The man has let his answering machine take the call.
    (B) The man's feet have become tangled in the phone cord.
    (C) The man is clearing his desk of papers.
    (D) The man has his feet on the desk while he talks.

6. W: (A) The man is shouting to the cyclist as he goes by.
    (B) The men are competing in a race on their bicycles.
    (C) The man is firing a shot to start the race.
    (D) The man is helping the cyclist on with his helmet.

7. M1: (A) The woman's pencils are scattered all around the top of the desk.
    (B) The artist is examining her photographs.
    (C) The woman is drawing a picture on her sketch pad.
    (D) The woman is presenting an advertising proposal to clients.

8. M2: (A) The woman has waded out into the lake.
    (B) The woman is sitting at the edge of the water and reading.
    (C) The water has risen high enough to cover the woman's legs.
    (D) The woman is calling out to her friends across the lake.

9. W: (A) The man and woman are shaking hands.
    (B) The woman is behind the desk.
    (C) The man is standing near the woman.
    (D) The woman is handing the man a paper.

10. M2: (A) The sign tells motorists to use seat belts.
    (B) The plane is in final preparation for takeoff.
    (C) The warning sign has been illuminated.
    (D) Cars are being checked at the intersection.

11. M1: (A) The woman is opening her umbrella.
    (B) The rain has canceled the performance.
    (C) The woman is checking for raindrops.
    (D) The woman is hailing a taxi in the rain.

12. W: (A) Cars may travel in every lane.
    (B) Pedestrians may use the left lane.
    (C) Cyclists must ride in the right-hand lane.
    (D) The arrow indicates the bicycle lane.

13. M2: (A) The man is taking notes from the textbook.
    (B) The man is delivering a lecture to the audience.
    (C) The man is removing the textbooks from their shelves.
    (D) The man is having his class notes copied.

14. M1: (A) The woman has taken her purchases to the cashier.
    (B) The woman is hanging the prices overhead.
    (C) The woman is pushing her cart through the market.
    (D) The woman is looking through the produce to select her items.

15. W: (A) The woman is taking the garbage outside.
    (B) The woman is washing the furniture in her office.
    (C) The woman is emptying the trash into another container.
    (D) The woman is sweeping the trash from the floor.

16. M1: (A) The man is passing out notes for his lecture.
    (B) The man is addressing his colleagues.
    (C) The schedule for the lecture has been posted.
    (D) The participants are taking notes on the lecture.

17. M2: (A) The man is showing the woman where to put her signature.
    (B) The man and woman are being introduced by mutual friends.
    (C) The contents of the package are being inspected by the supervisor.
    (D) The woman cannot cash the check without a signature.

TEST TWO

18. W: (A) She's paying her traffic fine to the attendant.
    (B) She's searching for coins to put in the meter.
    (C) She's looking for a parking space.
    (D) She's driving into the parking garage.

19. W: (A) The boat is nearing the starting line of the race.
    (B) The bridge has been raised to let boats pass through.
    (C) The boat's sail have been fully raised.
    (D) High winds have prevented the sails from being raised.

20. W: (A) The two motorcycles are traveling side by side.
    (B) The cyclists are riding double on a motorcycle.
    (C) The motorcyclist is stopping to pick up another passenger.
    (D) One cyclist is getting off the motorcycle.

Sample Question
W: Good morning, John. How are you?
M: (A) I am fine, thank you.
M: (B) I am in the living room.
M: (C) My name is John.

21. W: What time does the guided tour start?
    M: (A) At the information booth.
    M: (B) A week ago yesterday.
    M: (C) Every hour on the hour.

22. M: Should we eat lunch before the meeting or afterwards?
    W: (A) I'm starving. I'd love to go now.
    W: (B) At the restaurant downtown.
    W: (C) She never goes to meetings.

23. W: Why didn't you preregister for the conference?
    M: (A) It's cheaper, you know.
    M: (B) I wasn't sure I could go.
    M: (C) When I arrived.

24. M: How can I subscribe to that magazine?
    W: (A) Just fill out the enclosed card.
    W: (B) No, sorry. It's sold out.
    W: (C) Somewhere around five dollars.

25. W: Will you be moving closer to the office?
    M: (A) It's the third house on the left.
    M: (B) The bus leaves at seven.
    M: (C) If I can find an inexpensive apartment.

26. M: What about switching offices, so I can have the one with a window?
    W: (A) It's fine with me.
    W: (B) I'll see you tomorrow.
    W: (C) No, we need new computers.

27. M: Who's the author of this proposal?
    W: (A) Not me. I don't have a way with words.
    W: (B) Thank you. I'm glad you liked it.
    W: (C) Maybe we should read all his books.

28. W: Aren't you due for a promotion?
    M: (A) I returned all the library books.
    M: (B) It was two years ago Thursday.
    M: (C) It should be anytime soon.

29. M: Shall we go shopping or visit a museum?
    W: (A) I like your new coat.
    W: (B) I'd like to see the new exhibit.
    W: (C) Yes, I have.

30. W: How were the quarterly earnings?
    M: (A) They end tomorrow.
    M: (B) My salary stayed the same.
    M: (C) Down, I'm afraid.

31. M: Why don't we join the health club?
    W: (A) I can't seem to find any free time.
    W: (B) Maybe five kilograms.
    W: (C) Until next Friday.

32. W: How many people have to sign up for us to hold the seminar?
    M: (A) In room 217.
    M: (B) There's no minimum.
    M: (C) During lunch hour is fine.

33. M: Where will you take your summer vacation this year?
    W: (A) It's too hot in August.
    W: (B) The last two weeks in July.
    W: (C) In a cottage by a lake.

34. M: Are you really from Spain?
    W: (A) No, but I've lived there for five years.
    W: (B) No, it's not too painful.
    W: (C) I see it's difficult.

35. W: When is Mr. McDonald retiring?
    M: (A) His car is brand new.
    M: (B) The end of the month.
    M: (C) He's placed his order.

36. M: Where's the closest soda machine?
    W: (A) I was thirsty last night.
    W: (B) I thought it was open.
    W: (C) In the basement.

37. M: How much longer do you think it'll be before I hear from them?
    W: (A) Stand closer to the speaker.
    W: (B) Probably by the end of the week.
    W: (C) I think you can hear me now.

38. W: What do you suggest I order?
    M: (A) They're famous for their fried chicken.
    M: (B) The prices are always excellent.
    M: (C) I usually go to the supermarket.

39. M: How far is it to the airport from here?
    W: (A) The morning flights are usually less crowded.
    W: (B) I live three blocks from the subway.
    W: (C) It's a twenty-minute taxi ride.

40. W: Do I get the copier access card from you?
    M: (A) Sorry, I don't use credit cards.
    M: (B) I think Carol has it now.
    M: (C) It's easy to get to.

41. M: Call me before you leave the country.
    W: (A) I promise I won't forget.
    W: (B) I never use pay phones.
    W: (C) I live in a suburb.

42. W: Did you enjoy the guest speaker?
    M: (A) I joined a month ago.
    M: (B) No, all my guests left.
    M: (C) Yes, she was quite informative.

43. M: Do you often take the train?
    W: (A) Today I forgot my umbrella.
    W: (B) Actually, I prefer it to flying.
    W: (C) I usually take my time.

44. W: Can I have the check before four o'clock?
    M: (A) Stop by around two-thirty.
    M: (B) I checked at the bank.
    M: (C) I'll need four more.

45. M: Please fill out this form in pencil.
    W: (A) I'll have to borrow one of yours.
    W: (B) No, I didn't.
    W: (C) I don't draw very well.

46. W: Has the company taken a vote yet?
    M: (A) Yes, by about two-thirds.
    M: (B) The boat ride was wonderful.
    M: (C) No, it'll be next week.

47. M: When will you bring in the pictures from your ski trip?
    W: (A) I ski every winter.
    W: (B) Last winter in the Alps.
    W: (C) Sorry, I keep forgetting them.

48. W: Can I speak to the manager?
    M: (A) No, I left before she arrived.
    M: (B) She's out sick today.
    M: (C) The man speaks slowly.

49. M: Do you know any language tutors?
    W: (A) I know three languages.
    W: (B) Twenty dollars an hour.
    W: (C) My sister recommends her former teacher.

50. W: Is your landlord's name Tyler or Taylor?
    M: (A) It's the former.
    M: (B) No, he doesn't do alterations.
    M: (C) Don't let me tie you down.

51. W: Wasn't the meeting supposed to start at ten? How come we're the only two people here?
    M: I'd better go check with Mr. Lamar's secretary.
    W: I hope it's canceled. I have so much work to do.

52. W: Can I help you?
    M: I'd like some suits that I can wear at the office as well as on the weekends.
    W: Let me show you our new fall collection. There are several styles that are just what you're looking for.

53. M: Have you met the new office manager?
    W: She has to be better than Susan was. I swear, she lost every single purchase order I ever submitted.
    M: Well, you weren't alone. That's why Susan was fired.

54. M: Are you ready to order?
    W: I see the special of the day is salmon. How is it cooked?
    M: It's fried in a little oil with a lemon and garlic sauce.

55. W: I saw Mr. Kennedy walking with a cane.
    M: I heard he fell while walking his dog.
    W: Have you ever seen his dog? It's the size of a small horse.

56. W: John, please bring me the documents as soon as they get here.
    M: If they were sent by overnight delivery, they should get here about 9:30, Ms. Wilson.
    W: I hope so. I need to look them over before negotiations begin.

57. M: Is everyone in the export department working on commission?
    W: Sure, I thought the entire company was.
    M: We're thinking of changing domestic sales to straight salary plus a small commission.

58. W: Did you hear that at some airlines frequent-flyer miles expire after a certain amount of time?
    M: Yeah, and mine is one of them.
    W: What a joke. Mine too. I'll have to take ten international trips by December.

59. M: Can you tell me how much a subscription to the symphony costs?
    W: It depends on whether you want three concerts or four. Also, the price is lower on Wednesday evenings and Saturday and Sunday afternoons.
    M: Oh, I want two tickets for four concerts on Friday evenings.

60. W: Christine, do you think your department can manage without hiring temporary workers when people take their vacations this summer?
M: I'm sure we will be fine. We'll just make sure we all take different weeks off.
W: Good. We need to trim the budget wherever we can. Sales have been off this quarter.

61. M: After work do you want to come with me to that new golf store that opened where King's Department Store used to be?
W: Great. I heard they have an indoor putting green and a place where you can hit balls into a net.
M: We can pretend it's springtime.

62. M: I wish we could get some more of those talking dinosaur toys. The Learning Store could sell ten thousand in a day.
W: All day long people call asking if we're getting anymore in.
M: I hear other stores are out of stock, too. The company didn't produce enough of them to meet demand.

63. M: Excuse me, I'm looking for 115 Washington Street.
W: Well this is 120, so it's not too far from here.
M: Thanks. So many buildings around here don't have numbers.

64. W: Have you gotten a flu shot yet?
M: I keep meaning to. They're giving them free every night this week at the clinic on Twenty-third Street.
W: I'm debating what to do. I don't fit any of the high-risk groups.

65. M: I heard the elevator is being repaired today.
W: It's about time. I can't imagine having to walk up these ten flights of stairs another day.
M: Hey, think about all the exercise you've been getting.

66. W: When did you get this new desk?
M: It's not really new. When Bob moved to the third floor, he left this one behind.
W: I could really use a bigger one. Now that we all have computers, I have no room on mine for anything else.

67. M: I couldn't help noticing that new billboard on Market Street. The design is impressive.
W: You know, it's a form of advertising we've never tried.
M: Well, let's find out how much it costs and write up a proposal.

68. M: I wonder which of us will be moving to the new wing.
W: Well, I heard the design hasn't been approved by the building commissioner yet.
M: Once they get the green light from him, the contractors are ready to begin.

69. W: Look at the check-in line! It's going to take an hour.
M: There must be a convention in this hotel. Wouldn't you know it?
W: Let's see if we can leave our bags somewhere, go to lunch, and then come back.

70. W: I've never traveled for the company before. Do they give us money in advance for meals and transportation?
M: They give you a flat fee, and you keep all the receipts. In the end, either you owe them money or they owe you some.
W: So who do I speak to?

71. W: This year the company picnic is going to be at the amusement park for a change.
M: Wow! That's a first. My kids will be so excited.
W: I'm sure they will. I wish I had some.

72. M: Do you carry the *International Herald Tribune*?
W: Yes, but we're all out. The weekend edition is really popular.
M: Can you suggest someplace else that might still have it?

73. W: Have you tried the new health club on Broadway?
M: No, but I heard the company will pay the initiation fee.
W: And they'll pay fifty percent of the monthly fee. I guess they want us to stay in shape.

74. W: They promised to have my car fixed by 2:00, and now they say maybe not until tomorrow.
M: Do you need a ride home today?
W: I'd appreciate it. I was supposed to do some shopping for my mother and visit Mr. Johnston in the hospital, but now I won't be able to do either.

75. W: I heard you're getting your office painted. Have you picked out colors?
M: Well, the only thing they have is white. I had wanted blue, yellow, or peach.
W: I guess that makes it easy.

76. M: Are you going to refinance your condominium? The rates are the lowest they've been in twenty years.
W: I was told that if you plan to move in the next four years, it's not worth it.
M: Oh, and you're still dreaming of Australia, right?

77. W: Have you read anything good lately?
M: I just finished a marvelous book. The main character writes letters to an imaginary friend.
W: And it's not too sad? I need something light.

78. M: I bought my computer just three months ago, and now the same model is five hundred dollars less.
W: Did you try to get a refund?
M: They just laughed in my face. The lesson is don't buy anything electronic for at least a year after it comes out.

79. W: I applied for the administrative assistant's job in the president's office, and I haven't heard anything in three weeks.
M2: I wouldn't be too concerned. They have to advertise those positions, and it takes time.
W: Do you think I should speak to the personnel director?

80. M: Have you had your interview with the consultant yet?
W: No, have you? Everyone is optimistic he'll be able to bring about some changes.
M: I sure hope so. I spent two hours with him, and I gave him plenty of suggestions.

Questions 81–83 refer to the following announcement:
W: Big things come in small packages, including revolutionary advances in the travel industry. One of the biggest, and smallest, of these is the smart card, a plastic rectangle that looks like a conventional credit card but contains a microprocessor which transforms it into a mini-computer with impressive capabilities. A smart card can keep track of travel reservations and tickets, hotel reservations and information, bank debit and credit cards, as well as electronic money.

Questions 84–86 refer to the following announcement:
W: All employees will be mailed a vacation questionnaire this week. Please return it to Bonnie Carter by the end of the month. We have been asked by several individuals to examine the current vacation policy. Full-time employees with one year of service receive two weeks' paid vacation per year. After five years, employees get three weeks. After ten years, employees receive the maximum amount, or four weeks. Currently employees are not allowed to take more than one week at a time. Many of you have asked us to change this policy. We will change our policy based on your responses in this study. You will see the questionnaire asks about length of vacations, the feasibility of taking unpaid vacation time, and establishing a policy for requesting vacation weeks. Thank you for your consideration.

Questions 87–89 refer to the following bulletin:
M2: The province of Quebec will remain an official disaster area until Friday, the twelfth. Over 10 million people have been without power since Tuesday. All vehicles, except those used for emergencies, are asked to stay off the roads. The three days of freezing rain, which began last Saturday, quickly turned to ice, toppling trees and electric power lines. Emergency shelters have been set up throughout the province. Police are attempting to reach as many homes as possible to transport residents to these shelters, which are powered by generators. The shelters are crowded and noisy, but heat and food are available to all.

Questions 90–91 refer to the following report:
W: The Italian unions announced that the railroad strike, which had been scheduled for Monday, has been postponed. But union leaders announced that unless their salary demands were met by midnight on Monday, the 24-hour strike would begin Tuesday at 12:01 a.m. In addition, workers for the ferry companies would strike for 24 hours starting at 5:30 a.m. on Wednesday. On Thursday, airline ground workers would strike from 10:00 a.m. to 6:00 p.m. Traveling anywhere this week in Italy, unless on foot, promises to be difficult.

Questions 92–94 refer to the following advertisement:
M2: Spice is the key word to describe this year's collection of perfumes for men. At department store counters over the world, the smell is exotic. Labels advertise ingredients, such as pineapple, cinnamon bark, nutmeg, black pepper, Brazilian tea leaves, Lebanese cedar wood, and amber. One might easily think this season's new perfumes were really items from the kitchen.

Questions 95–97 refer to the following announcement:
M1: Welcome aboard today's flight. For your safety we suggest you follow these safety procedures today and whenever you fly. First. Be attentive to the flight attendant's predeparture announcements and safety demonstration. Second. Read the emergency card found in the seat pocket in front of you. Third. Locate the emergency exits closest to you. Fourth. Ask the flight attendant if you have any questions about safety procedures. Fifth. Even when the fasten seat belt sign is not lighted, we recommend you leave your seat belt fastened throughout the flight.

Questions 98–100 refer to the following introduction:
W: Welcome to the department head meeting. We are pleased to announce that Don Stevens has joined our company as a full-time technology specialist. He comes to us from the world of academia, having taught computer science at the University of Toronto for six years. But in those six years he did more than just lecture students. He oversaw the campus-wide installation of a networked computer system and served as the troubleshooter for students and staff. Here with us he will primarily be our troubleshooter. Please write down on the yellow form any problem you are having with your computer, software, or printer and Don will come to your rescue as soon as possible. If he is stopped in the hall or telephoned with a problem, he can't do his job. So please remember to use the yellow forms that you all received in your mailboxes, and join me in warmly welcoming Don.

ANSWERS & EXPLANATIONS

1. (A) *The man is taking something out of his bag.*
   Choice (B) is incorrect because the man is not working with his computer. Choice (C) is incorrect because the backpack is under the desk. Choice (D) is incorrect because the man is sitting at his desk; he is not at his locker.

2. (D) *A person is swimming alongside the lane marker.*
   Choice (A) is incorrect because the swimmer is swimming, not diving. Choice (B) is incorrect because there is a swimmer in the pool; it is not empty. Choice (C) is incorrect because there is water in the pool; it is not being drained.

3. (B) *The man is slicing the pie.*
   Choice (A) is incorrect because the man is cutting the pie, not serving it, and no guests can be seen. Choice (C) is incorrect because the pie is already out of the oven. Choice (D) is incorrect because the man is slicing the pie, not writing down a recipe.

4. (C) *The woman is cleaning the copy machine.*
   Choice (A) is incorrect because the woman is standing by the machine, not delivering copies. Choice (B) is incorrect because no one is waiting in line. Choice (D) is incorrect because there are no copies in the picture.

5. (D) *The man has his feet on the desk while he talks.*
   Choice (A) is incorrect because the man is talking; the answering machine has not taken the call. Choice (B) is incorrect because his feet are on the desk, not tangled in the cord. Choice (C) is incorrect because the man is not touching the papers on his desk.

6. (A) *A man is shouting to the bicyclist as he goes by.*
   Choice (B) is incorrect because only one man is riding on his bicycle; the second man is not competing. Choice (C) is incorrect because the man is shouting, not shooting. Choice (D) is incorrect because the cyclist already has his helmet on; the other man is not helping him on with it.

7. (C) *The woman is drawing a picture on her sketch pad.*
   Choice (A) is incorrect because the pencils are not scattered; they're in a box. Choice (B) is incorrect because the woman is drawing, not examining photographs. Choice (D) is incorrect because there are no clients in the picture; the woman is alone.

8. (B) *The woman is sitting on the edge of the water and reading.*
   Choice (A) is incorrect because the woman is not in the lake. Choice (C) is incorrect because the water has not risen high enough to cover her legs. Choice (D) is incorrect because the woman is looking at a book, not calling out to her friends.

9. (D) *The woman is handing the man a paper.*
   Choice (A) is incorrect because the woman is handing the man something, not shaking his hand. Choice (B) is incorrect because the man is behind the desk, not the woman. Choice (C) is incorrect because the woman is standing, not the man.

10. (A) *The sign tells motorists to use seat belts.*
    Choice (B) is incorrect because there is no plane in the picture. Choice (C) is incorrect because the sign is not lit up, or illuminated. Choice (D) is incorrect because there are no cars in the picture.

11. (C) *The woman is checking for raindrops.*
    Choice (A) is incorrect because the woman's umbrella is already open. Choice (B) is incorrect because there is no indication the performance has been canceled. Choice (D) is incorrect because the woman is looking up checking the rain, not hailing a cab.

12. (D) *The arrow indicates the bicycle lane.*
    Choice (A) is incorrect because the lane on the left is marked for bicycles only. Choice (B) is incorrect because the left lane is for bicycles, not pedestrians. Choice (C) is incorrect because bicyclists must ride in the left lane, not the right lane.

13. (A) *The man is taking notes from the textbook.*
    Choice (B) is incorrect because there is no audience in the picture. Choice (C) is incorrect because the man is reading from a textbook, not removing books from their shelves. Choice (D) is incorrect because the man is copying the notes himself, not having the notes copied.

14. (D) *The woman is looking through the produce to select her items.*
    Choice (A) is incorrect because the woman is standing by the produce, not a cashier. Choice (B) is incorrect because the prices are already hung overhead; she isn't hanging them. Choice (C) is incorrect because the woman is standing, not pushing a cart.

15. (C) *The woman is emptying the trash into another container.*
    Choice (A) is incorrect because the woman is indoors. Choice (B) is incorrect because the woman is emptying trash, not washing furniture. Choice (D) is incorrect because the woman is emptying trash, not sweeping it with a broom.

16. (B) *The man is addressing his colleagues.*
Choice (A) is incorrect because the man is reading from his notes, not passing them out. Choice (C) is incorrect because there is no schedule posted in the picture. Choice (D) is incorrect because the participants are not writing in the picture; they are looking at the speaker.

17. (A) *The man is showing the woman where to put her signature.*
Choice (B) is incorrect because the man and woman are the only ones in the picture; there are no friends in the picture. Choice (C) is incorrect because there is no package in the picture. Choice (D) is incorrect because there is no check in the picture.

18. (B) *She's searching for coins to put in the meter.*
Choice (A) is incorrect because there is no attendant in the picture. Choice (C) is incorrect because she has already found a parking space. Choice (D) is incorrect because she has a space on the street; she's not driving into a garage.

19. (C) *The boat sails have been fully raised.*
Choice (A) is incorrect because there is no starting line of a race in the picture. Choice (B) is incorrect because there is no bridge in the picture. Choice (D) is incorrect because the sails have been raised.

20. (B) *The cyclists are riding double on a motorcycle.*
Choice (A) is incorrect because the cyclists are riding on the same bike, not on separate ones side by side. Choice (C) is incorrect because the passenger has already been picked up. Choice (D) is incorrect because both cyclists are on the bike; one isn't getting off.

21. (C) *Every hour on the hour* answers when the tour starts. Choice (A) answers a *where* question. Choice (B) answers a past tense *when* question.

22. (A) *I'm starving. I'd love to go now* means the woman would like to eat before the meeting because she is very hungry. Choice (B) answers a *where* question. Choice (C) is an illogical response.

23. (B) *I wasn't sure I could go* explains why the man didn't preregister. Choice (A) is an illogical response. Choice (C) answers a *when* question.

24. (A) *Just fill out the enclosed card* tells what the man must do to subscribe to the magazine. Choice (B) would be a response if he asked to buy a magazine from a newsstand. Choice (C) answers a *how much* question.

25. (C) *If I can find an inexpensive apartment* means the man will move if he finds an apartment that is cheap. Choice (A) answers a *which* question. Choice (B) answers a *when* question.

26. (A) *It's fine with me* indicates the woman agrees to switch offices. Choice (B) is an illogical response. Choice (C) answers a *do you* question.

27. (A) *Not me. I don't have a way with words* means the woman didn't write the proposal because she's not a good writer. Choice (B) is a response to a compliment and is an illogical response. Choice (C) confuses *author* with a related word: *books*.

28. (C) *It should be anytime soon* indicates the man believes he'll soon be promoted. Choice (A) confuses *due* with related words: *library books*. Choice (B) answers a *when* question.

29. (B) *I'd like to see the new exhibit* means the woman would prefer to go to the museum. Choice (A) is an illogical response. Choice (C) answers a *have you* question.

30. (C) *Down, I'm afraid* indicates that earnings decreased this quarter. Choice (A) answers a *when* question. Choice (B) confuses *earnings* with a related word: *salary*.

31. (A) *I can't seem to find any time* explains why she hasn't joined the health club. Choice (B) answers a *how much* question. Choice (C) answers a *how long* question.

32. (B) *There's no minimum* means that the seminar will be held no matter how few people sign up for it. Choice (A) answers a *where* question. Choice (C) answers a *when* question and is an illogical response.

33. (C) *In a cottage by a lake* tells where she will vacation this year. Choice (A) confuses *summer vacation* with a related word: *August*. Choice (B) answers a *when* question.

34. (A) *No, but I've lived there for five years* answers whether or not the woman is Spanish. Choice (B) confuses *Spain* and *painful*. Choice (C) is an illogical response.

35. (B) *The end of the month* tells when Mr. McDonald is retiring. Choice (A) confuses re*tire*(ing) and a related word: *car*. Choice (C) is an illogical response.

36. (C) *In the basement* tells where the closest soda machine is. Choice (A) confuses *soda* with a related word: *thirsty*. Choice (B) confuses *closest* and *closed*, an antonym of *open*.

37. (B) *Probably by the end of the week* indicates when she thinks he'll hear from them. Choice (A) confuses *hear* with a related word: *speaker*. Choice (C) confuses *hear from them* and *hear me*.

38. (A) *They're famous for their fried chicken* means the man recommends the chicken. Choices (B) and (C) are illogical responses.

39. (C) *It's a twenty-minute taxi ride* tells how far it is to the airport; it takes twenty minutes by cab. Choice (A) confuses *airport* with a related word: *flights*. Choice (B) is an illogical response.

40. (B) *I think Carol has it now* means that Carol has the card the woman needs. Choice (A) confuses *access card* and *credit cards*. Choice (C) is an illogical response.

41. (A) *I promise I won't forget* indicates the woman will remember to call him before he leaves. Choice (B) confuses *call* with a related word: *phones*. Choice (C) confuses *country* (side) and *suburbs*.

42. (C) *Yes, she was quite informative* means the man learned a lot from the speaker. Choice (A) confuses *enjoy* and *joined*. Choice (B) confuses *guest speaker* and *guests* in a home, and is an illogical response.

43. (B) *Actually I prefer it to flying* means the man likes taking trains more than flying. Choice (A) is an illogical response confusing *train* and a word related to *umbrella*: *rain*. Choice (C) confuses *take the train* and *take my time*.

44. (A) *Stop by around two-thirty* tells the woman when she can pick up her check. Choice (B) confuses *check* and *checked*. Choice (C) confuses *four o'clock* and *four more*.

45. (A) *I'll have to borrow one of yours* means the woman needs to use one of the man's pencils to fill out the form. Choice (B) answers a *did you* question. Choice (C) confuses *pencil* with a related word: *draw*.

46. (C) *No, it'll be next week* answers that the vote hasn't happened yet, but it will be next week. Choice (A) is an illogical response. Choice (B) confuses *vote* and *boat*.

47. (C) *Sorry, I keep forgetting them* means the woman intends to bring in her pictures but is forgetful. Choice (A) answers a present tense *when* question. Choice (B) answers a past tense *when* question.

48. (B) *She's out sick today* means the woman can't speak to the manager because she's not working today. Choice (A) is an illogical response. Choice (C) confuses *speak to* and *speaks slowly*.

49. (C) *My sister recommends her former teacher* gives a recommendation for a language tutor. Choice (A) confuses *language tutor* and *three languages*. Choice (B) answers a *how much* question.

50. (A) *It's the former* means his landlord's name is Tyler, the first name she mentioned. Choice (B) confuses *Taylor* (tailor) with a related word: *alterations*. Choice (C) confuses *Tyler* and *tie*.

51. (D) The man says *I'd better go check with Mr. Lamar's secretary*. Choice (A) is incorrect because the woman says she hopes the meeting is canceled. Choice (B) is incorrect because the woman says she has so much work to do. Choice (C) is incorrect because the woman asks if the meeting was supposed to start at ten.

52. (B) They mention *suits, the new fall collection*, and *several styles*; the conversation takes place in a clothing store. Although the woman *wants suits she can wear at the office*, Choice (A) is incorrect. Choices (C) and (D) are not mentioned.

53. (C) Referring to lost purchase orders, the man says *that's why Susan was fired*. Choice (A) confuses *you weren't alone* with *worked all alone*. Choice (B) is incorrect because Susan was the last office manager, not the new one. Choice (D) is incorrect because Susan lost purchase orders; she didn't submit them.

54. (A) The man asks *Are you ready to order?* The woman answers *I see the special of the day is salmon*, meaning the conversation takes place in a restaurant. Choice (B) confuses *the food items* with *a supermarket* but the woman is *ordering food*, not *shopping for food*. Choice (C) confuses *salmon* with a related word: *boat*. Choice (D) is not mentioned.

55. (C) The man says *I heard he fell while walking his dog*. Choice (A) confuses *horseback riding* with *comparing the size of the dog to a small horse*. Choice (B) confuses *working* with *walking*. Choice (D) is not mentioned.

56. (D) The man says *if they were sent by overnight delivery, they should get here about 9:30*. Choice (A) is the name of the assistant. Choice (B) is the woman asking for the documents. Choice (C) confuses *negotiators* with *negotiations*.

57. (C) When the man asks *if everyone in the export department is working on commission*, the woman answers *Sure*, meaning, *of course*. Choice (A) is not mentioned. Choices (B) and (D) are what the company is thinking of changing domestic sales to.

58. (D) The woman says *Did you hear that some airlines' frequent flyer miles expire after a certain amount of time?*, to which the man says his is *one of them*. Choice (A) confuses the joke that she'll have to take ten international trips by December, not a funny joke. Choices (B) and (C) are not mentioned.

59. (C) The woman says *the price is lower on Wednesday evenings and Saturday and Sunday afternoons*. Choice (A) is incorrect because they are cheaper on Wednesday *evening*, not *afternoon*. Choice (B) is incorrect; the man requests tickets to Friday *evening* but not because they are cheaper. Tickets are cheaper on Sunday afternoon. so Choice (D) is incorrect.

60. (A) Christine is asked if her *department can manage without hiring temporary workers this summer*. Choice (B) is a cause for trimming the budget. Choice (C) is incorrect because Christine says *we'll make sure we all take different weeks off*. Choice (D) is not mentioned.

61. (B) The man asks the woman if she wants *to come to that new golf store*. Choice (A) is incorrect because the store *has only a putting green and a place to hit balls into a net*, not nine holes. Choice (C) is incorrect because it's *an indoor putting green*. Choice (D) is incorrect because they'll *pretend it's springtime*.

62. (C) The man says the company *didn't produce enough to meet demand*. Choice (A) is not mentioned. The man exaggerates and says that they could *sell ten thousand in a day*. They haven't already sold that many, so Choice (B) is incorrect. Choice (D) confuses *strike* and *stock*.

63. (D) The man says *I'm looking for 115 Washington Street;* he needs to get to that address. Choice (A) confuses the numbers *115 and 120 Washington Street* with the time. Choices (B) and (C) are not mentioned.

64. (C) The woman says *I'm debating* whether or not to get a flu shot because *I don't fit any of the high-risk groups,* she is not at high risk for getting flu. Choice (A) is not mentioned. Choice (B) confuses the *free (not requiring pay) shots* with *a free (available) evening*. Choice (D) is not mentioned.

65. (B) The man and woman are discussing walking up *ten flights of stairs*, so the conversation takes place on the stairs. Choice (A) confuses the *elevator's being repaired* with *a repair shop*. Choice (C) confuses all the exercise the woman has been getting walking up the stairs with exercising at a gym. Choice (D) is incorrect because the elevator is being repaired; that's why they are taking the stairs.

66. (D) The woman says *I could really use a bigger one*, meaning a bigger desk. Choice (A) is not mentioned; they already have computers. Choice (B) is incorrect because her desk is too small, not her room. Choice (C) is incorrect because Bob moved to a different floor, not her.

67. (B) The man says *Let's find out how much it costs*, referring to advertising on billboards. Choice (A) is where the new billboard is. Choices (C) and (D) are not mentioned.

68. (C) The woman says *the design hasn't been approved by the building commissioner yet*, meaning the commissioner is the one responsible for the delay. Choice (A) confuses *design* with *designers*. Choice (B) is incorrect because the contractors are ready to begin now. Choice (D) confuses *traffic engineer* with related words: *green light*.

69. (C) The woman suggests they leave their bags and *go to lunch*. Choice (A) is incorrect because they don't want to wait in line. Choice (B) is incorrect because they want to *leave* their bags, not take them. Choice (D) is incorrect because they are not attending the convention; they assume the long line is cause by one.

70. (C) The woman asks *do they give us money in advance for meals and transportation*. She doesn't know how expenses are reimbursed. Although she wants to know about money for meals, she doesn't ask about the amount, Choice (A). Choice (B) is incorrect; no travel has been arranged. Choice (D) is not mentioned.

71. (A) The woman says *I wish I had some*, referring to children. Choices (B) and (C) are not mentioned. Choice (D) is incorrect; the company picnic has not been held at the amusement park.

72. (B) The woman says *we're all out*; they've sold all their copies. Choice (A) is incorrect because the newsstand sells it. Choice (C) is incorrect because it has arrived already. Choice (D) is incorrect because the woman says *the weekend edition is really popular*.

73. (D) *The company will pay the initiation fee and fifty percent of the monthly fee*. Choices (A), (B), and (C) are contradicted by *The company will pay the initiation fee and fifty percent of the monthly fee*.

74. (C) The man asks *Do you need a ride home today?* Choices (A) and (B) are not offered by the man although the woman says she was supposed to do both. Choice (D) is not mentioned.

75. (C) The man says *I had wanted blue, yellow, or peach*. Choice (A) is not mentioned. Choice (B) is the color the office will be painted. Choice (D) confuses *apricot* with a related word: *peach*.

76. (B) The woman says *I was told if you plan to move in the next four years, it's not worth it*, meaning she won't refinance because she may move in that time. Choice (A) confuses *moving to Australia* with *dreaming of Australia*. Choices (C) and (D) are not mentioned.

77. (D) The woman says *And it's not too sad? I need something light,* meaning she's looking for a book that isn't too serious. Choice (A) confuses *light* (not serious) with *light* (easy to carry). Choice (B) is contradicted by *not too sad*. Choice (C) is incorrect because it is mentioned by the man.

78. (C) The man says *the same model is five hundred dollars less* and *the lesson is don't buy anything electronic for at least a year* because prices are falling. Choice (A) confuses trying to get a refund with how to get one. Choice (B) confuses *laughing in my face* with a related word: *humor*. Choice (D) is not mentioned.

79. (B) The woman asks *Do you think I should speak to the personnel director?* Choice (A) is not mentioned. Choice (C) confuses the man's saying *they have to advertise those positions* with *whether she should advertise the position*. Choice (D) confuses not hearing *in three weeks* with *waiting three weeks*.

80. (D) Referring to the consultant, the woman says *everyone is optimistic he'll be able to bring about some changes*. Choice (A) is incorrect; she hasn't had her interview yet. Choice (B) is incorrect because the man spent two hours with the consultant. Choice (C) is incorrect because the man gave him *plenty of suggestions*.

81. (B) *It looks like a card but contains a micro-processor which transforms it into a mini-computer*. Choice (A) is not mentioned. Choice (C) is contradicted by *one of the smallest is the smart card*. Choice (D) is incorrect because it confuses the fact that *a smart card can keep track of travel reservations* with *a travel agent*.

82. (D) *A micro-processor transforms it into a mini-computer*. Choice (A) is not mentioned. Choice (B) is incorrect because although the smart card is a plastic rectangle, *A micro-processor transforms it into a mini-computer*. Choice (C) is incorrect because it confuses what transforms the smart card with what the smart card is transformed into.

83. (C) *A smart card can keep track of hotel reservations*. Choice (A) confuses *travel reservations* with *travel directions*. Choice (B) is not mentioned. Choice (D) confuses *electronic money* with *electronic gadgets*.

84. (A) All employees are being mailed a questionnaire which states *Many of you have asked us to change this policy*. Choices (B) and (C) are not mentioned. Choice (D) is whom the questionnaire should be returned to.

85. (C) *After five years, employees get three weeks* and *after ten, four weeks*. Choice (A) is not mentioned. Choice (B) is incorrect because it is the amount *full-time employees with one-year of service receive*. Choice (D) is incorrect because it is the amount employees receive *after ten years*.

86. (B) Because *full-time employees with one-year of service receive two weeks vacation*, those who have worked less than one year receive no vacation. Choice (A) is incorrect because the questionnaire asks about *the feasibility of establishing a policy for requesting vacation weeks*, meaning no policy exists now. Choice (C) is contradicted by *Currently employees are not allowed to take more than one week at a time*. Choice (D) is incorrect because the questionnaire asks about *the feasibility of taking unpaid vacation time*. It is not in existence now.

87. (C) *The province of Quebec will remain an official disaster area until Friday*. Choice (A) is incorrect because it confuses the day that people lost power with the day until Quebec *will be a disaster area*. Choice (B) is not mentioned. Choice (D) is incorrect because it confuses the day the freezing rain began with the day until *Quebec will remain a disaster area*.

88. (C) *All vehicles, except those used for emergencies, are asked to stay off the roads*. Choices (A), (B), and (D) are not mentioned.

89. (B) *The shelters are crowded and noisy, but heat and food are available to all;* security is not mentioned. Choices (A), (C), and (D) are explicitly mentioned.

90. (B) *The railroad strike would begin Tuesday.* Choice (A) is incorrect because it confuses the day on which salary demands must be met with the day of the railroad strike. Choice (C) is incorrect because it confuses the day on which the ferry workers will strike with the day on which the railroad strike would begin. Choice (D) is incorrect because it confuses the day on which airline ground workers would strike with the day on which the railroad strike would begin.

91. (A) *Workers for ferry companies would strike for 24 hours.* Choice (B) confuses *airline ground workers* with *airline pilots*. Choices (C) and (D) are not mentioned.

92. (C) *Spice is the key word to describe this year's collection of perfumes for men*. Choices (A) and (B) are not mentioned. Choice (D) is only mentioned in *Labels advertise ingredients*, but it is not a key word.

93. (D) The advertisement reads *At department store counters the world over, the smell* (of men's perfumes) *is exotic*; therefore perfumes are sold at department stores. Choice (A) is incorrect because it confuses an ingredient, *Lebanese cedar wood* with a related word: *lumber mills*. Choices (B) and (C) are not mentioned.

94. (B) *The perfumes include ingredients such as black pepper, nutmeg, and amber; coffee* is not mentioned. Choices (A), (C), and (D) are mentioned.

95. (D) The announcement begins, *Welcome aboard today's flight*. Choices (A), (B), and (C) are contradicted by this statement.

96. (D) *Read the emergency card found in the seat pocket in front of you*. Choices (A), (B), and (C) are contradicted by this statement.

97. (B) *We recommend you leave your seat belt fastened throughout the flight.* Choices (A), (C), and (D) are contradicted by this statement.

98. (A) The introduction begins *Welcome to the department head meeting.* Choices (B), (C), and (D) are contradicted by this statement.

99. (C) *Don Stevens comes to us from the world of academia, having taught computer science at the University of Toronto;* he was a lecturer. Choice (A) is not mentioned. Choice (B) confuses *university teacher* with *university president.* Choice (D) confuses *selling computer systems* with *overseeing (the installation) of a computer system* as part of his job.

100. (D) Employers are told to *please write down on the yellow form any problem you are having with your computer.* Choices (A) and (B) are incorrect; employers are asked not to stop him *in the hall* or *call him.* Choice (C) is not mentioned.

101. (D) The relationship between these two independent clauses is one of opposition, so *although* is the correct conjunction. Choice (A) is illogical as it introduces a clause of reason. Choice (B) is either the subject of an independent clause or, if it precedes a subject, needs to be paired with *or.* Choice (C) is illogical as it introduces a result.

102. (C) *Taking early retirement* means *retiring before the official retirement age.* Choices (A), (B), and (D) are not used with *early retirement.*

103. (B) *Outnumber* means *exceed the number of* and is the only logical choice. Choice (A) means *list.* Choice (C) means *introduce something new.* Choice (D) means *designate.*

104. (A) The superlative form of the adjective follows *the, oldest,* which must be used with *most historic,* another superlative form. Choice (B) is a simple form of the adjective used only with people. Choice (C) is a simple form of the adjective. Choice (D) is the comparative form.

105. (C) *Inventory control* is the correct compound noun meaning *keeping track of the items in inventory.* Choices (A), (B), and (D) are not used with *control.*

106. (D) *At the forefront* is a prepositional phrase meaning *in the position of prominence.* Choices (A), and (C), although nouns, are illogical. Choice (B) is an adjective.

107. (A) *Based on* means *as measured by.* Choices (B), (C), and (D) are not used with *base.*

108. (B) *Surge* means *a sudden increase.* Choices (A), (C), and (D) are not logical.

109. (C) The correct word order for the causative passive form is *had;* direct object, *the market;* the past participle, *surveyed.* Choices (A), (B), and (D) are in the wrong order.

110. (D) The adjective *lonely* follows a linking verb. Choice (A) is usually an adverb or a conjunction. When used as an adjective, it must precede a noun. Choice (B) is a noun. Choice (C) is an adverb.

111. (A) *As well as* means *with equal effect.* Choice (B), the comparative form, must be used with *than.* Choice (C) needs to be preceded by *more* to be a comparative form. Choice (D), the adjective form, cannot follow an action verb.

112. (B) *Dozed off* is an idiom meaning *fell asleep lightly and for a short time.* Choice (A) would need to be *felt sleepy* to be correct. Choice (C) means *decreased.* Choice (D) means *used sleep as a way to get rid of something.*

113. (C) *Often* is an adverb used before the verb, *interviewed.* Choice (A) is an adverb usually used in questions. Choice (B) is an adjective. Choice (D) is an adverb meaning *extraordinarily.*

114. (D) The adjective form *increasing* follows the article and precedes the noun. Choice (A) is either a verb or a noun. Choice (B) is an adverb. Choice (C) is a noun.

115. (D) *Their* is the third-person plural possessive adjective which agrees with *trainees* and precedes *adjustment.* Choice (A) is the third-person singular possessive adjective. Choice (B) is the first-person plural possessive adjective. Choice (C) is the third-person singular object pronoun form.

116. (B) The base form of the verb, *pay,* must follow the modal *can.* Choices (A) and (C) cannot follow *can.* Choice (D) is the passive form which is incorrect in this sentence.

117. (A) *The true test* means *the real worth.* Choice (B) is frequently used to mean *a test of knowledge.* Choice (C) means *a theory.* Choice (D) frequently means *the total points in a sporting event.*

118. (C) *At times* means *occasionally.* Choices (A) and (B) are both used with the singular, *time,* not the plural form. Choice (D) is used when an adjective precedes *times.*

119. (D) *Mispronounce* is a verb meaning *say it incorrectly.* Choice (A) is a noun meaning *a minor legal offense.* Choices (B) and (C) are not logical.

120. (B) The adjective form *leading* follows the article and precedes the noun. Choice (A) is either a verb or a noun. Choice (C) is a past participle adjective meaning *made of lead.* Choice (D) is a noun.

121. (C) *On back order* is an idiom meaning *items that have been ordered, are out of stock, and will be shipped when available*. Choices (A) and (D) do not follow *back*. Choice (B), (on the) *back burner*, means *inactive status*.

122. (A) The correct word order is article, *a*; adjective, *two-night*; noun, *minimum;* compound noun, *reservation policy*. In Choices (B), (C), and (D), the word order is incorrect.

123. (D) The present perfect tense is needed, *the demand has risen*. Choice (A) is the relative pronoun, subject, and present tense. Choice (B) is the relative pronoun and present tense. Choice (C) is the present passive form.

124. (B) The permits *are no longer valid* meaning they are *not legally usable anymore*. Although Choices (A), (C), and (D) are all adjectives and are correct grammatically, they are not logical in this sentence.

125. (C) *Substituted* means *an acceptable alternative*. Choice (A) means *given acceptable reasons for an action*. Choice (B) means *put back in a former position*. Choice (D) means *accomplished something desired*.

126. (D) *Neither... nor* is a paired conjunction; *neither this year's software version nor last year's*. Choices (A), (B), and (C) cannot be paired with *neither*.

127. (A) *Beside* is the correct preposition meaning *next to*. Choice (B) indicates location *in a lower place*. Choice (C) indicates location *in a direction opposite to*. Choice (D) indicates location *in a lower place*.

128. (B) *Despite,* a preposition, precedes the noun *rates*. Choice (A) must be followed be a subject + verb. When Choice (C) begins a sentence, it must be followed by a subject + noun. Choice (D) cannot be followed by an object.

129. (C) *Medium of exchange* means *source of trade*. Although Choices (A), (B), and (D) are grammatically correct, they are illogical in this sentence.

130. (D) *Slash* means *reduce drastically*. Choice (A) means *make diagonal*. Choice (B) means *split*. Choice (C) means *clean or clear*.

131. (B) The third person feminine reflexive pronoun, *herself*, is needed to agree with *Ms. Sanchez*. Choice (A) is the third person reflexive pronoun used for things. Choice (C) is the third person plural reflexive pronoun. Choice (D) is a third person reflexive pronoun used to agree with the pronoun, *one*.

132. (A) The noun *feedback* means *information about a process*. Choice (B) *money gained*, Choice (C) *estimation of value*, and Choice (D) *act of doing math* are all nouns but are illogical.

133. (C) *In the order in which* means *in succession*. Although Choices (A), (B), and (D) are all nouns and are grammatically correct, they are not logical in this context.

134. (D) *Beforehand* is an adverb meaning *in advance*. Choice (A) is an adjective. When Choice (B) is an adverb, it means *frontward*. Although Choice (C) is an adverb, it means *once*.

135. (C) *A sense of* is an expression meaning *a feeling of*. Choice (A) is a noun which cannot precede the noun, *privacy*. Choice (B) uses the incorrect preposition, *to*. Choice (D) is not logical.

136. (B) The adjective, *financial* modifies a noun, *investment*. Choice (A) is a verb or a noun. Choice (C) is the active participle and is not logical in this sentence. Choice (D) is a noun.

137. (A) *Most airline companies* means *the majority of airline companies*. Choice (B) must be followed by *all*. Choice (C) must be followed by *the*. Choice (D) is an adverb which cannot precede a noun.

138. (C) *Undergo*, a verb, means *experience*. Choice (A) means *underestimate*. Choice (B), an adjective, means *performed in secret*. Choice (D), a noun, means *a person who learns another performer's lines in case that person needs a replacement*.

139. (D) *Whom* is a relative pronoun used with people, as with *the payroll manager*. Choice (A) is used to modify places. Choice (B) is a relative pronoun that refers to things. Choice (C) is an object pronoun.

140. (B) *Attract investors* means *arouse the attention of investors*. Choices (A) *attract*, (C) *stick to a surface*, and (D) *credit or give a reason for* must all be followed by *to*.

Part VI

141. (B) *Interest* is a singular noun, and therefore takes a singular verb — *depends*.

142. (A) *They* is not necessary because the sentence already has a subject: *states*.

143. (B) *The company,* a thing, takes the possessive adjective: *its*.

144. (D) The participle form of the verb is needed to make a correct passive form — *may be added*.

145. (C) The preposition is incorrect; *from* should be used.

146. (C) The correct expression is *make a reservation*.

147. (B) Without *the* preceding *workers, of* cannot be used.

148. (D) *Permitted,* the past participle from a reduced adjective clause, should be used.

149. (A) The sentence is missing a verb; *is* should precede *best*.

150. (D) Use the adjective form, *other*, before the noun, *buildings*.

151. (B) The adjective form is never in the plural: *two-day program*.

152. (B) The adjective form, *colored*, should be used before the compound noun, *refrigerator magnets*.

153. (C) The preposition *of* is needed following *on top*.

154. (B) *Hardly* and *rarely* give the same information and are redundant; use one word or the other.

155. (A) The passive verb form is incomplete; use either *has been* or *was appointed*.

156. (D) The noun form is needed: *options*.

157. (C) *Equipment* is a noncount noun and is always in the singular form.

158. (D) The preposition choice is incorrect; *in* should be used.

159. (C) The correct noun form is *insurance*.

160. (C) The adjective form is needed before the noun: *financial*.

161. (A) *The city's newest and most elegant shopping center*, which is another word for a *mall*. The announcement continues *The mall includes...* Choices (B), (C), and (D) are contradicted by *shopping center*.

162. (D) *On the first floor is a ten-screen movie theater*. Choices (A), (B), and (C) are contradicted by this information.

163. (D) *The mall is open Monday through Saturday from 9 a.m. to 10 p.m. and Sundays from noon to 6 p.m.*, so the mall closes early on Sunday. Choices (A), (B), and (C) are contradicted by these statements.

164. (C) *Why study theory for several years when you learn all the basics of television and radio broadcasting in six months?* Therefore, the California School of Broadcasting is a training site. Although students can do an internship at a television studio, Choice (A), the school is not a station. Choice (B) confuses *real studios* with *movie studios*. Choice (D) is contradicted by *why study theory?*

165. (C) *You can learn all the basics... in six months*. Choice (A) confuses *the length of the program* with *the length of an externship*. Choice (B) confuses *the length of the program* with *the length of time in the studios*. Choice (D) confuses *the length of the program* with *why study for several years*.

166. (C) *You can learn all the basics of broadcasting*. Choices (A), (B), and (D) are not mentioned or implied.

167. (B) The length is mentioned: *in six months*; the location is mentioned: *suburban Pacific Palisades*; the facilities are mentioned: *state-of-the-art facilities*. Only *the cost* is NOT discussed. Choices (A), (C), and (D) are explicitly mentioned.

168. (B) *The mailing address for payments is shown to the right*. Choices (A), (C), and (D) are contradicted by this statement.

169. (C) *Payments received after 12:00 noon or on weekends or holidays may not be credited until the next business day*, so a payment made *at 9:00 a.m.* would be credited on the same business day. Choices (A), (B), and (D) are all after noon, on a weekend or a holiday, so would be credited the next business day.

170. (A) *Your maximum liability is $50 should you fail to report loss or theft*. Choices (B), (C), and (D) are contradicted by this statement.

171. (B) *A leader in the retailing of classic apparel for business women*; *apparel* means *clothing*. Choices (A), (C), and (D) are contradicted by this statement.

172. (C) *Working Women* has *experienced poor holiday sales due to shoppers buying... items instead of clothes*. Choice (A) is not mentioned. Choice (B) is confused with *post-holiday sale*; the sales did not begin later this year. Choice (D) is not mentioned.

173. (C) *See our two- and three-bedroom condominium models;* Boca East is a condominium complex. Choice (A) is contradicted by Boca East is *adjacent to the Boca Raton Resort and Club*. Choice (B) is contradicted by Boca East is *nearby fine dining*. Choice (D) is contradicted by Boca East is *nearby the Atlantic Ocean;* it is not stated that it is either a high rise or on the ocean.

174. (D) *There is a spectacular on-site work-out facility*, which is a *health club*. Choice (A) is contradicted by *adjacent to (next to) the golf course*. Choice (B) is not mentioned; there is shopping in downtown Boca Raton. Choice (C) is contradicted by *adjacent to tennis courts*.

175. (C) *The world's best daily* means the *Sun Star* is a newspaper. Choice (A) is not mentioned. Choice (B) confuses the *Sun Star* with its advertising supplement, *WORLDMARKET*. Choice (D) confuses *a market* with the name of advertising supplement, *WORLDMARKET*.

176. (B) *Wednesday* is *automotive*, the day to sell *a car*. Choices (A), (C), and (D) are contradicted by this information.

177. (C) *Friday* is *Residential Real Estate;* the day to *find an apartment*. Choices (A) and (D) are contradicted by this information. Choice (B) confuses the day for *Residential Real Estate* with the day for *Commercial Real Estate*.

178. (D) *Call, fax, or e-mail Sarah Perry.* Contacting *by letter* is not mentioned. Choices (A), (B), and (C) are all explicitly mentioned.

179. (A) *3% of U.S. companies export to more than five foreign markets*. Choices (B) and (D) confuse *only 15% of U.S. exporters account for 85% of the value of U.S.-manufactured exports* with the percentage of U.S. companies that sell to more than five markets abroad. Choice (C) confuses the fact that *20% of exporters export to more than five foreign markets* with the fact that *only 3% of U.S companies* do so.

180. (D) The announcement recommends that businesses should *continue to pursue export business even when the U.S. market is healthy*. Choices (A), (B), and (C) are contradicted by this statement.

181. (B) The announcement recommends that businesses should *be willing to adapt products to meet regulations of other countries*, meaning change products to meet local standards. Choices (A), (C) and (D) are not mentioned.

182. (D) *Below you will find names of agencies which can assist you.* Choices (A), (B), and (C) are contradicted by this statement.

183. (C) *For a long time it has been Sable's desire to retire at 62.* Choice (A) is incorrect because it is the age Sable is now: *retire at 62*, which is two years away. Choices (B) and (D) are not mentioned.

184. (B) *The vitamin company.* Choice (A) confuses *retirement advice* with the fact that the company president plans to retire. Choice (C) confuses *recruitment service* with the *recruitment efforts* the company is engaged in to find a successor to the president. Choice (D) confuses *biotechnology* with the company name *Biolife*.

185. (C) *Firm is seeking an administrator to... manage... the firm.* Choice (A) is not mentioned. Choice (B) confuses the fact the company is a *law firm* with its seeking *a manager*. Although the manager's responsibilities will include accounting, the firm is not seeking a billing clerk, Choice (D).

186. (A) *Small, expanding law firm is seeking...; expanding* means *growing*. Choice (B) is not mentioned. Choice (C) is incorrect; it is *a five-lawyer firm*. Choice (D) is incorrect; it is a *small, expanding firm*.

187. (D) *Please send salary requirements, a resume, and two letters of recommendation; a cover letter* is not mentioned. Choices (A), (B), and (C) are explicitly mentioned.

188. (D) *Your business name can be one of your most effective and least expensive marketing tools.* Choices (A), (B), and (C) are not mentioned.

189. (B) *Another mistake is choosing a name that is hard to spell*, so *Kind Kar Kare* would misspell *car* and *care*. Choices (A), (C), and (D) are by contradicted this information.

190. (A) *Another mistake is choosing a name that is hard to pronounce*, so easy pronunciation makes a good choice. Choices (B), (C), and (D) are all mentioned as things not to do: *another mistake is choosing a name that is hard to spell*; it is also a mistake to select a name that is *too general, others may create an obscure name* and *as a result the name might end up costing them money*.

191. (B) *As more and more workers moved from manufacturing to white collar jobs, it was believed they would toil in a vastly healthier work environment.* Office jobs are one kind of white collar job. Choices (A), (C), and (D) are not mentioned.

192. (D) *The first reports... were greeted with disbelief.* Choices (A), (B), and (C) are contradicted by this statement.

193. (A) *Workers have reported headaches, shortness of breath, and dizziness. Vomiting* is not mentioned. Choices (B), (C), and (D) are explicitly mentioned.

194. (C) *Michael Lane, the author of a widely-used accounting program;* he is a software programmer. Choices (A), (B), and (D) are contradicted by this information.

195. (B) *Four pirated versions are made for every one program sold*, so for twenty-eight pirated ones, 7 legitimate ones are sold. Choices (A), (C), and (D) are contradicted by this statement.

196. (D) *Any employee who copies software will be immediately disciplined.* Choice (A) may happen after *a hearing* is held. Choices (B) and (C) are not mentioned.

197. (B) *No special underwater suit is required*; therefore *a special diving suit is required* is NOT true. Choices (A), (C), and (D) are explicitly mentioned.

198. (C) The most logical place where this report would probably appear is in a magazine. There is no mention of this report being a fantasy, Choice (A). There is no mention of this report's being a movie scenario, Choice (B). There is no mention of any medical jargon, Choice (D).

199. (B) *Movies originated in the late 1800s.* Choices (A) is not mentioned. Choice (C) confuses when motion pictures began with when *specialized techniques and artistic theories* were developed. Choice (D) confuses when motion pictures began with when movies began to generate *scholarly attention*.

200. (D) *Movies generated little scholarly attention until the 1960s*, not throughout the century; therefore, Choice (D) is not correct. Choices (A) *there are thousands of books about film*, (B) *universities and colleges offer... advanced degrees*, and (C) *universities and colleges offer individual film courses* are all explicitly mentioned.

TEST
three

TEST OF ENGLISH FOR INTERNATIONAL COMMUNICATION

General Directions

This is a test of your ability to use the English language. The total time for the test is approximately two and a half hours. It is divided into seven parts. Each part of the test begins with a set of specific directions. Be sure you understand what you are to do before you begin to work on a part.

You will find that some of the questions are harder than others, but you should try to answer every one. There is no penalty for guessing. Do not be concerned if you cannot answer all of the questions.

Do not mark your answers in this test book. **You must put all of your answers on the separate answer sheet** that you have been given. When putting your answer to a question on your answer sheet, be sure to fill in the answer space corresponding to the letter of your choice. Fill in the space so that the letter inside the oval cannot be seen, as shown in the example below.

EXAMPLE

Mr. Palmer _____ with the president last month.
(A) meet
(B) meeting
(C) met
(D) to meet

Sample Answer: (A)   (B)   ●   (D)

The sentence should read, "Mr. Palmer met with the president last month." Therefore, you should choose answer (C). Notice how this has been done in the example given.

Mark only **ONE** answer for each question. If you change your mind about an answer after you have marked it on your answer sheet, completely erase your old answer and then mark your new answer. You must mark the answer sheet carefully so that your score can be recorded accurately.

LISTENING COMPREHENSION

In this section of the test, you will have the chance to show how well you understand spoken English. There are four parts to this section, with special directions for each part.

Directions

For each question, you will see a picture in your test book and you will hear four short statements. The statements will be spoken just one time. They will not be written in your test book; therefore, you must listen carefully in order to understand what the speaker says.

When you hear the four statements, look at the picture in your test book and choose the statement that best describes what you see in the picture. Then, on your answer sheet, find the number of the question and mark your answer. Look at the sample picture.

EXAMPLE

Now listen to the four statements.

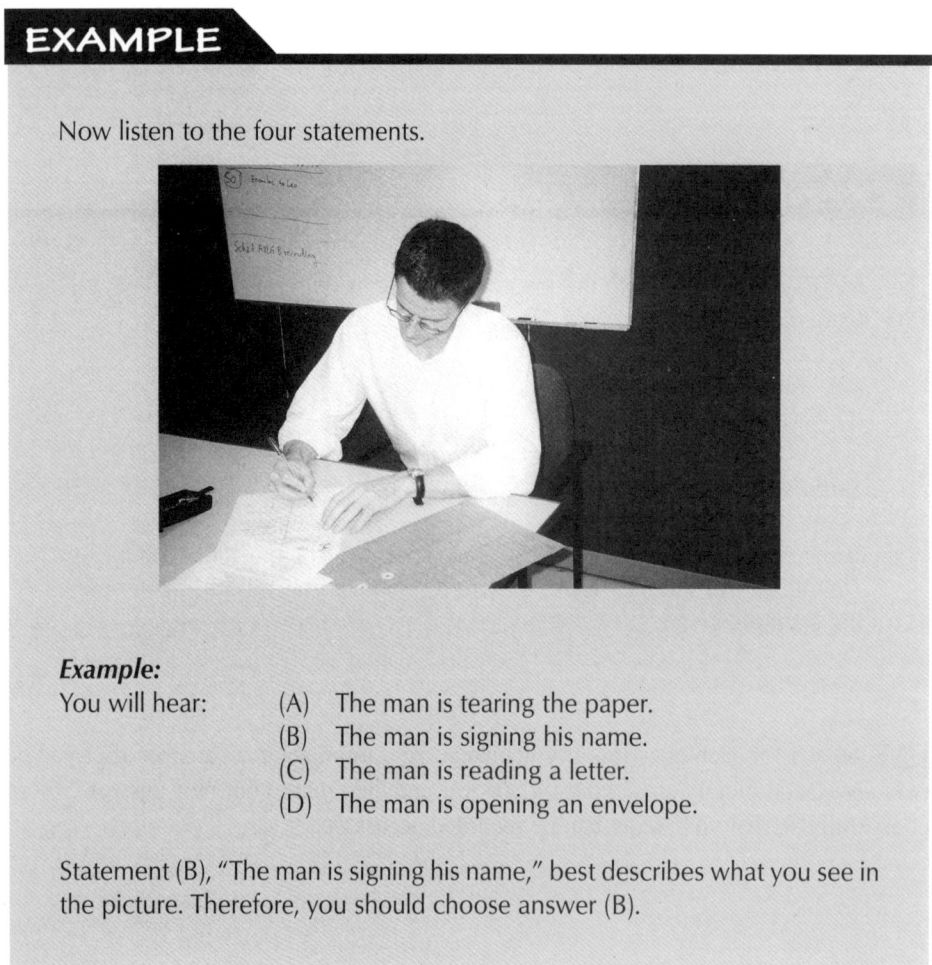

Example:
You will hear:
(A) The man is tearing the paper.
(B) The man is signing his name.
(C) The man is reading a letter.
(D) The man is opening an envelope.

Statement (B), "The man is signing his name," best describes what you see in the picture. Therefore, you should choose answer (B).

1

2

3

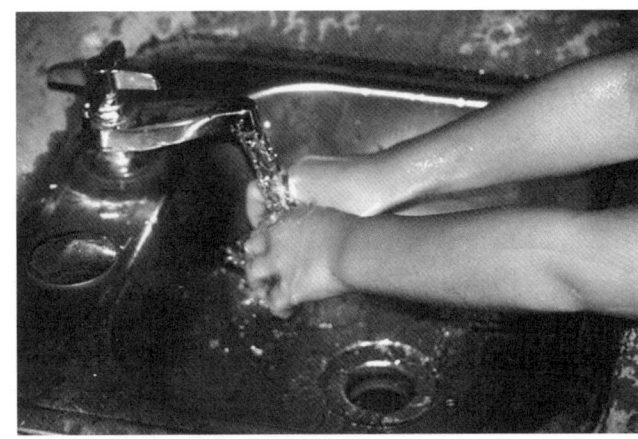

TEST THREE

13

14

15

▶ 16

▶ 17

TEST THREE

18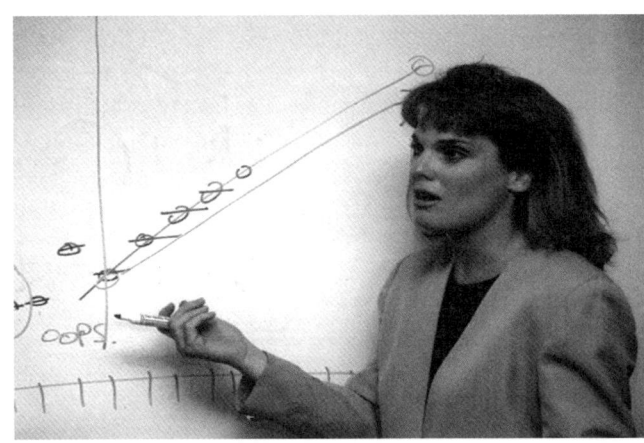

19

20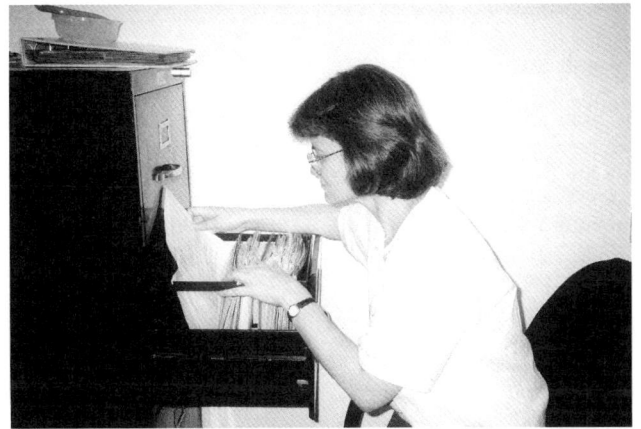

Directions

In this part of the test, you will hear a question spoken in English, followed by three responses, also spoken in English. The question and the responses will be spoken just one time. They will not be written out for you; therefore, you must listen carefully to understand. You are to choose the best response to each question.

EXAMPLE

Now listen to a sample question.

You will hear: Good morning, John. How are you?

You will also hear: (A)   I am fine, thank you.
                            (B)   I am in the living room.
                            (C)   My name is John.

The best response to the question "How are you?" is choice (A), "I am fine, thank you." Therefore, you should choose answer (A).

21. Mark your answer on your answer sheet.
22. Mark your answer on your answer sheet.
23. Mark your answer on your answer sheet.
24. Mark your answer on your answer sheet.
25. Mark your answer on your answer sheet.
26. Mark your answer on your answer sheet.
27. Mark your answer on your answer sheet.
28. Mark your answer on your answer sheet.
29. Mark your answer on your answer sheet.
30. Mark your answer on your answer sheet.
31. Mark your answer on your answer sheet.
32. Mark your answer on your answer sheet.
33. Mark your answer on your answer sheet.
34. Mark your answer on your answer sheet.
35. Mark your answer on your answer sheet.
36. Mark your answer on your answer sheet.
37. Mark your answer on your answer sheet.
38. Mark your answer on your answer sheet.
39. Mark your answer on your answer sheet.
40. Mark your answer on your answer sheet.
41. Mark your answer on your answer sheet.
42. Mark your answer on your answer sheet.
43. Mark your answer on your answer sheet.
44. Mark your answer on your answer sheet.
45. Mark your answer on your answer sheet.
46. Mark your answer on your answer sheet.
47. Mark your answer on your answer sheet.
48. Mark your answer on your answer sheet.
49. Mark your answer on your answer sheet.
50. Mark your answer on your answer sheet.

Directions

In this part of the test, you will hear short conversations between two people. The conversations will not be written in your test book. You will hear the conversations only once; therefore, you must listen carefully.

In your test book, you will read a short question about each conversation. The question will be followed by four short answers. You are to choose the best answer to each question and mark it on your answer sheet.

51. What does the woman want to know?
    (A) The address of Prime Computer
    (B) If the company has any job openings
    (C) If she can fax her materials
    (D) Where to send the check

52. What does the man want to do?
    (A) Get a new printer
    (B) Put his theories into practice
    (C) Be able to use the copy machine for back-to-back copies
    (D) Use the copy machine to print from his computer

53. What is said about the new postal rate?
    (A) Prices vary from country to country.
    (B) The claims are reliable.
    (C) Its delivery to the Far East is great.
    (D) It can only be used for Singapore.

54. Where is the conversation taking place?
    (A) In an office
    (B) At the post office
    (C) On the telephone
    (D) At a furniture store

55. What does the woman suggest?
    (A) That they head out of town
    (B) That they try a different route
    (C) That they take a vacation
    (D) That they get a traffic report

56. What will the man probably do?
    (A) Continue advertising on TV
    (B) Return to using the newspaper
    (C) Inherit a small fortune
    (D) Make another commercial

57. What is happening in six weeks?
    (A) The telephone area code is changing.
    (B) New postal codes will be announced.
    (C) The woman will pick up her stationery.
    (D) New business cards will be printed.

58. What does the woman suggest?
    (A) The man can make them dinner.
    (B) She'll cook them spaghetti.
    (C) She'll teach him how to cook.
    (D) They can eat in a restaurant.

59. Where does this conversation take place?
    (A) In Seattle
    (B) At a travel agency
    (C) On an airplane
    (D) At an airport

60. What does the man want to do?
    (A) Get a license
    (B) Change some money
    (C) Cash a check
    (D) Open an account

61. What is said about Carmen Lopez?
    (A) She's the new credit manager.
    (B) She's leaving at 5:00.
    (C) She doesn't get paid enough.
    (D) She thinks her job is too demanding.

62. Why was the man embarrassed?
    (A) Because Michael no longer works there
    (B) Because he mistook the person's name
    (C) Because Karen answered the phone
    (D) Because he had the wrong number

GO ON TO THE NEXT PAGE

63. What does the woman need?
    (A) Help filling out an application
    (B) To have a check signed
    (C) A ride to the man's home
    (D) To use an electric typewriter

64. What does the man offer to do?
    (A) Help decorate
    (B) Speak to the president
    (C) Call the country club
    (D) Plan the retirement party

65. What does the woman want to buy?
    (A) Painting supplies
    (B) Beach blankets
    (C) Outdoor film
    (D) Photo albums

66. What is the man's problem?
    (A) He does not know whose signature he needs.
    (B) He's in pain from his last trip.
    (C) His travel plans are frequently made at the last minute.
    (D) His expenses are not always authorized.

67. What does the woman want to do?
    (A) Drive the company's truck
    (B) Transport her purchases
    (C) Pay for the couch and dresser
    (D) Shop for some new furniture

68. What does the woman suggest?
    (A) That he meet her college roommate
    (B) That he lend her an umbrella
    (C) That the three of them see the match
    (D) That they go out some other time

69. What will the woman probably do?
    (A) Ask someone else from work for a ride
    (B) Leave before rush hour
    (C) Drop off her suitcase at the station earlier
    (D) Walk to the station

70. What did the woman learn about the company?
    (A) Hiring will soon take place
    (B) The quarter was profitable
    (C) That people will be laid off
    (D) That profits were down again

71. What does the woman advise?
    (A) To enter at the front
    (B) To get off at 67th Street
    (C) To use the side entrance
    (D) To walk to the interview

72. What does the man want to know?
    (A) Where the woman's neighbor has been relocated
    (B) If she's heard from her neighbor
    (C) How many apartments are vacant in the building
    (D) If her neighbor's apartment has been rented

73. What does Suzy want to know?
    (A) If she can get her hair cut
    (B) If she can fit into the parking space
    (C) If her appointment is at 4:00
    (D) If there are any cancellations

74. What is Janet being asked to do?
    (A) Select some puppets
    (B) Buy a glass to replace a broken one
    (C) Attend a conference in Prague
    (D) Pick up the man's prescription glasses

75. What's the problem?
    (A) No one is returning calls.
    (B) There are too many messages.
    (C) Message lights will not stop flashing.
    (D) The telephones have no dial tone.

76. When does this conversation take place?
    (A) On Monday
    (B) On Wednesday
    (C) On Thursday
    (D) On Friday

TEST THREE

77. What does the woman want to buy?
    (A) Boots
    (B) An umbrella
    (C) Leather shoes
    (D) A rubber hose

78. What are they discussing?
    (A) A change machine
    (B) Renovating the lobby
    (C) Converting money
    (D) A drink machine

79. What does the man need to know?
    (A) The number of games
    (B) If she will go with him
    (C) Practice times
    (D) When tryouts are

80. What does the man suggest?
    (A) That high school students visit their workplace
    (B) That they organize some demonstrations
    (C) That computers be outfitted with new software
    (D) That the company donate some computers

GO ON TO THE NEXT PAGE

Part IV

Directions

In this part of the test, you will hear several short talks. Each will be spoken just one time. They will not be written out for you; therefore, you will have to listen carefully in order to understand and remember what is said.

In your test book, you will read two or more questions about each short talk. The questions will be followed by four answers. You are to choose the best answer to each question and mark it on your answer sheet.

81. Where is this announcement being made?
    (A) In Nashville
    (B) At a radio station
    (C) In an airport
    (D) Aboard a plane

82. What are the people on flight 312 requested to do?
    (A) Reschedule their flight
    (B) Listen to the weather report
    (C) Leave for home
    (D) Remain in the airport

83. Who will attend the luncheon?
    (A) Retirees
    (B) Employees
    (C) Investment bankers
    (D) Financial planners

84. What are participants asked to do?
    (A) Submit questions to Ms. Chu
    (B) Contact Mr. Almquist before the luncheon
    (C) Raise concerns during the lecture
    (D) Write to Mr. Almquist

85. How much money does the auction hope to raise?
    (A) $100
    (B) $2,000
    (C) $20,000
    (D) $30,000

86. How long will the first vocal auction last?
    (A) 30 minutes
    (B) 60 minutes
    (C) 90 minutes
    (D) 120 minutes

87. How will someone know if he/she wins an item from the silent auction?
    (A) His/Her name will be announced.
    (B) He/She can check the bid sheet.
    (C) Winners will be notified in writing during the second vocal auction.
    (D) A banner will announce all winners.

88. Where are the people who are listening to this talk?
    (A) In a rainstorm
    (B) On a ship
    (C) On a trolley
    (D) On the Pacific Ocean

89. How long is the tour?
    (A) 20 minutes
    (B) 1 hour
    (C) 2 hours
    (D) 3 hours

90. How much will a $100 purchase be discounted during the sale?
    (A) $10
    (B) $20
    (C) $25
    (D) $50

TEST THREE

91. How long has the establishment been in business?
    (A) 1 year
    (B) 2 years
    (C) 5 years
    (D) 10 years

92. What is the job being advertised?
    (A) A marketing director
    (B) A graphic designer
    (C) A Spanish translator
    (D) A tour guide

93. How much experience is needed for the job?
    (A) 6 months
    (B) 1 year
    (C) 2 years
    (D) 3 years

94. How will the salary be determined?
    (A) By the salary history
    (B) By the amount of sales
    (C) By the number of markets
    (D) By the number of educational degrees

95. How many runners are in this year's field?
    (A) 100
    (B) 1000
    (C) 7000
    (D) 10,000

96. What is the function of the computer chip?
    (A) It verifies that a runner completes the race.
    (B) It records each runner's actual time.
    (C) It keeps track of the number of runners.
    (D) It divides the runners into groups.

97. Who will be first behind the starting line?
    (A) Runners without computer chips
    (B) Previous marathon runners with fast times
    (C) Residents of the city of Dublin
    (D) Registrants whose applications arrived first

98. Where does this introduction take place?
    (A) At a retirement party
    (B) At a luncheon meeting
    (C) At a recruitment seminar
    (D) At a hiring interview

99. What was Ms. Arthur's last position?
    (A) A secretary
    (B) An editor
    (C) A librarian
    (D) A typesetter

100. How long has Ms. Arthur worked at the company?
    (A) 5 years
    (B) 10 years
    (C) 25 years
    (D) 40 years

This is the end of the Listening Comprehension portion of the test. Turn to Part V in your test book.

GO ON TO THE NEXT PAGE

YOU WILL HAVE ONE HOUR AND FIFTEEN MINUTES TO COMPLETE PARTS V, VI, AND VII OF THE TEST.

READING

In this section of the test, you will have the chance to show how well you understand written English. There are three parts to this section, with special directions for each part.

Directions

This part of the test has incomplete sentences. Four words or phrases, marked (A), (B), (C), (D), are given beneath each sentence. You are to choose the **ONE** word or phrase that best completes the sentence. Then, on your answer sheet, find the number of the question and mark your answer.

EXAMPLE

Because the equipment is very delicate, it must be handled with _____ .
(A) caring
(B) careful
(C) care
(D) carefully

The sentence should read, "Because the equipment is very delicate, it must be handled with care." Therefore, you should choose answer (C).

Now begin work on the questions.

101. When the car radio was first introduced, people thought of it as a dangerous _____ .
   (A) accommodation
   (B) living
   (C) surrounding
   (D) luxury

102. Now you can purchase a seat and pick up your boarding pass at the airport on the day of departure _____ simply showing appropriate identification.
   (A) together
   (B) for
   (C) by
   (D) with

103. According to many interior designers, the wastebasket may be the most _____ piece of equipment in your office.
    (A) interrogative
    (B) indispensable
    (C) instantaneous
    (D) involuntary

104. Mr. Johnson's _____ will be named at the executive meeting on Friday.
    (A) successor
    (B) succinctness
    (C) subsequence
    (D) substance

105. _____ the cost, many companies are choosing to renovate rather than relocate.
    (A) But
    (B) Although
    (C) Despite
    (D) In spite of the fact that

106. No one was surprised that Mr. Lee _____ to retire.
    (A) deciding
    (B) is being decided
    (C) had been decided
    (D) decided

107. Not only the management _____ the customers are delighted with the new fall designs.
    (A) and
    (B) but also
    (C) yet
    (D) neither

108. Rarely _____ seen such a quick turnaround.
    (A) have we
    (B) have
    (C) we have
    (D) that we have

109. Many publishing companies _____ their own artists to design advertising materials.
    (A) run into
    (B) look up
    (C) rely on
    (D) browse through

110. Numerous _____ textile manufacturers in the Northeast have gone out of business recently.
    (A) lead
    (B) leader
    (C) leaden
    (D) leading

111. If the tapes do not meet with your satisfaction, you can return _____ within sixty days for a full refund.
    (A) it
    (B) them
    (C) him
    (D) yourselves

112. Each department suggested _____ the firm could implement immediately.
    (A) cutbacks
    (B) cutouts
    (C) cuttings
    (D) cutaways

113. She took the suit _____ to the dressmaker's to be altered.
    (A) bought it
    (B) that she bought it
    (C) that she bought
    (D) it that she bought

114. _____ business school graduates pursue employment in business-related fields.
    (A) The students of
    (B) The maximum of
    (C) The number of
    (D) The majority of

115. One must _____ an overnight compartment in advance.
    (A) to reserve
    (B) reserve
    (C) reserved
    (D) be reserved

GO ON TO THE NEXT PAGE

116. The sales force was encouraged by the _____ program.
    (A) intention
    (B) incision
    (C) incentive
    (D) infringement

117. Mr. Jeffries was _____ to hear you're leaving so soon.
    (A) surrendered
    (B) surprised
    (C) surfaced
    (D) surpassed

118. There is no _____ that negotiations will resume anytime soon.
    (A) sign
    (B) check
    (C) mark
    (D) symptom

119. Each country has its own regulations _____ fruit and vegetable imports.
    (A) pertaining
    (B) against
    (C) allowable
    (D) regarding

120. Additional _____ need to be installed in each office before the new computers can be used.
    (A) numbers
    (B) supplies
    (C) outlets
    (D) factions

121. Originally ocean liners _____ for commerce and transportation.
    (A) have built
    (B) that they build
    (C) that built
    (D) were built

122. For your _____, you can call our customer service representatives 24 hours a day.
    (A) desire
    (B) convenience
    (C) accuracy
    (D) permission

123. The participants were dismayed when the negotiations reached a _____.
    (A) standstill
    (B) finite
    (C) transaction
    (D) position

124. Carry-on baggage must be placed in the overhead compartments or _____ the seat in front of you during takeoff and landing.
    (A) parallel
    (B) down
    (C) underneath
    (D) lower

125. The critics found little _____ in the recently released comedy.
    (A) amusingly
    (B) to amuse
    (C) amused
    (D) amusing

126. Since item 612B is out of stock, we hope you will consider _____ item.
    (A) other
    (B) another
    (C) each other
    (D) one another

127. Recording devices _____ in the concert hall.
    (A) are not permitted
    (B) will have no admission
    (C) cannot be made
    (D) have no allowance

128. A _____ for Dr. Spack has not yet been found.
    (A) displacement
    (B) separation
    (C) dismissal
    (D) replacement

129. Everyone was surprised to learn that Mr. Takahara cuts his hair _____ .
    (A) hisself
    (B) him
    (C) himself
    (D) it

130. It is expected that one be nervous _____ one's boss for the first time.
    (A) meet
    (B) meeting
    (C) met
    (D) meets

131. We _____ your account for the defective merchandise.
    (A) crediting
    (B) to be credited
    (C) will have credited
    (D) will credit

132. Gasoline prices are lower due to the _____ of oil on the market.
    (A) glut
    (B) hike
    (C) greed
    (D) fullness

133. _____ the two publishing houses to merge, they would control all textbook production worldwide.
    (A) Providing
    (B) With
    (C) Were
    (D) Planning

134. The Drake Hotel in downtown Chicago sits _____ Lake Michigan.
    (A) overhearing
    (B) overlooking
    (C) overcrowding
    (D) overseeing

135. The Hong Kong biotechnology firm is one _____ .
    (A) is watched
    (B) watch
    (C) watching
    (D) to watch

136. Repairing the office copier _____ is of utmost concern to all.
    (A) immediately
    (B) currently
    (C) relatively
    (D) respectively

137. Outdoor billboards are the most cost-effective way of _____ the consumer.
    (A) noticing
    (B) reaching
    (C) contracting
    (D) gaining

138. Mr. Vigriolo _____ his lecture with a humorous remark.
    (A) receded
    (B) seceded
    (C) preceded
    (D) conceded

139. The popular suitcase comes in _____ colors and fabrics.
    (A) numerous of
    (B) amounts of
    (C) multitude of
    (D) dozens of

140. For passengers traveling into the city, taxis and car services charge _____ 50 dollars.
    (A) imminently
    (B) approximately
    (C) relatively
    (D) decreasingly

GO ON TO THE NEXT PAGE

Directions

In this part of the test, each sentence has four words or phrases underlined. The four underlined parts of the sentence are marked (A), (B), (C), (D). You are to identify the **ONE** underlined word or phrase that should be corrected or rewritten. Then, on your answer sheet, find the number of the question and mark your answer.

EXAMPLE

All <u>employee</u> are required <u>to wear</u> their <u>identification</u> badges <u>while</u> at work.
    A   B   C   D

Choice (A), the underlined word "employee," is not correct in this sentence. The sentence should read, "All employees are required to wear their identification badges while at work." Therefore, you should choose answer (A).

Now begin work on the questions.

141. <u>Our</u> next flight <u>with seats available</u> <u>leave</u> at
     A   B   C
ten o'clock <u>this evening</u>.
                D

142. The firm that <u>submitted</u> the <u>most cheapest</u>
                A   B
estimate <u>also</u> has <u>the best</u> recommendations.
        C   D

143. <u>All</u> new hires <u>must to submit</u> a resume, two
    A   B
<u>reference</u> letters, and results <u>from</u> a medical
   C   D
check-up.

144. <u>While</u> Mrs. Alcaron is <u>on</u> vacation, <u>his</u>
   A   B   C
assistant will answer the telephone and
<u>respond to</u> all inquiries.
   D

145. Although the sole <u>bases</u> of the state's economy
                   A
is tourism, <u>vast</u> sums <u>have been invested</u> <u>in</u>
          B   C   D
farming.

146. <u>A</u> one-hour lecture <u>will precede</u> the <u>viewing</u>
   A   B   C
of the film "Architecture in the Workplace"
next Tuesday <u>on</u> the first-floor auditorium.
            D

147. Every two weeks a meeting <u>among</u> <u>the senior</u>
                           A   B
partners of the firm <u>is held</u> to discuss and to
                 C
analyze <u>differently</u> issues.
        D

148. The accounting department is looking forward to organization(A) the annual(B) picnic which will be held on(C) August 4 at Crater Lake from(D) noon to dusk.

149. As we move into the new office suites(A) this month, we remind all employees of the decision not to take(B) any(C) furnitures(D) from the old building.

150. Most brochure(A) are now designed and printed by the design department, saving(B) the company thousands(C) of dollars annually(D).

151. Anyone(A) who visits Boston in(B) the next two years will find(C) driving downtown a nightmare due to the highway construction has(D) detours.

152. Because(A) the factory plans to remain open during(B) the summer holiday period, supervisors will no(C) be allowed to take more than two consecutive weeks(D) of vacation.

153. Several computers problems(A) have been caused(B) recently by the spilling(C) of soft drinks onto(D) keyboards.

154. Numerous retailers report(A) that consumer demand for small stuffed animals between(B) teenagers has resulted(C) in increased(D) sales this quarter.

155. Public(A) telephones can be found(B) on the first, fifth, and tenth floors, as well as(C) in basement(D).

156. A(A) registration sheet for noontime(B) aerobic classes it is(C) posted in room 321 until classes fill(D).

157. Once(A) you have checked the drafting(B) of the soon-to-be-published(C) phone directory, initial your name, indicating accuracy(D), or make the necessary corrections in red ink.

158. Paychecks can picked(A) up at(B) the personnel(C) office every Friday between(D) 2:00 and 4:00.

159. In the next(A) century a shortage trained(B) workers in the fields of information technology(C), health care, and engineering has(D) been predicted.

160. As(A) we were unable to fill all requests for the annual banquet, either(B) accept the number of tickets you have allotted(C) or request a refund by the end of(D) the week.

GO ON TO THE NEXT PAGE

Directions

The questions in this part of the test are based on a variety of reading material, such as notices, letters, newspaper and magazine articles, and advertisements. You are to choose the **ONE** best answer, (A), (B), (C), or (D), to each question. Then, on your answer sheet, find the number of the question and mark your answer. Answer all questions following a passage on the basis of what is **stated** or **implied** in that passage.

EXAMPLE

Read the following example.

> The Museum of Technology is designed for people to experience science at work. Visitors are encouraged to use, test, and handle the objects on display. Special demonstrations are scheduled for the first and second Wednesdays of each month at 1:30 p.m. Open Tuesday-Friday, 2:30-4:30 p.m., Saturday 11:00 a.m. -4:30 p.m., and Sunday 1:00-4:30 p.m.

When during the month can visitors see special demonstrations?
(A) Every weekend
(B) The first two Wednesdays
(C) One afternoon a week
(D) Every other Wednesday

The passage says that the demonstrations are scheduled on the first and second Wednesdays of the month. Therefore, you should choose answer (B).

Now begin work on the questions.

Questions 161-162 refer to the following offer.

Looking for a great promotional item?

Put your company's logo on our watches.

- Unlimited colors at no extra charge.
- No minimum quantity.
- Best prices. Over 25 years of experience.
- 23K gold-plated, water-resistant, leather strap.

Brochures and prices available upon request.
Call, write, fax, or visit us on the web.

YOUR LOGO WATCH COMPANY

161. Where would this advertisement most likely appear?
 (A) In a magazine
 (B) On a news telecast
 (C) In a manual
 (D) On a banner

162. What can be said about the watches the advertisement promotes?
 (A) They are solid gold.
 (B) They have a variety of straps.
 (C) They can be worn in the rain.
 (D) There's a minimum quantity in stock.

GO ON TO THE NEXT PAGE

Questions 163-164 refer to the following invitation.

You are kindly invited to the groundbreaking ceremony for the Abraham and Sarah Miller Memorial production plant, which replaces the one destroyed in the 1997 fire. Come view our facility, examine our state-of-the-art equipment, and enjoy our luncheon buffet. Shuttle buses will run every ten minutes from the downtown bus terminal.

11:30–12:30	Tour
12:30–1:30	Groundbreaking ceremony Welcome remarks Video highlighting the past, present, and future
1:30	Luncheon
3:00	Last shuttle bus departs

163. Why was the new facility constructed?
 (A) To increase production capability
 (B) To meet federal codes for its equipment
 (C) To replace the previous one
 (D) To be closer to downtown

164. How long will the luncheon last?
 (A) One hour
 (B) One and a half hours
 (C) Two hours
 (D) Three and a half hours

Questions 165-167 refer to the following document.

Rental Agreement

I hereby attest to an agreement between

_____ and UCA
(your full name, you are the lessee)

Realty. The lessee agrees to a one-year lease

for the property at _____.
(fill in exact address, include apartment number)

The lessee agrees to pay for all utilities and telephone charges. The lessee will, upon signing, pay the first and last month's rent, as well as a one-month security deposit which will be held in a 5% annual interest-bearing account. Upon cessation of the lease and a check of the apartment, the deposit will be returned in full, minus any damage charges incurred by the lessee.

165. This agreement is to be made between UCA Realty and what other party?
 (A) An accountant
 (B) A banker
 (C) A tenant
 (D) A lawyer

166. Which of the following does the lessee NOT have to pay upon signing?
 (A) The first month's rent
 (B) A security deposit
 (C) The last month's rent
 (D) The first month's utilities

167. If no damage occurred, how much money would be returned on a $500 deposit?
 (A) $505
 (B) $525
 (C) $550
 (D) $2500

GO ON TO THE NEXT PAGE

Questions 168-169 refer to the following news notice.

WHAT MEETS THE EYE ISN'T ENOUGH FOR SOME ARTISTS. REARRANGING REALITY IN HAND-PAINTED PHOTOGRAPHS IS THE SPECIALTY OF NINA DWYER, WHO PHOTOGRAPHS VIBRANT SCENES WITH BLACK-AND-WHITE FILM, THEN HAND PAINTS HER IMAGES WITH OIL COLORS.

HER WORKS ARE ON DISPLAY, AND FROM MARCH 12-APRIL 5, SELECTED ONES MAY BE PURCHASED AT THE NELSON GALLERY, 178 CENTRAL STREET.

168. What can be said about Ms. Dwyer?
 (A) First she paints her pictures.
 (B) She is strictly a photographer.
 (C) She primarily produces portraits.
 (D) She works with two mediums.

169. Which of the following does the passage support?
 (A) One need not purchase a work of Ms. Dwyer's at the gallery.
 (B) All of Ms. Dwyer's works will be for sale.
 (C) Ms. Dwyer's work will be on display for two months.
 (D) Using black-and-white film is less expensive.

Questions 170-171 refer to the following advertisement.

Don't miss the newly redesigned
NETWORKS EXPO BOSTON,
the interactive forum for real-world networking solutions!

**HEALTH CARE
FINANCE
EDUCATION**

Networking Communications Technologies and Solutions in the Heart of these Powerful New England Markets:

✔ **Networking**: Internet, multimedia, video-conferencing and more.

✔ **Security:** Detecting break-ins, security audits, fraud and more.

✔ **Communications:** Computer telephone systems and products.

✔ **Health care:** Technologies for every facet of the health care industry.

✔ **Financial:** Networking application products for the banking, insurance, and accounting fields.

**WORLD TRADE CENTER/BOSTON, MASSACHUSETTS
JUNE 2–4**

170. To which of the following is the advertisement addressed?
(A) Telephone operators
(B) Banking executives
(C) Veterinarians
(D) Fashion merchandisers

171. Which of the following is true about the Expo?
(A) It is permanently located at the World Trade Center.
(B) Its registration fees are extremely high.
(C) Its format has been revised.
(D) It showcases British merchandise.

Questions 172-175 refer to the following news report.

The Federal Aviation Administration grounded scores of planes manufactured before 1970 for inspections to fuel pump wiring. Damage was found in half of the first 80 inspected. Saying engine vibration was probably the cause, agency officials added that they feared that frayed insulation could lead to a spark from the 110-volt wires that could cause a fire or explosion. Several national and international flights were canceled as a result.

172. What probably caused the damage?
 (A) Defective fuel pumps
 (B) Faulty wiring
 (C) Vibrations from the engine
 (A) Frayed insulation

173. In how many planes was damage found?
 (A) 40
 (B) 80
 (C) 110
 (D) 160

174. What did agency officials fear might happen?
 (A) The engine could fall out.
 (B) An airplane could explode.
 (C) Passengers could get sick on flights.
 (D) Flight schedules could be disrupted.

175. What effect did the grounding have on passengers?
 (A) Flights were rerouted.
 (B) Flights were delayed.
 (C) Flights were called off.
 (D) Flights were combined.

Questions 176-178 refer to the following advertisement.

PLANT THE FUTURE

GLOBAL ReLEAF 2002

You can plant trees with GLOBAL ReLEAF and make an important difference in the new millennium.

Every tree cleans the air, purifies the water, furnishes the earth with oxygen, and provides shade to reduce not only energy bills, but the effects of global warming.

Our goal is to plant 20 million trees by the year 2002 — trees urgently needed to restore damaged forest ecosystems.

Please dig in. If you can't plant your own tree, or if you want to do more, GLOBAL ReLEAF will plant 10 trees for every $10 you donate, which is only one dollar per tree. We'll also send you a personalized certificate. Just call us today or visit our web site.

GLOBAL ReLEAF 2002 is a campaign of American Forests, the nation's oldest citizen conservation organization, founded in 1875.

176. Which of the following is NOT mentioned as a benefit of trees?
   (A) A decrease in the effects of global warming
   (B) Reduced pollution
   (C) Purer water and air
   (D) Lower energy costs

177. If someone donates $100, how many trees will be planted?
   (A) 10
   (B) 100
   (C) 1,000
   (D) 10,000

178. What is true about the program?
   (A) Whoever wishes to plant a tree must do it by him/herself.
   (B) The government is overseeing this program.
   (C) Everyone's certificate will say the same thing.
   (D) The sponsoring organization was founded in the nineteenth century.

Questions 179-181 are based on the following news item.

A computer glitch at Bank of Toronto's automated teller machines yesterday raised the eyebrows and blood pressure of hundreds of customers who were told that their checking accounts had been closed or could not be found. The mishap, which bank spokeswoman Diane Larson said affected all of Bank of Toronto's 1,550 ATMs in the greater Toronto area, occurred when a routine computer program designed to expand file space sent false information to the network. The problem began at approximately 6:30 a.m. and lasted until 8:00 a.m. At 8:00, customers could finally get cash but not account information. The glitch did not affect savings or other accounts. Larson said the bank found out about the problem as soon as it began and that all ATMs were fully functional by 8:45 a.m.

179. What caused the Bank of Toronto's ATM problem?
 (A) An overload of information
 (B) Excessive demand
 (C) Expanded file space
 (D) A computer error

180. What happened when customers used an ATM machine at 7:00 a.m.?
 (A) They could access all their accounts.
 (B) They could check their savings account balance.
 (C) They could get cash from their checking account.
 (D) They could verify their recent checking account transactions.

181. At what time were the ATMs able to perform all their functions?
 (A) 6:30 a.m.
 (B) 8:00 a.m.
 (C) 8:30 a.m.
 (D) 8:45 a.m.

Questions 182-184 are based on the following advertisement.

LAMP SHADES
A Unique Retail Concept That Outshines the Rest

Own an *A SHADE BETTER* franchise, a one-of-a-kind retail opportunity. Our enormous selection of 2,000 lamp shades and 500 lamps gives you the edge in a retail market with little or no competition.

In just two years we've opened stores in Chicago, Cleveland, Dallas, Milwaukee, and Phoenix. Why not open a store in your hometown?

Benefits include exclusive territory rights, extensive training, access to volume buying, and high profile marketing.

The Home Furnishings market is booming and NOW is the best time to invest. Call now to bring an *A SHADE BETTER* franchise to your city.

182. What product does *A Shade Better* sell?
    (A) Sunglasses
    (B) Home furniture
    (C) Lamp coverings
    (D) Shoeshine kits

183. What can a franchisee expect from the company?
    (A) Financing
    (B) Market exclusivity
    (C) An incentive program
    (D) Annual bonuses

184. What city does not yet have an *A Shade Better* franchise?
    (A) Miami
    (B) Cleveland
    (C) Dallas
    (D) Phoenix

GO ON TO THE NEXT PAGE

Questions 185-187 refer to the following article.

Give Credit Where Credit Is Due
10 ways to praise employees

Positive reinforcement is an important part of employee motivation — yet praising good work is not as simple as it seems. "The last time many people heard applause was at their high school graduation," says Peter Brookstone in his book *Peter Brookstone on People Management*. So how do you reward your employees' good performance? Start by using these tactics to help you compliment them more effectively.

1. Praise behavior you want to reinforce.
2. Avoid insincere or superficial remarks.
3. Give specific compliments.
4. Reward people immediately.
5. When possible, make a public compliment.
6. Make it personal.
7. Put it in writing.
8. Start your compliment with the word *I*. A simple *I appreciate it* is invaluable.
9. Never follow with *but*, *however*, or *except*.
10. Just do it!

185. What is true about giving positive reinforcement?
    (A) It is motivational for the work force.
    (B) It is more effective when given orally.
    (C) It is best done in private.
    (D) It is very easy to do.

186. Which of the following remarks would Brookstone most endorse?
    (A) Except for some typing mistakes, your report is excellent.
    (B) I am very appreciative of your extra work on the design project, Paul.
    (C) Good job, everyone, on last year's profit margins.
    (D) You have done a great job, but last month's totals were not so good.

187. To what does the word *it* in item number ten refer?
    (A) Use the word *but*.
    (B) Applaud a recent graduate.
    (C) Give a compliment.
    (D) Read Brookstone's book.

Questions 188-190 refer to the following brochure.

From the air, metropolitan Phoenix looks like a mirage — a glistening, shimmering city of 2.3 million, spreading across a vast expanse of desert. Its sprawl is stopped only by mountain ranges to the north, south, east, and west. Get down into it, though, and you'll quickly see why visitors keep coming back for more, and why so many have moved to Phoenix since the mid-1940s and the dawn of air conditioning. It's friendly, relaxed, and outdoorsy. With 300 days of sun a year, people don't stay cranky very long. The Valley of the Sun, as Phoenix and the 22 smaller surrounding cities are nicknamed, lures visitors with obvious possibilities. Golf is a huge draw, with more than 140 courses in the area. The area also entices sports fans with four professional teams. Rent a car, for everything is spread out, and public transportation is in its infancy.

188. How does Phoenix look from the sky?
 (A) Like a mountain range
 (B) Like an oasis
 (C) Like an illusion
 (D) Like a golf course

189. Why did so many people move to Phoenix after the mid-1940s?
 (A) To watch the sports teams
 (B) Because of air conditioning
 (C) To play golf
 (D) Because of the sunshine

190. What can be said about Phoenix?
 (A) Golfing is a seasonal sport.
 (B) It has a developed public transportation system.
 (C) The sun shines about half the time.
 (D) It is surrounded by mountains.

Questions 191-193 refer to the following advertisement.

INTRODUCING THE BIGGEST, MOST EXPENSIVE CRUISE SHIP EVER BUILT

IMAGINE AN ENTERTAINMENT AND DINING EXTRAVAGANZA TO RIVAL THE CITY THAT NEVER SLEEPS. $450 million and four years in the making, Grand Duchess is home to more excitement than most cities. In every way she's the absolute pinnacle of grand cruising. With over 700 private balconies — more than any other cruise ship — you enjoy cruising as it was truly meant to be. Dine any time, day or night, at nine different onboard locations. Choose from three different shows every single night. Accompany Grand Duchess as she embarks on her historic fall Caribbean debut, fresh from her triumphant European tour.

FOR DETAILS, CALL 1-800-DUCHESS OR YOUR TRAVEL AGENT TODAY.

191. What is the Grand Duchess?
 (A) An apartment house
 (B) A ship
 (C) A balcony
 (D) A restaurant

192. How long did it take to build the Grand Duchess?
 (A) 3 years
 (B) 4 years
 (C) 7 years
 (D) 9 years

193. What is true about the Grand Duchess?
 (A) She has already been to the Caribbean.
 (B) There are nine nightly shows.
 (C) A travel agent can make the reservation.
 (D) There are 450 balconies.

Questions 194-195 refer to the following notice.

The Seventh California International Piano Competition

JULY 6-10

Contestants from around the globe
Internationally renowned judges
$25,000 in prizes plus
A Carnegie Hall recital debut

194. Where is the competition held every year?
  (A) In a different location
  (B) Outside the United States
  (C) At Carnegie Hall
  (D) Somewhere in California

195. What is true about the competition?
  (A) It lasts five days.
  (B) The judges are from California.
  (C) The competitors are American.
  (D) This year marks its debut.

Questions 196-198 refer to the following advertisement.

Brilliant, Articulate, Persuasive
PHYSICAL or SOCIAL SCIENTIST

Positions available for recent Ph.D. or M.S. level with some professional work experience, and a degree in computer science, psychology, or one of the physical or social sciences to join a marketing research company studying consumer choice behavior. Emphasis on development of fundamental theory in conjunction with major real-life experiments.

Exceptional personal qualifications required. Prior experience in marketing research unnecessary. Competitive starting salary. Unlimited potential; ideal opportunity for person with the right mix of ambition, initiative, and commitment to intellectual pursuits.

Send resume, including starting salary requirements to:
Jane Durkin, President
Durkin and Durkin Associates

---

196. A graduate in which field should apply for the job?
(A) Accounting
(B) Biology
(C) Marketing
(D) Finance

197. What will the employee be studying?
(A) Results of experiments
(B) Developmental theory
(C) Customer selections
(D) Computer applications

198. What was NOT mentioned as a characteristic the candidate should possess?
(A) Brilliance
(B) Persuasiveness
(C) Commitment
(D) Originality

Questions 199-200 refer to the following announcement.

199. What can be concluded from this announcement?
 (A) That the employee must work until retirement age to receive any benefits
 (B) That the employee should check the statement for inaccuracies from all previous years
 (C) That the employee's payments will differ depending upon the age of retirement
 (D) That the employee is at retirement age and should file for benefits

200. What is included in this mailing?
 (A) The correct amount contributed last year
 (B) The total amount contributed last year
 (C) A history of the recipient's contributions
 (D) Penalty amounts for early withdrawals

TAPESCRIPT

Sample Item
M: (A) The man is tearing the paper.
(B) The man is signing his name.
(C) The man is reading a letter.
(D) The man is opening an envelope.

1. M2: (A) The man is driving his golf cart onto the green.
(B) The man is swinging his bat to hit the ball.
(C) The man has just swung his golf club.
(D) The man has thrown his golf club into the air.

2. W: (A) The woman is accessing the library online.
(B) The woman has taken all the books down from the shelves.
(C) The woman is stacking the books in a single pile.
(D) The woman is searching for some information.

3. M2: (A) The woman is being photographed on the rocks.
(B) The woman is crouching down to take a photograph.
(C) The woman is positioning the camera on one of the rocks.
(D) The woman is shooting a picture of her friends.

4. M1: (A) The men are admiring the view from the window.
(B) The men are shaking hands near the window.
(C) The men are looking at suits in the shop window.
(D) The men are observing each other through the window.

5. W: (A) No vehicles are allowed to park in this space longer than twenty minutes.
(B) A truck must be under a certain length to park here.
(C) Parking is prohibited at certain times of the day.
(D) Only vehicles over twenty feet long can park here.

6. M2: (A) The woman is dropping off her laundry with the attendant.
(B) The basket of clothes has spilled out onto the street.
(C) The woman is hanging up her clothes outdoors.
(D) The woman is loading the basket onto the back seat.

7. M1: (A) The person's hands are under a running faucet.
(B) The sink is overflowing with water.
(C) The person is unclogging the drain of the sink.
(D) The bathtub has not been filled with water yet.

8. W: (A) The boy is swinging his arms as he skates.
(B) The boy has fallen down on the skaters.
(C) The boy is climbing over the fence with his skates on.
(D) The boy is hanging on the fence with both hands.

9. M1: (A) The woman has no money to put in the meter.
(B) The people have parked their car in a metered space.
(C) The parking garage entrance only accepts coins.
(D) The woman is turning the key in the ignition.

10. M2: (A) The man is watering his newly planted shrubs.
(B) The man is digging up the roots of a tree.
(C) The man is planting something in the garden.
(D) The man is plowing the garden with a tractor.

11. W: (A) The woman is lighting a candle with a match.
(B) The woman is turning on the lights over the table.
(C) The woman is reading by candlelight.
(D) The woman is watching the candles burn on the table.

12. M1: (A) The man is catching up with the other riders.
(B) The man has taken off his bicycle helmet.
(C) The man is locking up his bicycle for safety.
(D) The man is riding his bicycle on the street.

13. M2: (A) The man is resting his head against the back of the chair.
(B) The man is taking down an order as he listens.
(C) The man is taking a call on his cordless phone.
(D) The phone receiver doesn't reach the man's ear.

14. W: (A) The food is being placed on the grill from a platter.
(B) The chef is in the kitchen preparing dinner for his family.
(C) The man is grilling some food outdoors.
(D) The man is ordering take-out food for dinner.

15. M2: (A) The woman is taking her bags out of the cart.
(B) The woman is selecting her groceries.
(C) The woman is pushing a shopping cart into the supermarket.
(D) The woman is loading her groceries into the trunk.

16. M1: (A) The woman is fastening her seat belt before driving.
(B) The woman is instructing the passengers to use their seat belts.
(C) The woman is looking for a belt to match her outfit.
(D) The officer is checking to see if the woman's seat belt is fastened.

17. W: (A) The man is drinking his coffee.
(B) The man is leaving a tip for the waiter.
(C) The man has just placed his order.
(D) The man is eating in the cafeteria.

18. M2: (A) The woman is erasing the figures from the board.
    (B) The woman is explaining the diagram she has drawn.
    (C) The woman is weighing herself on the scale.
    (D) The woman is giving her presentation with the aid of a projector.

19. M1: (A) The passengers are boarding the bus.
    (B) The passengers are getting off the bus.
    (C) The bus driver is collecting fares beside the bus.
    (D) The bus is closing its doors before the passengers can board.

20. W: (A) The woman has put the documents into the courier pouch.
    (B) The woman is stacking the folders on the floor.
    (C) The woman is looking through some files in the drawer.
    (D) The woman is measuring the space behind her file cabinet.

Sample Question
W: Good morning, John. How are you?
M: (A) I am fine, thank you.
M: (B) I am in the living room.
M: (C) My name is John.

21. W: Nice to meet you, Mr. Lee. How do you like Tokyo?
    M: (A) So far so good.
    M: (B) I'm fine, thank you.
    M: (C) I leave after work.

22. M: You got that raise, didn't you?
    W: (A) No, the window is stuck.
    W: (B) Yes, I need my sunglasses.
    W: (C) Yes, now I'm the supervisor.

23. W: How do you spend your Sundays?
    M: (A) I won't have any money until next week.
    M: (B) I sometimes visit my family.
    M: (C) Thanks for inviting me.

24. W: Why aren't you taking the 8:00 a.m. flight?
    M: (A) I couldn't get a seat.
    M: (B) Yes, that's right.
    M: (C) When I took the call.

25. M: Who should sign the purchase order?
    W: (A) Perhaps you missed the sign.
    W: (B) Not me — check with Sue Daniels.
    W: (C) I didn't order any signs.

26. M: What time was the conference call?
    W: (A) When John gets back.
    W: (B) In the office or at home.
    W: (C) At 9:00. I'm sorry you missed it.

27. W: Do you spell your name with an "i" or an "e?"
    M: (A) I can't remember.
    M: (B) I see what you mean.
    M: (C) It's Ching, with an "i."

28. M: Can you tell me a good place for a haircut?
    W: (A) Try the salon in the mall.
    W: (B) It closes at six.
    W: (C) Use the bandages in the first aid box.

29. W: Is the vice president looking for a secretary or a receptionist?
    M: (A) Yes, he is.
    M: (B) Both, I think.
    M: (C) He found it.

30. M: How much does a light portable computer weigh?
    W: (A) Mine weighs only four kilos.
    W: (B) Sure, it's the right one.
    W: (C) When it needs recharging, the lights flash.

31. W: Where will you move when your lease is up?
    M: (A) Maybe I'll rearrange my office.
    M: (B) Perhaps at the end of July.
    M: (C) Probably I'll move downtown.

32. M: Do you ever take your car to work?
    W: (A) Yes, it does.
    W: (B) Only if I'm running late.
    W: (C) It's on Main Street.

33. M: Would you rather take your vacation in July or August?
    W: (A) I'll take them both.
    W: (B) No, not this year.
    W: (C) August — most of my friends are off then.

34. W: What about ordering that software we talked about?
    M: (A) I can't. It's too expensive.
    M: (B) No, I didn't order it.
    M: (C) Yes, I know everyone's wearing it.

35. M: Don't you find the climate in the capital too humid?
    W: (A) Yes, I had two caps to choose from.
    W: (B) Surprisingly I don't mind it.
    W: (C) No, I haven't located it yet.

36. M: Who are we waiting for?
    W: (A) Someone from marketing.
    W: (B) Yes, I can wait a while.
    W: (C) Another twenty minutes.

37. W: What did you think of the movie?
    M: (A) I thought it had a matinee.
    M: (B) I saw it last week.
    M: (C) The ending was a complete surprise.

38. M: Would you like a cup of coffee?
    W: (A) Yes, I'll copy the report.
    W: (B) Oh no, I've had enough for today.
    W: (C) Yes, I do drink coffee.

39. W: When did you start the night shift?
    M: (A) At the factory.
    M: (B) Every Tuesday.
    M: (C) Two weeks ago.

40. M: *Do you prefer editing at the computer or on paper?*
    W: (A) No, I don't.
    W: (B) Only when it's an important document.
    W: (C) Paper and pencil for me.

41. W: *Haven't you finished the budget projections yet?*
    M: (A) Don't rush me. I need another week.
    M: (B) Sorry, I don't have time to help you.
    M: (C) Believe it or not, I need a microphone.

42. M: *You were supposed to update the e-mail accounts, weren't you?*
    W: (A) The mail should be picked up at noon.
    W: (B) Yes, but I was out of town all last week.
    W: (C) I stopped counting.

43. W: *Should I run the proposal by the home office?*
    M: (A) It won't be necessary.
    M: (B) I jog every evening after work.
    M: (C) No one's working at home.

44. M: *Is the firm planning to hire an interior decorator?*
    W: (A) Only the exterior one.
    W: (B) It keeps getting higher.
    W: (C) I sure hope so.

45. W: *Should we get the rates for the new overnight service?*
    M: (A) Yes, it should be served.
    M: (B) It can't hurt.
    M: (C) No, it's only noon.

46. M: *Do you think they'll accept our offer?*
    W: (A) Only if we're the lowest.
    W: (B) Yes, everyone except us.
    W: (C) No, I didn't think so.

47. W: *Wasn't your check-up supposed to last only an hour?*
    M: (A) I'll check for you.
    M: (B) That's what I thought.
    M: (C) It's every hour on the hour.

48. M: *Could you fax this memo for me when you get a chance?*
    W: (A) Yes, it was all by chance.
    W: (B) No, I don't have all the facts.
    W: (C) Sorry, all the phone lines are down.

49. W: *How can I ever thank you?*
    M: (A) Don't worry about it.
    M: (B) It's welcome.
    M: (C) Thanks, but no thanks.

50. M: *Is Hong Kong one or two hours ahead?*
    W: (A) Either one.
    W: (B) It's two.
    W: (C) It's right ahead.

51. W: Hello, Prime Computer? Are you accepting resumes by fax?
    M: That would be fine. Please send a cover page identifying which position you're applying for.
    W: Thanks. Let me double check the fax number I have.

52. M: Aren't we supposed to be able to print from our computers via the copy machine now?
    W: In theory, yes — in practice, no.
    M: So what was that copy machine guy doing back here last Friday?

53. W: Did you hear about the new international rate for letters?
    M: Yeah, but I heard it's only good for Singapore.
    W: That's a shame. The post office advertises great delivery to all the Far East.

54. M: Would you look at these office furniture catalogs with me?
    W: Sure. What are you ordering? Anything major?
    M: I've finally gotten approval for a new desk and chair.

55. W: I thought since it's a holiday there wouldn't be so much traffic tonight.
    M: Just the opposite! Everyone's heading out of town.
    W: Maybe we should get off this road then.

56. M: I thought that by running some local TV ads I'd get some new customers, but so far no luck.
    W: Too bad. Didn't it cost a small fortune to make that commercial?
    M: It sure did. I guess it's back to the newspaper for me.

57. W: Can you believe it? We all got new business cards, and our telephone area code is changing in six weeks.
    M: Don't print new ones. I heard they're changing the postal code soon as well.
    W: And I just got new personal stationery.

58. W: How do you know so much about cooking?
    M: My parents had a restaurant while I was growing up, so I spent every dinner there.
    W: Well, since all I can make is spaghetti, let's eat at your place.

59. W: Any word on the 7:00 a.m. flight to Seattle?
    M: I'm sorry. Haven't you heard? It's been rescheduled for 8:30.
    W: You mean I didn't have to get up at 4:00?

60. M: Can I cash a check if I don't have an account here?
    W: If you have two picture IDs and the amount is under $250, it's OK.
    M: Great. I've got a license and my work badge.

61. W: At 5:00 there's a reception to meet the new credit manager, Carmen Lopez.
    M: I hope she stays longer than the last two.
    W: I don't know exactly what the problem is, but either they don't pay enough or the job is too demanding.

62. M: Hello. I'm trying to reach Karen Michaels in customer service.
    W: Oh, you must mean Michael Kareen.
    M: Oops. You're right. Can you connect me, please?

63. W: Do you think anyone in your department still has an electric typewriter? I need to fill out an application.
    M: Everyone got rid of theirs, but I think I have one at home.
    W: Would you check? I'd really appreciate it.

64. M: Is Lisa Flanagan's retirement party going to be at the country club?
    W: Is that what you heard? I thought Sheila said it would be in the President's office.
    M: Oh, really? Well, let me know if I can help with the decorations.

65. W: I need some film to take pictures on my vacation.
    M: Will you be shooting mainly indoors or outdoors?
    W: Outdoors. I'll be on the beach every day.

66. M: Can you believe this memo about reimbursements?
    W: Yeah. Now we have to get signatures before we travel to authorize all meals, hotels, and car rentals.
    M: What a pain. Sometimes I don't know I have to travel until the day before.

67. W: Do you know anyone with a pick-up truck or a van? I bought a great dresser and couch from a friend that I need to get to my apartment.
    M: Let's see, I could ask to use one of the company's delivery trucks on Saturday.
    W: Oh, that would be wonderful. I promise I'll pay you back somehow.

68. M: If I can get two tickets to Saturday's soccer match, would you like to go with me?
    W: I'll take a rain check. This Saturday my college roommate will be in town for a conference and I'm taking her sightseeing.
    M: Have fun. We'll see a match some other time.

69. W: What's the best way to get to the train station at rush hour?
    M: Definitely not by car. I'd probably walk.
    W: Except I'll have a heavy suitcase. I guess I'll try to leave earlier.

70. M: The quarterly earnings report came out today.
    W: I'm afraid to look. Were profits down again?
    M: No, and you can stop looking for another job. We're in the black.

71. W: When you come for the interview, use the side door. The front entrance is blocked due to construction.
    M: Do I still get off at 67th Street?
    W: It's probably closer to get off at 66th and walk up Third Avenue.

72. M: Did I hear you say your next-door neighbor is moving out?
    W: Yes, she's been relocated to Montreal.
    M: I've always loved your building. Do you know if her apartment's been rented yet?

73. W: This is Suzy Parker. I don't have an appointment, but could Diego fit me in for a haircut this afternoon?
    M: Let me check. If you can get here by four, he'll squeeze you in.
    W: Thanks so much, I'm on my way.

74. M: Janet, is your conference in Prague? Could I ask you a huge favor?
    W: Sure, as long as it doesn't involve picking out marionettes for all your relatives.
    M: No. I broke a crystal drinking glass I bought there. I want you to get me as many matching ones as they have.

75. W: What's with the telephones?
    M: Everyone's message light is flashing even when there are no messages.
    W: It makes me crazy. I check it fifty times a day.

76. M: I'll need the budget projections by Friday at the latest.
    W: But it's Wednesday. I can't possibly do them in two days.
    M: OK, but I have to have them on Monday.

77. W: I'm looking for rain boots.
    M: Let me see. Then you don't want leather, right?
    W: Right. What do you have in rubber?

78. M: Did you see we got a new juice machine in the lobby?
    W: Great. I was really tired of soda.
    M: And this one takes bills, not just change.

79. W: Tryouts for the company volleyball team are tomorrow. Will you go with me?
    M: Do you know when the practices will be?
    W: I heard something about every Tuesday and Thursday, but it's not definite.

80. M: All those computers we aren't using are going to be donated to the local high school.
    W: I'm so glad. I was wondering what would become of them.
    M: Maybe you and I could organize some software demonstrations. What do you say?

Questions 81–82 refer to the following announcement:
W: Flight 312, scheduled to depart for Nashville at 6:30, has been delayed due to a tornado watch in that region. We will keep you posted on weather conditions and projected time of departure, so please do not leave the airport.

Questions 83–84 refer to the following announcement:
M1: On August 7 we will welcome financial planner Adam Almquist as our keynote speaker for the annual employee appreciation luncheon. Mr. Almquist, a specialist in retirement savings plans, will shed valuable light on investment options for the twenty-first century. His speech, entitled "Your Age Determines Your Contribution," promises to be relevant to all employees, no matter what year you were born. Please leave questions you wish Mr. Almquist to address in writing with Ms. Chu in the Human Resource office on the fifth floor.

Questions 85–87 refer to the following speech:
M2: Thank you all for attending and contributing to this year's auction. So far this evening we have raised over $2,000 for scholarships and salaries. Before the night is through, we plan to raise a total of $20,000. I hope you're all enjoying the delicious meal, donated by La Groceria restaurant. The owners' two children attend our school. Please patronise this noteworthy establishment located at 100 Main Street downtown. Here's the schedule of tonight's events: After dinner we will hold the first part of the vocal auction from 7:00 to 8:00. During dinner and the vocal auction, you can write down bids for items in the silent auction. This will end at 8:30. Once we collect all the bid sheets from the silent auction items, a 30-minute second vocal auction will take place. At its conclusion, we will unfurl a banner announcing the winners of the silent auction.

Questions 88–89 refer to the following talk:
W: Welcome aboard our land and water tour of San Francisco. We hope you've brought your raincoats for the ocean leg of the trip. This two-hour journey will cover twenty different downtown locations on land before we head to the water in our multi-purpose trolley, which transforms itself into a floating ship as it cruises the Pacific for the second hour. Sit back and relax, but have those cameras ready!

Questions 90–91 refer to the following announcement:
M2: Attention, shoppers. Beginning in five minutes, at 2:00, Newton's Department Store will discount all purchases over $100 by 25%. This special unannounced sale will last for only one hour, until 3:00. Purchases may be made in cash, by check, or credit card. Today marks our tenth anniversary of serving you, our loyal customers, and we wish to say thank you.

Questions 92–94 refer to the following notice:
M1: Graphic Writer, a leading graphic design company, is currently seeking a director for international marketing. The successful candidate will have completed three years in a similar capacity. Familiarity with South American markets and mastery of Spanish or Portuguese is desired. The position demands extensive travel approximately six months out of the year. Please fax resume, two letters of reference, and your salary history, which will determine your salary range, to the Director of Personnel at 631-3809.

Questions 95–97 refer to the following announcement:
W: Hello, athletes! Congratulations on being among the 7,000 at the tenth running of the Dublin Marathon. This year's field is the largest to date. We are aware that the sheer number of runners will make it impossible for everyone to begin at the same time. In order to accurately measure each runner's time, make sure you pick your computer chip, which should be attached to your right shoe. It will automatically activate as you cross the starting line. Our volunteers will organize the runners into groups of one hundred, which will line up behind the starting line. The first runners are those with the fastest times earned at an international marathon this year. Good luck to you all and remember to drink plenty of water.

Questions 98–100 refer to the following introduction:
M2: We have all gathered here tonight to pay tribute to Christine Arthur, who is retiring after forty years of devoted service to R & S Publishing. She began as a secretary, typing on a manual typewriter and taking shorthand. After five years she was promoted to typesetting, where she remained for ten years until she was hired as an acquisition editor, specializing in children's literature. She has excelled in this position for the last twenty-five years. What will R & S do without her? We know Ms. Arthur has great plans for her next decade, which include worldwide travel, gourmet cooking, and reading every bestseller she can get her hands on. I am honored to call her forward to share with you her recollections and thoughts at this emotional time.

ANSWERS & EXPLANATIONS

Part 1

1. (C) *The man has just swung his golf club.*
   Choice (A) is incorrect because there is no golf cart in the picture. Choice (B) is incorrect because the man is holding a golf club, not a bat. Choice (D) is incorrect because the man is holding the golf club; he has not thrown it.

2. (D) *The woman is searching for some information.*
   Choice (A) is incorrect because the woman is not working at a computer. Choice (B) is incorrect because all the books, except for one, are still on the shelves. Choice (C) is incorrect because the books are not stacked in a single pile; they are on the shelves.

3. (B) *The woman is crouching down to take a photograph.*
   Choice (A) is incorrect because the woman is taking a photograph, not being photographed. Choice (C) is incorrect because the woman is holding the camera; not placing it on the rocks. Choice (D) is incorrect because there are no other people in the picture; who or what she is photographing is unknown.

4. (B) *The men are shaking hands near the window.*
   Choice (A) is incorrect because the men are not admiring the view; they are looking at each other. Choice (C) is incorrect because the men are not looking in a shop window. Choice (D) is incorrect because the men are on the same side of the window; they are not observing each other through the window.

5. (B) *A truck must be under a certain length to park here.*
   Choice (A) is incorrect because the sign says 20 feet; not 20 minutes. Choice (C) is incorrect because the sign does not mention times of the day. Choice (D) is incorrect because only vehicles under twenty feet long can park here.

6. (D) *The woman is loading the basket onto the back seat.*
   Choice (A) is incorrect because there is no attendant in the picture. Choice (B) is incorrect because the clothes are all in the basket; none are on the street. Choice (C) is incorrect because the woman is putting her clothes into the car, not hanging them up.

7. (A) *The person's hands are under a running faucet.*
   Choice (B) is incorrect because the sink is not overflowing; the water is going down the drain. Choice (C) is incorrect because the person's hands are under the water; the hands are not unclogging the sink. Choice (D) is incorrect because there is a sink in the picture, not a bathtub.

8. (D) *The boy is hanging on the fence with both hands.*
   Choice (A) is incorrect because the boy's hands are on the fence; the arms are not swinging. Choice (B) is incorrect because there is no other skaters in the picture. Choice (C) is incorrect because the boy is not climbing the fence; he is holding onto it.

9. (B) *The people have parked their car in a metered space.*
   Choice (A) is incorrect because the woman is putting money into the meter. Choice (C) is incorrect because the car is on the street, not in a garage. Choice (D) is incorrect because the woman is outside the car, not turning the ignition.

10. (C) *The man is planting something in the garden.*
    Choice (A) is incorrect because the man is not watering the plants; he is holding a plant. Choice (B) is incorrect because the man is not digging up tree roots. Choice (D) is incorrect because the man is bending down; he is not on a tractor.

11. (A) *The woman is lighting a candle with a match.*
    Choice (B) is incorrect because the woman is lighting a candle, not turning on the lights. Choice (C) is incorrect because the woman is not reading. Choice (D) is incorrect because the woman is not watching the candles burn; she is lighting a candle.

12. (D) *The man is riding his bicycle on the street.*
    Choice (A) is incorrect because there are no other riders in the picture. Choice (B) is incorrect because the man has not removed his helmet; he is wearing it. Choice (C) is incorrect because the man is riding his bicycle, not locking it up.

13. (A) *The man is resting his head against the back of the chair.*
    Choice (B) is incorrect because the man is not taking an order. Choice (C) is incorrect because the telephone has a cord; it is not cordless. Choice (D) is incorrect because the receiver is against the man's ear.

14. (C) *The man is grilling some food outdoors.*
    Choice (A) is incorrect because the food is already on the grill; there is no platter in the picture. Choice (B) is incorrect because the chef is outdoors, not in the kitchen. Choice (D) is incorrect because the man is cooking the food for dinner, not ordering take-out.

15. (C) *The woman is pushing a shopping cart into the supermarket.*
    Choice (A) is incorrect because there are no bags in the woman's cart. Choice (B) is incorrect because the woman is pushing the cart, not selecting groceries. Choice (D) is incorrect because the woman is pushing the cart, not loading bags into her car trunk.

TEST THREE

16. (A) *The woman is fastening her seat belt before driving.* Choice (B) is incorrect because there are no passengers in the picture. Choice (C) is incorrect because she is not looking for a belt; she is fastening a seat belt. Choice (D) is incorrect because there is no officer in the picture.

17. (D) *The man is eating in the cafeteria.* Choice (A) is incorrect because the man is eating, not drinking coffee. Choice (B) is incorrect because there is no money on the table; he's eating and hasn't left a tip. Choice (C) is incorrect because the man has already received his food; his order was placed some time ago.

18. (B) *The woman is explaining the diagram she has drawn.* Choice (A) is incorrect because the woman is pointing to something, not erasing the board. Choice (C) is incorrect because the woman is not on a scale. Choice (D) is incorrect because there is no projector visible in the picture.

19. (A) *The passengers are boarding the bus.* Choice (B) is incorrect because the passengers are getting on the bus, not off it. Choice (C) is incorrect because the bus driver is not visible in the picture. Choice (D) is incorrect because the bus doors are open, not closing.

20. (C) *The woman is looking through some files in the drawer.* Choice (A) is incorrect because there is no courier pouch in the picture. Choice (B) is incorrect because the woman is not stacking the folders on the floor. Choice (D) is incorrect because the woman is in front of the file cabinet; she is not measuring space behind it.

21. (A) *So far so good* means until now everything has been good. Choice (B) answers the question *how are you.* Choice (C) answers a *when* question.

22. (C) *Yes, now I'm the supervisor* indicates that the man got a raise and a new position. Choice (A) confuses *raise* or *pay increase,* with a related word: *window.* Choice (B) is an illogical response.

23. (B) *I sometimes visit my family* tells how the man spends his Sundays. Choice (A) confuses *spend* with a related word: *money.* Choice (C) is an illogical response.

24. (A) *I couldn't get a seat* answers why the man didn't take an 8:00 a.m. flight. Choice (B) confuses *flight* with a similarly sounding word: *right.* Choice (C) is an illogical response and confuses *take a call* with *take a flight.*

25. (B) *Not me, check with Sue Daniels* means the woman shouldn't sign the purchase order, and the man should ask Sue Daniels. Choice (A) confuses *sign the purchase order* and *the sign.* Choice (C) confuses *sign the purchase order* and *any signs.*

26. (C) *At 9:00. I'm sorry you missed it* tells when the call was and that the woman is sorry the man missed the call. Choice (A) answers a *what time* future tense question. Choice (B) answers a *where* question.

27. (C) *It's Ching, with an "i"* answers how he spells his name. Choice (A) is an illogical response. Choice (B) confuses *"i",* a homonym for *eye,* with a related word: *see.*

28. (A) *Try the salon in the mall* is the woman's recommendation of a good place for a haircut. Choice (B) answers a *when* question. Choice (C) confuses *(hair) cut* with a related word: *bandages.*

29. (B) *Both I think* means the man thinks the vice president is looking for both a secretary and a receptionist. Choice (A) does not respond to the choice the question asked. Choice (C) confuses *looking for* with a related word: *found.*

30. (A) *Mine weighs only four kilo* tells how much the woman's computer weighs. Choice (B) confuses *light* with a similarly sounding word: *right.* Choice (C) confuses *light,* meaning not heavy, with a flashing *light.*

31. (C) *Probably I'll move downtown* indicates where he'll move. Choice (A) is an illogical response and confuses *move* with a related word: *rearrange.* Choice (B) answers a *when* question.

32. (B) *Only if I'm running late* means that the man drives only when he's late. Choice (A) answers a *does it* question. Choice (C) answers a *where* question.

33. (C) *August — most of my friends are off then* tells when she prefers to take her vacation and why. Choice (A) confuses *take your vacation* and *take* objects. Choice (B) is an illogical response and doesn't answer a *would you rather* question requiring the respondent to make a choice.

34. (A) *I can't. It's too expensive* explains why the man isn't going to order the software. Choice (B) answers a *did you* question. Choice (C) confuses *(soft)ware* with *wear(ing).*

35. (B) *Surprisingly, I don't mind it* means the humidity doesn't bother the woman. Choice (A) confuses *capital* and *caps.* Choice (C) confuses *don't you find the climate,* meaning *isn't the climate for you* with a related word: *located.*

36. (A) *Someone from marketing* tells who they are waiting for. Choice (B) answers a *yes/no* question, not a *who* question. Choice (C) answers a *how long* question.

37. (C) *The ending was a complete surprise* tells the man's opinion of the movie. Choice (A) does not answer an opinion question and confuses *movie* with a related word: *matinee*. Choice (B) answers a *when* question.

38. (B) *Oh no, I've had enough for today* means the woman does not want any more coffee. Choice (A) is illogical and confuses *coffee* with the similar sounding *copy*. Choice (C) answers the question *do (or don't) you drink coffee*.

39. (C) *Two weeks ago* tells when he started the night shift. Choice (A) answers a *where* question. Choice (B) answers a *how often* or present tense *when* question.

40. (C) *Paper and pencil for me* means the woman prefers to edit on paper, not at the computer. Choices (A) and (B) are not responses to a question with a choice.

41. (A) *Don't rush me; I need another week* indicates the man hasn't finished yet and needs more time. Choice (B) is an illogical response. The woman did not request help. Choice (C) confuses *projection(s)* with a related word: *microphone*.

42. (B) *Yes, but I was out of town all week* says that the woman was responsible and explains why she was unable to update the accounts. Choice (A) confuses *(e-)mail* and *the mail*. Choice (C) confuses *accounts* and *counting*.

43. (A) *It won't be necessary* means the woman doesn't have to show the proposal to the home office. Choice (B) confuses *run* with a related word: *jog*. Choice (C) confuses *home office* and *at home*.

44. (C) *I sure hope so* means the woman hopes the firm plans to hire an interior decorator. Choice (A) confuses *interior* with *exterior*. Choice (B) confuses *hire* with *higher*.

45. (B) *It can't hurt* means the man thinks they should go ahead and have the extra information, to be safe. Choice (A) confuses *service* and *served*. Choice (C) is an illogical response.

46. (A) *Only if we're the lowest* means the woman thinks their offer will be accepted if they submit the lowest one. Choice (B) confuses *accept* and *except*. Choice (C) answers a *did you think* question.

47. (B) *That's what I thought* tells that the man thought that the check-up was supposed to be only an hour. Choice (A) confuses *check-up* and *check for*. Choice (C) is an illogical response that confuses *an hour* with *every hour on the hour*.

48. (C) *Sorry, all the phone lines are down* tells why the woman can't fax the memo. Choice (A) confuses *a chance* with *by chance*. Choice (B) confuses *fax* with *facts*.

49. (A) *Don't worry about it* indicates the man doesn't need to be thanked. Choice (B) confuses *thank you* with a related word: *welcome*. Choice (C) is an illogical response and confuses *thank you* with *thanks but no thanks*.

50. (B) *It's two* tells how many hours Hong Kong is ahead. Choice (A) answers a *which one* question. Choice (C) confuses *two hours ahead* and *right ahead*.

51. (C) The woman asks *Are you accepting resumes by fax?* Choice (A) is not mentioned. Choice (B) is incorrect; she knows there are job openings. Choice (D) confuses *check the fax number* with *send the check*.

52. (D) The man asks *Aren't we supposed to be able to print from our computers via the copy machine?* Choice (A) is not mentioned. Choice (B) confuses *in theory yes; in practice no* with *putting theories into practice*. Choice (C) confuses *back here* with *back-to-back*.

53. (D) The woman says *it's only good for Singapore*. Choice (A) is not mentioned. Choices (B) and (C) are contradicted by the woman's response upon hearing that only Singapore has new rates, *That's a shame. The post office advertises great delivery to all the Far East.*

54. (A) The man asks the woman to *look at these office furniture catalogs* with him because he has *gotten approval for a new desk and chair*, so the conversation takes place in an office. Therefore, Choices (B), (C), and (D) are incorrect.

55. (B) The woman suggests *maybe we should get off this road*, meaning they should try a different route. Choice (A) is incorrect because the man says *everyone's heading out of town*, but there is no indication that they are. Choice (C) confuses *vacation* with a related word: *holiday*. Choice (D) is not mentioned.

56. (B) The man says *it's back to the newspaper for me*. Choices (A) and (D) are contradicted by *it's back to the newspaper for me*, meaning he will go back to advertising in the newspaper. Choice (C) confuses *cost a small fortune* with *inherit a small fortune*.

57. (A) The woman says *our telephone area code is changing in six weeks*. Choice (B) is incorrect because the postal code will change *soon*, not *in six weeks*. Choice (C) is incorrect; she has gotten new personal stationary. Choice (D) is contradicted by *we all got new business cards*.

58. (A) The woman suggests to the man *let's eat at your place*, meaning he'll cook dinner for her. Although the woman admits *all I can make is spaghetti*, Choice (B) is contradicted by *let's eat at your place*. Choice (C) is not mentioned. Choice (D) confuses *having a restaurant* with *eating* in one.

TEST THREE

59. (D) The woman asks *Any word on the 7:00 a.m. flight* and is told *It's been rescheduled;* therefore, the conversation takes place in an airport. Choice (A) is incorrect because the flight is *to Seattle*. Choices (B) and (C) are contradicted by the information that the flight was rescheduled.

60. (C) The man asks *Can I cash a check?* Choice (A) confuses *getting* (obtaining) *a license* with *I've got* (having) *a license*. Choice (B) is incorrect because he wants to cash a check to get some money, not change any. Choice (D) confuses *having an account* with *opening an account*.

61. (A) The woman says *there's a reception to meet the new credit manager, Carmen Lopez*. Choice (B) confuses *the reception at 5* with *leaving at five*. Choices (C) and (D) are incorrect because they mention why the last two credit managers may have left.

62. (B) The man asked for *Karen Michaels* and is told the name is *Michael Kareen*. Choice (A) is not mentioned. Choice (C) is incorrect because Karen didn't answer the phone. Choice (D) is incorrect; the number was correct but the name was wrong.

63. (D) The woman asks the man if *anyone in the department still has an electric typewriter*. Choice (A) confuses *filling out an application* with *needing help filling out an application*. Choice (B) confuses *checking to see if he has a typewriter* with *signing a check*. Choice (C) is not mentioned.

64. (A) The man offers *let me know if I can help decorate*. Choice (B) confuses *being in the President's office* with *speaking to him*. Choice (C) confuses *being at the country club* with *calling the country club*. Choice (D) is incorrect because the party is already planned.

65. (C) When asked if she'll be taking pictures indoors or outdoors the woman replies *outdoors*. Choice (A) confuses *pictures* with a related word: *painting*. Choice (B) confuses *being on the beach* with *beach blankets*. Choice (D) confuses *pictures* with a related word: *photo albums*.

66. (C) The man says *What a pain. Sometimes I don't know I have to travel until the day before,* meaning at the last minute. Choice (A) is not mentioned. Choice (B) confuses the expression *what a pain* with *being in pain*. Choice (D) is not mentioned.

67. (B) The woman says she needs *a pick-up truck or van* because she *bought a great dresser and couch* that she needs to get to her apartment. Choice (A) is contradicted by the man's saying he *could use one of the company's trucks*. Choice (C) is incorrect; they are already paid for. Choice (D) is not mentioned.

68. (D) The woman says *I'll take a rain check* which means let's go out some other time. Choice (A) is incorrect; she says her roommate is in town but doesn't suggest he meet her. Choice (B) confuses *rain check* with a related word: *umbrella*. Choice (C) is not mentioned.

69. (B) The woman says *I'll try and leave earlier.* Choice (A) is not mentioned. Choice (C) is not mentioned and cannot be inferred. Choice (D) is contradicted by her saying to the man's suggestion of walking, *except I'll have a heavy suitcase*.

70. (B) The man says *the quarterly earning report came out today and we're in the black,* meaning we're showing a profit. Choices (A) and (C) are not mentioned. Choice (D) is contradicted by *we're in the black*.

71. (C) The woman says *use the side door*. Choice (A) is contradicted by *use the side door*. Choice (B) is contradicted by *get off at 66th*. Choice (D) is confused with *walk up Third Avenue*. She is not advised, though, to walk to the interview.

72. (D) The man asks *do you know if her apartment's been rented yet?* Choice (A) is incorrect; the woman tells the man her neighbor has been relocated to Montreal, but he doesn't ask for this information. Choice (B) confuses *hear you say* with *hear from*. Choice (C) is not mentioned.

73. (A) Suzy asks if Diego could fit her in *for a haircut*. Choice (B) confuses *fit her in for a haircut* with *fit into a parking space*. Choice (C) is incorrect because Suzy is told to be there *by four*; she says *I don't have an appointment*. Choice (D) is not mentioned.

74. (B) The man says *I broke a crystal drinking glass I bought there* and *get me as many matching ones as they have*. Choice (A) is what the woman says she won't do for the man. Choice (C) is incorrect; she is already planning to attend the conference. Choice (D) confuses *drinking glasses* with *prescription glasses*.

75. (C) The man says the *message light is flashing even when there are no messages*. Choices (A), (B), and (D) are not mentioned.

76. (B) The woman says *But it's Wednesday*. Choice (A) is incorrect because it is the day he finally agrees to have the budget projections done by. Choice (C) is not mentioned. Choice (D) is the day he first wanted the budget projections done by.

77. (A) The woman says *I'm looking for rain boots*. Choice (B) confuses *rain* with a related word: *umbrella*. Choice (C) is contradicted by *you don't want leather*. Choice (D) confuses *rubber boots* with *a rubber hose*.

78. (D) The man asks *Did you see we got a new juice machine?* Choice (A) confuses the machine taking bills and *change* with *a change machine*. Choice (B) confuses *in the lobby* with *renovating the lobby*. Choice (C) is not mentioned.

79. (C) The man asks *Do you know when the practices will be?* Choice (A) is not mentioned. Choice (B) is contradicted by her asking him *Will you go with me?* Choice (D) is contradicted by her telling him the *try-outs are tomorrow*.

80. (B) The man suggests *Maybe you and I could organize some software demonstrations*. Choice (A) is not mentioned. Choice (C) is incorrect; the computers have software now; new software in not mentioned. Choice (D) is contradicted by his telling her that *all those computers are going to be donated*.

81. (C) The announcement ends with *please do not leave the airport*. Choice (A) is incorrect because the flight is leaving for Nashville. Choice (B) is not mentioned. Choice (D) is incorrect because no one has boarded the plane yet.

82. (D) People on flight 312 are told *please do not leave the airport*. Choices (A), (B), and (C) are not mentioned.

83. (B) Mr. Almquist is the *speaker for the annual employee appreciation luncheon*. Choice (A) is incorrect because the attendees are not *retirees* yet; they are still employees. Choice (C) confuses *investment bankers* with what will be discussed: *investment options*. Choice (D) is incorrect because the speaker is a *financial planner*.

84. (A) Employees are asked to *please leave questions in writing with Ms. Chu*. Choices (B) and (C) are not mentioned. Choice (D) confuses *write to Mr. Almquist* with *address (questions) in writing*.

85. (C) *We plan to raise a total of $20,000*. Choice (A) confuses *100 Main Street* with the amount of money. Choice (B) confuses the amount *raised so far this evening*. Choice (D) is not mentioned.

86. (B) *We will hold the first part of the vocal auction from 7:00 to 8:00*, or 60 minutes. Choice (A) is how long the second vocal auction will be. Choices (C) and (D) are not mentioned.

87. (D) *At its* (the auction's) *conclusion, we will unfurl a banner announcing the winners of the silent auction*. Choices (A), (B), and (C) are contradicted by this statement.

88. (C) The passengers are told *Welcome aboard our land and water tour... in our multi-purpose trolley*. Choice (A) confuses *rainstorm* with a related word: *raincoats*. Although the trolley transforms itself into a floating ship Choice (B), it is a trolley. Choice (D) is incorrect because *the trolley will cruise the Pacific for the second hour*.

89. (C) The tour is a *two-hour journey*. Choice (A) confuses *twenty minutes* with *twenty locations*. Choice (B) confuses how long the land-based portion of the tour is with the entire tour length. Choice (D) is not mentioned.

90. (C) *All purchases over $100* will be discounted *by 25%*, so a $100 purchase will be discounted by $25. Choices (A), (B), and (D) are contradicted by this statement.

91. (D) Shoppers are told *Today marks our tenth anniversary*. Choice (A) confuses *one hour* with *one year*. Choice (B) confuses *two o'clock* with *two years*. Choice (C) confuses *five minutes* with *five years*.

92. (A) *Graphic Writer is currently seeking a director for marketing*. Choice (B) confuses the fact that Graphic Writer is a *graphic design company* with *a graphic designer*. Choice (C) confuses *Spanish translator* with the fact that the candidate should speak Spanish. Choice (D) is not mentioned.

93. (D) *The successful candidate will have completed three years in a similar capacity*. Choice (A) confuses the number of months of travel with the amount of experience. Choice (B) confuses the number of *letters of reference* with the amount of experience. Choice (C) is not mentioned.

94. (A) *Your salary history will determine your salary range*. Choices (B), (C), and (D) are not mentioned.

95. (C) *Congratulations on being among the 7,000 at the Dublin Marathon*. Choice (A) confuses the fact that runners are organized into groups of one hundred with the number of runners. Choice (B) is not mentioned. Choice (D) confuses the tenth running of the marathon (ten thousand) with the number of runners.

96. (B) *In order to accurately measure each runner's time, make sure you pick up your computer chip*. Choices (A), (C), and (D) are contradicted by this statement.

97. (B) *The first runners are those with the fastest times earned at an international marathon*. Choices (A), (C), and (D) are not mentioned.

98. (A) *We have all gathered here tonight to pay tribute to Christine Arthur, who is retiring*. Choice (B) is incorrect because *we have gathered here tonight*. Choices (C) and (D) are not mentioned.

99. (B) *She was hired as an acquisition editor*, a position *she has excelled in for the last twenty-five years*. Choice (A) is incorrect because *she began as a secretary*. Choice (C) confuses *librarian* with a related word: *bestseller*. Choice (D) is incorrect because it is the position she held *until she was hired as an acquisition editor*.

100. (D) *Christine Arthur is retiring after forty years of devoted service.* Choice (A) confuses the number of years she worked as a secretary with the total number of years. Choice (B) confuses the number of years she worked as a typesetter with the total number of years. Choice (C) confuses the number of years she worked as an editor with the total number of years.

101. (D) *Luxury* means *something inessential but pleasurable.* Choice (A) means *adjustment.* Choice (B) is not logical. Choice (C) is a preposition and does not follow an adjective.

102. (C) The gerund form *showing* is preceded by the preposition *by,* explaining *how.* Choice (A) is not a preposition. Choices (B) and (D) are not used to explain *how.*

103. (B) *Indispensable* means *essential.* Choice (A) means *asking a question.* Choice (C) means *occurring without delay.* Choice (D) means *acting against or without one's will.*

104. (A) *Successor* means *one that succeeds another.* Choice (B) means *brevity and clearness.* Choice (C) means *happening later* and is not used with people. Choice (D) means *something one can touch; material matter.*

105. (C) *Despite,* a preposition, precedes the noun *cost.* Although Choice (A) can be a preposition, in this context it is illogical. Choice (B) needs to be followed by a subject + verb. Choice (D) needs to be followed by a subject + verb.

106. (D) The active past tense, *decided* is the correct verb form. Choice (A) is a gerund or present participle. Choice (B) is the present progressive passive form. Choice (C) is the past perfect passive form.

107. (B) *Not only... but also* is a paired conjunction; *not only the management but also the customers.* Choices (A), (C), and (D) are not paired with *not only.*

108. (A) Following *rarely* the correct word order is helping verb, *have;* subject, *we;* past participle, *seen.* Choice (B) is missing a subject. Choice (C) is in the wrong word order. Choice (D) includes a relative pronoun and is in the wrong word order.

109. (C) *Rely on* means *depend on.* Choice (A) means *meet by chance.* Choice (B) means *search for in a reference book.* Choice (D) means *read superficially.*

110. (D) The adjective form *leading* precedes the noun, *manufacturers.* Choice (A) is either a verb or a noun. Choice (B) is a person noun. Choice (C), although an adjective, means *containing lead.*

111. (B) *Them* is the third-person plural object pronoun which agrees with *tapes.* Choice (A) is the third-person singular object pronoun used for things. Choice (C) is the third-person masculine singular object pronoun. Choice (D) is the second person plural reflexive pronoun.

112. (A) *Cutbacks* means *items to be decreased.* Choice (B) means *items physically cut out from something.* Choice (C) means *parts cut out from the main body.* Choice (D) means *formal daytime men's coats.*

113. (C) The correct word order is relative pronoun, *that;* subject, *she;* verb, *bought.* Choices (A), (B), and (D) all include an unnecessary object pronoun, *it.*

114. (D) *The majority of* means *most.* Choices (A), (B), and (C) are not logical in this sentence.

115. (B) The base form, *reserve,* follows the modal, *must.* Choice (A) is the infinitive. Choice (C) is the past tense. Choice (D) can follow *must* but is the passive form.

116. (C) *Incentive* means *something that motivates action.* Choice (A) means *a plan.* Choice (B) means *a cut into body tissue.* Choice (D) means *a violation.*

117. (B) *Surprised,* the predicate adjective, means *caught unaware.* Choices (A), (C), and (D) are past participles, not predicate adjectives.

118. (A) *Sign* means *indication.* Choices (B), (C), and (D) are not logical.

119. (D) *Regarding,* a preposition, means *concerning.* Choice (A) must be used with *to.* Choice (B) is not logical. Choice (C) is an adjective.

120. (C) *Outlets* means *receptacles for electrical plugs.* Choices (A), (B), and (D) are not logical.

121. (D) The passive form of the verb is needed: *ocean liners were built for commerce and transportation.* Choice (A) is the active present perfect tense. Choice (B) is the active simple present tense preceded by a relative pronoun. Choice (C) is the active past tense preceded by a relative pronoun.

122. (B) The expression *For your convenience* means *for your personal comfort and ease.* Choices (A), (C), and (D) are not logical.

123. (A) *Standstill,* a noun, is used with *reach* to mean *come to a halt.* Choice (B) is an adjective. Although Choices (C) and (D) are nouns, they are not used with *reach.*

124. (C) *Underneath,* a preposition meaning under, precedes the noun, *seat.* Choices (A) and (D) are not prepositions. Although Choice (B) can be a preposition, it is illogical in this sentence.

125. (D) The adjective, *amusing,* follows the pronoun, *little.* Choice (A) is an adverb. Choice (B) is an infinitive. Choice (C) is the past participle adjective form.

126. (B) *Another item* means *an additional item*. Choice (A), when used without a preceding *the*, must be followed by a plural noun or a noncount noun. Choices (C) and (D) are pronouns indicating a reciprocal arrangement.

127. (A) The passive form, *are not permitted*, is necessary in this sentence. Choice (B) is a future tense active verb. Although Choice (C) is passive, it is illogical. Choice (D) is a present simple active verb.

128. (D) *Replacement* means *substitute*. Choice (A) means *the movement from the usual place*. Choice (B) means *the act of setting apart*. Choice (C) means *the act of ending the employment of*.

129. (C) *Himself* is the third person masculine singular reflexive pronoun which agrees with Mr. Takahara. Choice (A) is not a word. Choice (B) is the third person singular object pronoun. Choice (D) is the third person singular object pronoun used for things.

130. (B) The prepositional phrase, *upon meeting*, can be reduced, leaving only the gerund, *meeting*. Choice (A) is either a verb or a noun. Choice (C) is the past tense verb. Choice (D) is a verb.

131. (D) *Will credit* is the future tense verb needed in this sentence. Choice (A) is a gerund. Choice (B) is an infinitive and a past participle. Choice (C) is the future perfect tense.

132. (A) *Glut* means *oversupply*. Choice (B) means *price increase*. Choice (C) means *excessive desire to acquire more than one needs*. Choice (D) means *the state of being whole or complete*.

133. (C) *Were the two publishing houses to merge* means if the two publishing houses were to merge. Choices (A), (B), and (D) cannot precede *to* and are incorrect.

134. (B) *Overlooking* means *looking at from a higher place*. Choice (A) means *hearing something without the speaker's awareness*. Choice (C) means *causing to have too many people in one place*. Choice (D) means *supervising*.

135. (D) The infinitive, *to watch*, is used as an adjective, modifying the pronoun, *one*. Choice (A) is a present tense passive form. Choice (B) is either a noun or a present tense verb. Choice (C) is a gerund.

136. (A) *Immediately* means *at once*. Choice (B) means *for the time being*. Choice (C) means *in comparison with something else*. Choice (D) means *singly in the order designated*.

137. (B) *Reaching the consumer* means *getting the consumer's attention*. Choices (A), (C), and (D) are not logical.

138. (C) *Preceded* means *introduced*. Choice (A) means *move back from a point*. Choice (B) means *withdraw formally from membership*. Choice (D) means *admitting*.

139. (D) *Dozens of* means *a large number of*. Choice (A) should not include *of*. Choice (B) would require an adjective before *numerous*. Choice (C) would require the article *a* before *multitude*.

140. (B) *Approximately* means *about*. Choice (A) means *soon*. Choice (C) means *in comparison with something else*. Choice (D) means *in the act of decreasing*.

141. (C) The singular form *leaves* is needed to agree with *flight*.

142. (B) The correct superlative form is *cheapest*.

143. (B) Use the simple base form of the verb after the modal *must*: *must submit*.

144. (C) *Mrs. Alcaron*, a woman, takes the feminine possessive adjective: *her*.

145. (A) The singular noun *basis* is needed to agree with the singular verb *is*.

146. (D) The correct preposition is *in*: *in the first-floor auditorium*.

147. (D) The adjective form *different* is needed before a noun.

148. (A) The gerund form *organizing* is needed after looking forward to: *looking forward to organizing*.

149. (D) *Furniture* is a noncount noun and is always in the singular form.

150. (A) The plural form *brochures* is needed to agree with *are*.

151. (D) The verb *has* cannot follow the preposition *due to*; the clause should read *due to the highway construction detours*.

152. (C) The adverb *not* follows *will* and precedes *be allowed*: *will not be allowed*.

153. (A) In a compound noun, the first noun, acting as an adjective, is never in the plural: *computer problems*.

154. (B) For more than two items the preposition *among* should be used: *among teenagers*.

155. (D) The article *the* should precede *basement*: *in the basement*.

156. (C) *It* is not necessary because the sentence already has a subject: *sheet*.

157. (B) *Draft* is the correct noun form.

158. (A) The passive form of the verb is needed: *can be picked up.*

159. (B) The preposition *of* is needed following *a shortage: a shortage of trained workers.*

160. (C) The passive form of the verb is needed: *have been allotted.*

161. (A) *A promotional item* most likely appears in a magazine. Therefore, Choices (B), (C), and (D) are incorrect.

162. (C) Because they are *water-resistant*, they can be *worn in the rain* without harming them. Choice (A) is incorrect; they are *gold-plated* only. Choice (B) is incorrect; only a *leather strap* is mentioned. Choice (D) is incorrect; there is *no minimum quantity* required when ordering.

163. (C) *The plant replaces the one destroyed in the 1997 fire.* Choices (A), (B), and (D) are not mentioned.

164. (B) The luncheon begins at 1:30, and the last shuttle bus departs at 3:00, meaning *one and a half hours*. Choice (A) is incorrect because it is the length of the tour. Choice (C) is incorrect because it is the length of the tour and the ceremony. Choice (D) is incorrect because it is the length of the entire day.

165. (C) The agreement is made *between UCA Realty and the lessee*, meaning the *tenant*. Choices (A), (B), and (D) are not mentioned.

166. (D) *Upon signing the lessee will pay the first and last month's rent as well as a one-month security deposit; the first month's utilities* is not mentioned. Choices (A), (B), and (C) are explicitly mentioned.

167. (B) *A one-month security deposit will be held in a 5% annual interest-bearing account*; on a $500 deposit, $525 would be returned. Choices (A), (C), and (D) are therefore incorrect.

168. (D) Ms. Dwyer takes *photographs*, one medium, and *then hand paints her images*, another medium. Choices (A) and (B) are contradicted by *Dwyer photographs vibrant scenes, then hand paints her images*. Choice (C) is not mentioned.

169. (A) *Selected ones may be purchased*, meaning one is able to purchase but doesn't have to. Choice (B) is contradicted by *selected ones may be purchased*. Choice (C) is contradicted by *March 12–April 5*, less than one month. Choice (D) is not mentioned.

170. (B) One of the markets advertised is *financial*, including the *banking field*. Choice (A) is contradicted by *telephone systems* being addressed, not *telephone operators*. Choices (C) and (D) are not mentioned.

171. (C) *Don't miss the newly redesigned NETWORKS EXPO BOSTON*. Choice (A) is contradicted by *June 2–4*. Choices (B) and (D) are not mentioned.

172. (C) The report says *engine vibration was probably the cause*. Choices (A) and (B) are contradicted by *inspections to fuel pump wiring*. This is where the damage is; it is not the cause. Although there is fear *that frayed insulation could lead to a spark*, Choice (D) is contradicted by *engine vibration was probably the cause*.

173. (A) *Damage was found in half of the 80 inspected*, meaning *40* planes. Choices (B), (C), and (D) are contradicted by this information.

174. (B) *Officials added they feared that frayed insulation could cause an explosion*. Choices (A), (C), and (D) are not mentioned.

175. (C) *National and international flights were canceled*, or *called off*. Choices (A), (B), and (D) are not mentioned.

176. (B) *Every tree cleans the air, purifies the water, furnishes the earth with oxygen, and provides shade to reduce not only energy bills, but the effects of global warming; Reduced pollution* is NOT mentioned. Choices (A), (C), and (D) are explicitly mentioned.

177. (B) *Global ReLeaf will plant 10 trees for every $10,* so $100 will plant 100 trees. Choices (A), (C), and (D) are contradicted by this statement.

178. (D) *Global ReLeaf... the nations' oldest citizen conservation organization... founded in 1875,* meaning the *nineteenth century.* Choice (A) is contradicted by *if you can't plant your own tree... Global ReLeaf will plant...* Choice (B) is contradicted by *citizen... organization.* Choice (C) is contradicted by *personalized certificate.*

179. (D) *The mishap... occurred when a routine computer program... sent false information.* Choices (A) and (B) are not mentioned. Choice (C) is confused with what the computer program was designed to do, but it is not the cause of the problem.

180. (B) *The glitch did not affect savings... accounts,* so at 7:00 a.m. customers could check their savings account balances. Choices (A) and (D) are contradicted by *customers were told that their checking accounts had been closed or could not be found.* Choice (C) is contradicted by *at 8:00, customers could finally get cash.*

181. (D) *All ATMs were fully functional by 8:45 a.m.* Choices (A), (B), and (C) are contradicted by this statement.

182. (C) The advertisement begins *LAMP SHADES*, meaning lamp coverings. Choices (A), (B), and (D) are not mentioned.

183. (B) *Benefits include exclusive territory rights*, meaning *market exclusivity*. Choices (A), (C), and (D) are not mentioned.

184. (A) *In just two years we've opened stores in Chicago, Cleveland, Dallas, and Phoenix; Miami* is not mentioned. Choices (B), (C) and (D) are explicitly mentioned.

185. (A) *Positive reinforcement is an important part of employee motivation.* Choice (B) is contradicted by *put it in writing.* Choice (C) is contradicted by *when possible, make a public compliment.* Choice (D) is contradicted by *praising... is not as simple as it seems.*

186. (B) *Start your compliment with "I", give specific compliments; I am very appreciative of your extra work on the design project, Paul* begins with *I* and is *specific*. Choice (A) is contradicted by disregarding *Never follow with "except."* Choice (C) is contradicted by disregarding *Reward people immediately.* Choice (D) is contradicted by disregarding *Never follow with "but."*

187. (C) *It* refers to helping one *compliment more effectively*; "just do it" means *give a compliment*. Choices (A), (B), and (D) are contradicted by this information.

188. (C) *From the air, metropolitan Phoenix looks like a mirage,* meaning an *oasis*. Choices (A), (B), and (D) are contradicted by this information.

189. (B) *So many have moved to Phoenix since the mid-1940s and the dawn of air conditioning,* meaning air conditioning, has made Phoenix more attractive. Choices (A), (C), and (D) are contradicted by this.

190. (D) *Its sprawl is stopped only by mountain ranges to the north, south, east, and west,* meaning Phoenix is *surrounded by mountains*. Choice (A) is not mentioned. Choice (B) is contradicted by *public transportation is in its infancy*. Choice (C) is contradicted by *300 days of sun a year*.

191. (B) *Introducing the biggest, most expensive cruise ship.* Choices (A), (C), and (D) are contradicted by this.

192. (B) *The ship was four years in the making.* Choice (A) confuses the number of years with the number of nightly shows. Choice (C) is not mentioned. Choice (D) confuses the number of years with the number of dining locations.

193. (C) *Call your travel agent today.* Choice (A) is contradicted by *her historic fall Caribbean debut.* Choice (B) is contradicted by *three different shows every night.* Choice (D) is contradicted by *700 private balconies.*

194. (D) The notice begins *The Seventh California International Piano Competition.* Choices (A) and (B) are contradicted by *California International Piano Competition.* Choice (C) is contradicted by *A Carnegie Hall recital debut* for the winner.

195. (A) The competition is from *July 6–10,* meaning five days. Choice (B) is contradicted by *internationally renowned judges.* Choice (C) is contradicted by *contestants from around the globe.* Choice (D) is contradicted by *Seventh... Competition.*

196. (B) *Positions available for recent Ph.D. or M.S. level... in one of the physical... sciences; biology* is a physical science. Choices (A), (C), and (D) are not mentioned.

197. (C) *Join a marketing research company studying consumer choice,* meaning *customer selections.* Choices (A), (B), and (D) are contradicted by this statement.

198. (D) The candidate should be *brilliant* and *persuasive... with the right mix of commitment. Originality* is not mentioned. Choices (A), (B), and (C) are explicitly mentioned.

199. (C) *Also included are the different monthly projected payments you would receive if you keep working at the same rate until the age of 62, 65, or 70,* meaning *employee's payments will differ depending upon the age of retirement.* Choice (A) is not mentioned. Choice (B) is contradicted by *note that last year's total may not accurately reflect your total income.* Choice (D) is not mentioned.

200. (C) *Please check the following summary of your contributions.* Choice (A) is not mentioned. Choice (B) is contradicted by *note that last year's total may not accurately reflect your total income.* Choice (D) is not mentioned.

TEST ONE — ANSWER SHEET

Listening Comprehension

1. Ⓐ Ⓑ Ⓒ Ⓓ
2. Ⓐ Ⓑ Ⓒ Ⓓ
3. Ⓐ Ⓑ Ⓒ Ⓓ
4. Ⓐ Ⓑ Ⓒ Ⓓ
5. Ⓐ Ⓑ Ⓒ Ⓓ
6. Ⓐ Ⓑ Ⓒ Ⓓ
7. Ⓐ Ⓑ Ⓒ Ⓓ
8. Ⓐ Ⓑ Ⓒ Ⓓ
9. Ⓐ Ⓑ Ⓒ Ⓓ
10. Ⓐ Ⓑ Ⓒ Ⓓ
11. Ⓐ Ⓑ Ⓒ Ⓓ
12. Ⓐ Ⓑ Ⓒ Ⓓ
13. Ⓐ Ⓑ Ⓒ Ⓓ
14. Ⓐ Ⓑ Ⓒ Ⓓ
15. Ⓐ Ⓑ Ⓒ Ⓓ
16. Ⓐ Ⓑ Ⓒ Ⓓ
17. Ⓐ Ⓑ Ⓒ Ⓓ
18. Ⓐ Ⓑ Ⓒ Ⓓ
19. Ⓐ Ⓑ Ⓒ Ⓓ
20. Ⓐ Ⓑ Ⓒ Ⓓ
21. Ⓐ Ⓑ Ⓒ Ⓓ
22. Ⓐ Ⓑ Ⓒ Ⓓ
23. Ⓐ Ⓑ Ⓒ Ⓓ
24. Ⓐ Ⓑ Ⓒ Ⓓ
25. Ⓐ Ⓑ Ⓒ Ⓓ
26. Ⓐ Ⓑ Ⓒ Ⓓ
27. Ⓐ Ⓑ Ⓒ Ⓓ
28. Ⓐ Ⓑ Ⓒ Ⓓ
29. Ⓐ Ⓑ Ⓒ Ⓓ
30. Ⓐ Ⓑ Ⓒ Ⓓ
31. Ⓐ Ⓑ Ⓒ Ⓓ
32. Ⓐ Ⓑ Ⓒ Ⓓ
33. Ⓐ Ⓑ Ⓒ Ⓓ
34. Ⓐ Ⓑ Ⓒ Ⓓ
35. Ⓐ Ⓑ Ⓒ Ⓓ
36. Ⓐ Ⓑ Ⓒ Ⓓ
37. Ⓐ Ⓑ Ⓒ Ⓓ
38. Ⓐ Ⓑ Ⓒ Ⓓ
39. Ⓐ Ⓑ Ⓒ Ⓓ
40. Ⓐ Ⓑ Ⓒ Ⓓ
41. Ⓐ Ⓑ Ⓒ Ⓓ
42. Ⓐ Ⓑ Ⓒ Ⓓ
43. Ⓐ Ⓑ Ⓒ Ⓓ
44. Ⓐ Ⓑ Ⓒ Ⓓ
45. Ⓐ Ⓑ Ⓒ Ⓓ
46. Ⓐ Ⓑ Ⓒ Ⓓ
47. Ⓐ Ⓑ Ⓒ Ⓓ
48. Ⓐ Ⓑ Ⓒ Ⓓ
49. Ⓐ Ⓑ Ⓒ Ⓓ
50. Ⓐ Ⓑ Ⓒ Ⓓ
51. Ⓐ Ⓑ Ⓒ Ⓓ
52. Ⓐ Ⓑ Ⓒ Ⓓ
53. Ⓐ Ⓑ Ⓒ Ⓓ
54. Ⓐ Ⓑ Ⓒ Ⓓ
55. Ⓐ Ⓑ Ⓒ Ⓓ
56. Ⓐ Ⓑ Ⓒ Ⓓ
57. Ⓐ Ⓑ Ⓒ Ⓓ
58. Ⓐ Ⓑ Ⓒ Ⓓ
59. Ⓐ Ⓑ Ⓒ Ⓓ
60. Ⓐ Ⓑ Ⓒ Ⓓ
61. Ⓐ Ⓑ Ⓒ Ⓓ
62. Ⓐ Ⓑ Ⓒ Ⓓ
63. Ⓐ Ⓑ Ⓒ Ⓓ
64. Ⓐ Ⓑ Ⓒ Ⓓ
65. Ⓐ Ⓑ Ⓒ Ⓓ
66. Ⓐ Ⓑ Ⓒ Ⓓ
67. Ⓐ Ⓑ Ⓒ Ⓓ
68. Ⓐ Ⓑ Ⓒ Ⓓ
69. Ⓐ Ⓑ Ⓒ Ⓓ
70. Ⓐ Ⓑ Ⓒ Ⓓ
71. Ⓐ Ⓑ Ⓒ Ⓓ
72. Ⓐ Ⓑ Ⓒ Ⓓ
73. Ⓐ Ⓑ Ⓒ Ⓓ
74. Ⓐ Ⓑ Ⓒ Ⓓ
75. Ⓐ Ⓑ Ⓒ Ⓓ
76. Ⓐ Ⓑ Ⓒ Ⓓ
77. Ⓐ Ⓑ Ⓒ Ⓓ
78. Ⓐ Ⓑ Ⓒ Ⓓ
79. Ⓐ Ⓑ Ⓒ Ⓓ
80. Ⓐ Ⓑ Ⓒ Ⓓ
81. Ⓐ Ⓑ Ⓒ Ⓓ
82. Ⓐ Ⓑ Ⓒ Ⓓ
83. Ⓐ Ⓑ Ⓒ Ⓓ
84. Ⓐ Ⓑ Ⓒ Ⓓ
85. Ⓐ Ⓑ Ⓒ Ⓓ
86. Ⓐ Ⓑ Ⓒ Ⓓ
87. Ⓐ Ⓑ Ⓒ Ⓓ
88. Ⓐ Ⓑ Ⓒ Ⓓ
89. Ⓐ Ⓑ Ⓒ Ⓓ
90. Ⓐ Ⓑ Ⓒ Ⓓ
91. Ⓐ Ⓑ Ⓒ Ⓓ
92. Ⓐ Ⓑ Ⓒ Ⓓ
93. Ⓐ Ⓑ Ⓒ Ⓓ
94. Ⓐ Ⓑ Ⓒ Ⓓ
95. Ⓐ Ⓑ Ⓒ Ⓓ
96. Ⓐ Ⓑ Ⓒ Ⓓ
97. Ⓐ Ⓑ Ⓒ Ⓓ
98. Ⓐ Ⓑ Ⓒ Ⓓ
99. Ⓐ Ⓑ Ⓒ Ⓓ
100. Ⓐ Ⓑ Ⓒ Ⓓ

Reading Comprehension

#	A	B	C	D		#	A	B	C	D		#	A	B	C	D
101.	Ⓐ	Ⓑ	Ⓒ	Ⓓ		135.	Ⓐ	Ⓑ	Ⓒ	Ⓓ		169.	Ⓐ	Ⓑ	Ⓒ	Ⓓ
102.	Ⓐ	Ⓑ	Ⓒ	Ⓓ		136.	Ⓐ	Ⓑ	Ⓒ	Ⓓ		170.	Ⓐ	Ⓑ	Ⓒ	Ⓓ
103.	Ⓐ	Ⓑ	Ⓒ	Ⓓ		137.	Ⓐ	Ⓑ	Ⓒ	Ⓓ		171.	Ⓐ	Ⓑ	Ⓒ	Ⓓ
104.	Ⓐ	Ⓑ	Ⓒ	Ⓓ		138.	Ⓐ	Ⓑ	Ⓒ	Ⓓ		172.	Ⓐ	Ⓑ	Ⓒ	Ⓓ
105.	Ⓐ	Ⓑ	Ⓒ	Ⓓ		139.	Ⓐ	Ⓑ	Ⓒ	Ⓓ		173.	Ⓐ	Ⓑ	Ⓒ	Ⓓ
106.	Ⓐ	Ⓑ	Ⓒ	Ⓓ		140.	Ⓐ	Ⓑ	Ⓒ	Ⓓ		174.	Ⓐ	Ⓑ	Ⓒ	Ⓓ
107.	Ⓐ	Ⓑ	Ⓒ	Ⓓ		141.	Ⓐ	Ⓑ	Ⓒ	Ⓓ		175.	Ⓐ	Ⓑ	Ⓒ	Ⓓ
108.	Ⓐ	Ⓑ	Ⓒ	Ⓓ		142.	Ⓐ	Ⓑ	Ⓒ	Ⓓ		176.	Ⓐ	Ⓑ	Ⓒ	Ⓓ
109.	Ⓐ	Ⓑ	Ⓒ	Ⓓ		143.	Ⓐ	Ⓑ	Ⓒ	Ⓓ		177.	Ⓐ	Ⓑ	Ⓒ	Ⓓ
110.	Ⓐ	Ⓑ	Ⓒ	Ⓓ		144.	Ⓐ	Ⓑ	Ⓒ	Ⓓ		178.	Ⓐ	Ⓑ	Ⓒ	Ⓓ
111.	Ⓐ	Ⓑ	Ⓒ	Ⓓ		145.	Ⓐ	Ⓑ	Ⓒ	Ⓓ		179.	Ⓐ	Ⓑ	Ⓒ	Ⓓ
112.	Ⓐ	Ⓑ	Ⓒ	Ⓓ		146.	Ⓐ	Ⓑ	Ⓒ	Ⓓ		180.	Ⓐ	Ⓑ	Ⓒ	Ⓓ
113.	Ⓐ	Ⓑ	Ⓒ	Ⓓ		147.	Ⓐ	Ⓑ	Ⓒ	Ⓓ		181.	Ⓐ	Ⓑ	Ⓒ	Ⓓ
114.	Ⓐ	Ⓑ	Ⓒ	Ⓓ		148.	Ⓐ	Ⓑ	Ⓒ	Ⓓ		182.	Ⓐ	Ⓑ	Ⓒ	Ⓓ
115.	Ⓐ	Ⓑ	Ⓒ	Ⓓ		149.	Ⓐ	Ⓑ	Ⓒ	Ⓓ		183.	Ⓐ	Ⓑ	Ⓒ	Ⓓ
116.	Ⓐ	Ⓑ	Ⓒ	Ⓓ		150.	Ⓐ	Ⓑ	Ⓒ	Ⓓ		184.	Ⓐ	Ⓑ	Ⓒ	Ⓓ
117.	Ⓐ	Ⓑ	Ⓒ	Ⓓ		151.	Ⓐ	Ⓑ	Ⓒ	Ⓓ		185.	Ⓐ	Ⓑ	Ⓒ	Ⓓ
118.	Ⓐ	Ⓑ	Ⓒ	Ⓓ		152.	Ⓐ	Ⓑ	Ⓒ	Ⓓ		186.	Ⓐ	Ⓑ	Ⓒ	Ⓓ
119.	Ⓐ	Ⓑ	Ⓒ	Ⓓ		153.	Ⓐ	Ⓑ	Ⓒ	Ⓓ		187.	Ⓐ	Ⓑ	Ⓒ	Ⓓ
120.	Ⓐ	Ⓑ	Ⓒ	Ⓓ		154.	Ⓐ	Ⓑ	Ⓒ	Ⓓ		188.	Ⓐ	Ⓑ	Ⓒ	Ⓓ
121.	Ⓐ	Ⓑ	Ⓒ	Ⓓ		155.	Ⓐ	Ⓑ	Ⓒ	Ⓓ		189.	Ⓐ	Ⓑ	Ⓒ	Ⓓ
122.	Ⓐ	Ⓑ	Ⓒ	Ⓓ		156.	Ⓐ	Ⓑ	Ⓒ	Ⓓ		190.	Ⓐ	Ⓑ	Ⓒ	Ⓓ
123.	Ⓐ	Ⓑ	Ⓒ	Ⓓ		157.	Ⓐ	Ⓑ	Ⓒ	Ⓓ		191.	Ⓐ	Ⓑ	Ⓒ	Ⓓ
124.	Ⓐ	Ⓑ	Ⓒ	Ⓓ		158.	Ⓐ	Ⓑ	Ⓒ	Ⓓ		192.	Ⓐ	Ⓑ	Ⓒ	Ⓓ
125.	Ⓐ	Ⓑ	Ⓒ	Ⓓ		159.	Ⓐ	Ⓑ	Ⓒ	Ⓓ		193.	Ⓐ	Ⓑ	Ⓒ	Ⓓ
126.	Ⓐ	Ⓑ	Ⓒ	Ⓓ		160.	Ⓐ	Ⓑ	Ⓒ	Ⓓ		194.	Ⓐ	Ⓑ	Ⓒ	Ⓓ
127.	Ⓐ	Ⓑ	Ⓒ	Ⓓ		161.	Ⓐ	Ⓑ	Ⓒ	Ⓓ		195.	Ⓐ	Ⓑ	Ⓒ	Ⓓ
128.	Ⓐ	Ⓑ	Ⓒ	Ⓓ		162.	Ⓐ	Ⓑ	Ⓒ	Ⓓ		196.	Ⓐ	Ⓑ	Ⓒ	Ⓓ
129.	Ⓐ	Ⓑ	Ⓒ	Ⓓ		163.	Ⓐ	Ⓑ	Ⓒ	Ⓓ		197.	Ⓐ	Ⓑ	Ⓒ	Ⓓ
130.	Ⓐ	Ⓑ	Ⓒ	Ⓓ		164.	Ⓐ	Ⓑ	Ⓒ	Ⓓ		198.	Ⓐ	Ⓑ	Ⓒ	Ⓓ
131.	Ⓐ	Ⓑ	Ⓒ	Ⓓ		165.	Ⓐ	Ⓑ	Ⓒ	Ⓓ		199.	Ⓐ	Ⓑ	Ⓒ	Ⓓ
132.	Ⓐ	Ⓑ	Ⓒ	Ⓓ		166.	Ⓐ	Ⓑ	Ⓒ	Ⓓ		200.	Ⓐ	Ⓑ	Ⓒ	Ⓓ
133.	Ⓐ	Ⓑ	Ⓒ	Ⓓ		167.	Ⓐ	Ⓑ	Ⓒ	Ⓓ						
134.	Ⓐ	Ⓑ	Ⓒ	Ⓓ		168.	Ⓐ	Ⓑ	Ⓒ	Ⓓ						

ANSWER SHEET

TEST TWO — ANSWER SHEET

Listening Comprehension

1. Ⓐ Ⓑ Ⓒ Ⓓ
2. Ⓐ Ⓑ Ⓒ Ⓓ
3. Ⓐ Ⓑ Ⓒ Ⓓ
4. Ⓐ Ⓑ Ⓒ Ⓓ
5. Ⓐ Ⓑ Ⓒ Ⓓ
6. Ⓐ Ⓑ Ⓒ Ⓓ
7. Ⓐ Ⓑ Ⓒ Ⓓ
8. Ⓐ Ⓑ Ⓒ Ⓓ
9. Ⓐ Ⓑ Ⓒ Ⓓ
10. Ⓐ Ⓑ Ⓒ Ⓓ
11. Ⓐ Ⓑ Ⓒ Ⓓ
12. Ⓐ Ⓑ Ⓒ Ⓓ
13. Ⓐ Ⓑ Ⓒ Ⓓ
14. Ⓐ Ⓑ Ⓒ Ⓓ
15. Ⓐ Ⓑ Ⓒ Ⓓ
16. Ⓐ Ⓑ Ⓒ Ⓓ
17. Ⓐ Ⓑ Ⓒ Ⓓ
18. Ⓐ Ⓑ Ⓒ Ⓓ
19. Ⓐ Ⓑ Ⓒ Ⓓ
20. Ⓐ Ⓑ Ⓒ Ⓓ
21. Ⓐ Ⓑ Ⓒ Ⓓ
22. Ⓐ Ⓑ Ⓒ Ⓓ
23. Ⓐ Ⓑ Ⓒ Ⓓ
24. Ⓐ Ⓑ Ⓒ Ⓓ
25. Ⓐ Ⓑ Ⓒ Ⓓ
26. Ⓐ Ⓑ Ⓒ Ⓓ
27. Ⓐ Ⓑ Ⓒ Ⓓ
28. Ⓐ Ⓑ Ⓒ Ⓓ
29. Ⓐ Ⓑ Ⓒ Ⓓ
30. Ⓐ Ⓑ Ⓒ Ⓓ
31. Ⓐ Ⓑ Ⓒ Ⓓ
32. Ⓐ Ⓑ Ⓒ Ⓓ
33. Ⓐ Ⓑ Ⓒ Ⓓ
34. Ⓐ Ⓑ Ⓒ Ⓓ
35. Ⓐ Ⓑ Ⓒ Ⓓ
36. Ⓐ Ⓑ Ⓒ Ⓓ
37. Ⓐ Ⓑ Ⓒ Ⓓ
38. Ⓐ Ⓑ Ⓒ Ⓓ
39. Ⓐ Ⓑ Ⓒ Ⓓ
40. Ⓐ Ⓑ Ⓒ Ⓓ
41. Ⓐ Ⓑ Ⓒ Ⓓ
42. Ⓐ Ⓑ Ⓒ Ⓓ
43. Ⓐ Ⓑ Ⓒ Ⓓ
44. Ⓐ Ⓑ Ⓒ Ⓓ
45. Ⓐ Ⓑ Ⓒ Ⓓ
46. Ⓐ Ⓑ Ⓒ Ⓓ
47. Ⓐ Ⓑ Ⓒ Ⓓ
48. Ⓐ Ⓑ Ⓒ Ⓓ
49. Ⓐ Ⓑ Ⓒ Ⓓ
50. Ⓐ Ⓑ Ⓒ Ⓓ
51. Ⓐ Ⓑ Ⓒ Ⓓ
52. Ⓐ Ⓑ Ⓒ Ⓓ
53. Ⓐ Ⓑ Ⓒ Ⓓ
54. Ⓐ Ⓑ Ⓒ Ⓓ
55. Ⓐ Ⓑ Ⓒ Ⓓ
56. Ⓐ Ⓑ Ⓒ Ⓓ
57. Ⓐ Ⓑ Ⓒ Ⓓ
58. Ⓐ Ⓑ Ⓒ Ⓓ
59. Ⓐ Ⓑ Ⓒ Ⓓ
60. Ⓐ Ⓑ Ⓒ Ⓓ
61. Ⓐ Ⓑ Ⓒ Ⓓ
62. Ⓐ Ⓑ Ⓒ Ⓓ
63. Ⓐ Ⓑ Ⓒ Ⓓ
64. Ⓐ Ⓑ Ⓒ Ⓓ
65. Ⓐ Ⓑ Ⓒ Ⓓ
66. Ⓐ Ⓑ Ⓒ Ⓓ
67. Ⓐ Ⓑ Ⓒ Ⓓ
68. Ⓐ Ⓑ Ⓒ Ⓓ
69. Ⓐ Ⓑ Ⓒ Ⓓ
70. Ⓐ Ⓑ Ⓒ Ⓓ
71. Ⓐ Ⓑ Ⓒ Ⓓ
72. Ⓐ Ⓑ Ⓒ Ⓓ
73. Ⓐ Ⓑ Ⓒ Ⓓ
74. Ⓐ Ⓑ Ⓒ Ⓓ
75. Ⓐ Ⓑ Ⓒ Ⓓ
76. Ⓐ Ⓑ Ⓒ Ⓓ
77. Ⓐ Ⓑ Ⓒ Ⓓ
78. Ⓐ Ⓑ Ⓒ Ⓓ
79. Ⓐ Ⓑ Ⓒ Ⓓ
80. Ⓐ Ⓑ Ⓒ Ⓓ
81. Ⓐ Ⓑ Ⓒ Ⓓ
82. Ⓐ Ⓑ Ⓒ Ⓓ
83. Ⓐ Ⓑ Ⓒ Ⓓ
84. Ⓐ Ⓑ Ⓒ Ⓓ
85. Ⓐ Ⓑ Ⓒ Ⓓ
86. Ⓐ Ⓑ Ⓒ Ⓓ
87. Ⓐ Ⓑ Ⓒ Ⓓ
88. Ⓐ Ⓑ Ⓒ Ⓓ
89. Ⓐ Ⓑ Ⓒ Ⓓ
90. Ⓐ Ⓑ Ⓒ Ⓓ
91. Ⓐ Ⓑ Ⓒ Ⓓ
92. Ⓐ Ⓑ Ⓒ Ⓓ
93. Ⓐ Ⓑ Ⓒ Ⓓ
94. Ⓐ Ⓑ Ⓒ Ⓓ
95. Ⓐ Ⓑ Ⓒ Ⓓ
96. Ⓐ Ⓑ Ⓒ Ⓓ
97. Ⓐ Ⓑ Ⓒ Ⓓ
98. Ⓐ Ⓑ Ⓒ Ⓓ
99. Ⓐ Ⓑ Ⓒ Ⓓ
100. Ⓐ Ⓑ Ⓒ Ⓓ

Reading Comprehension

101.	Ⓐ	Ⓑ	Ⓒ	Ⓓ	135.	Ⓐ	Ⓑ	Ⓒ	Ⓓ	169.	Ⓐ Ⓑ Ⓒ Ⓓ
102.	Ⓐ	Ⓑ	Ⓒ	Ⓓ	136.	Ⓐ	Ⓑ	Ⓒ	Ⓓ	170.	Ⓐ Ⓑ Ⓒ Ⓓ
103.	Ⓐ	Ⓑ	Ⓒ	Ⓓ	137.	Ⓐ	Ⓑ	Ⓒ	Ⓓ	171.	Ⓐ Ⓑ Ⓒ Ⓓ
104.	Ⓐ	Ⓑ	Ⓒ	Ⓓ	138.	Ⓐ	Ⓑ	Ⓒ	Ⓓ	172.	Ⓐ Ⓑ Ⓒ Ⓓ
105.	Ⓐ	Ⓑ	Ⓒ	Ⓓ	139.	Ⓐ	Ⓑ	Ⓒ	Ⓓ	173.	Ⓐ Ⓑ Ⓒ Ⓓ
106.	Ⓐ	Ⓑ	Ⓒ	Ⓓ	140.	Ⓐ	Ⓑ	Ⓒ	Ⓓ	174.	Ⓐ Ⓑ Ⓒ Ⓓ
107.	Ⓐ	Ⓑ	Ⓒ	Ⓓ	141.	Ⓐ	Ⓑ	Ⓒ	Ⓓ	175.	Ⓐ Ⓑ Ⓒ Ⓓ
108.	Ⓐ	Ⓑ	Ⓒ	Ⓓ	142.	Ⓐ	Ⓑ	Ⓒ	Ⓓ	176.	Ⓐ Ⓑ Ⓒ Ⓓ
109.	Ⓐ	Ⓑ	Ⓒ	Ⓓ	143.	Ⓐ	Ⓑ	Ⓒ	Ⓓ	177.	Ⓐ Ⓑ Ⓒ Ⓓ
110.	Ⓐ	Ⓑ	Ⓒ	Ⓓ	144.	Ⓐ	Ⓑ	Ⓒ	Ⓓ	178.	Ⓐ Ⓑ Ⓒ Ⓓ
111.	Ⓐ	Ⓑ	Ⓒ	Ⓓ	145.	Ⓐ	Ⓑ	Ⓒ	Ⓓ	179.	Ⓐ Ⓑ Ⓒ Ⓓ
112.	Ⓐ	Ⓑ	Ⓒ	Ⓓ	146.	Ⓐ	Ⓑ	Ⓒ	Ⓓ	180.	Ⓐ Ⓑ Ⓒ Ⓓ
113.	Ⓐ	Ⓑ	Ⓒ	Ⓓ	147.	Ⓐ	Ⓑ	Ⓒ	Ⓓ	181.	Ⓐ Ⓑ Ⓒ Ⓓ
114.	Ⓐ	Ⓑ	Ⓒ	Ⓓ	148.	Ⓐ	Ⓑ	Ⓒ	Ⓓ	182.	Ⓐ Ⓑ Ⓒ Ⓓ
115.	Ⓐ	Ⓑ	Ⓒ	Ⓓ	149.	Ⓐ	Ⓑ	Ⓒ	Ⓓ	183.	Ⓐ Ⓑ Ⓒ Ⓓ
116.	Ⓐ	Ⓑ	Ⓒ	Ⓓ	150.	Ⓐ	Ⓑ	Ⓒ	Ⓓ	184.	Ⓐ Ⓑ Ⓒ Ⓓ
117.	Ⓐ	Ⓑ	Ⓒ	Ⓓ	151.	Ⓐ	Ⓑ	Ⓒ	Ⓓ	185.	Ⓐ Ⓑ Ⓒ Ⓓ
118.	Ⓐ	Ⓑ	Ⓒ	Ⓓ	152.	Ⓐ	Ⓑ	Ⓒ	Ⓓ	186.	Ⓐ Ⓑ Ⓒ Ⓓ
119.	Ⓐ	Ⓑ	Ⓒ	Ⓓ	153.	Ⓐ	Ⓑ	Ⓒ	Ⓓ	187.	Ⓐ Ⓑ Ⓒ Ⓓ
120.	Ⓐ	Ⓑ	Ⓒ	Ⓓ	154.	Ⓐ	Ⓑ	Ⓒ	Ⓓ	188.	Ⓐ Ⓑ Ⓒ Ⓓ
121.	Ⓐ	Ⓑ	Ⓒ	Ⓓ	155.	Ⓐ	Ⓑ	Ⓒ	Ⓓ	189.	Ⓐ Ⓑ Ⓒ Ⓓ
122.	Ⓐ	Ⓑ	Ⓒ	Ⓓ	156.	Ⓐ	Ⓑ	Ⓒ	Ⓓ	190.	Ⓐ Ⓑ Ⓒ Ⓓ
123.	Ⓐ	Ⓑ	Ⓒ	Ⓓ	157.	Ⓐ	Ⓑ	Ⓒ	Ⓓ	191.	Ⓐ Ⓑ Ⓒ Ⓓ
124.	Ⓐ	Ⓑ	Ⓒ	Ⓓ	158.	Ⓐ	Ⓑ	Ⓒ	Ⓓ	192.	Ⓐ Ⓑ Ⓒ Ⓓ
125.	Ⓐ	Ⓑ	Ⓒ	Ⓓ	159.	Ⓐ	Ⓑ	Ⓒ	Ⓓ	193.	Ⓐ Ⓑ Ⓒ Ⓓ
126.	Ⓐ	Ⓑ	Ⓒ	Ⓓ	160.	Ⓐ	Ⓑ	Ⓒ	Ⓓ	194.	Ⓐ Ⓑ Ⓒ Ⓓ
127.	Ⓐ	Ⓑ	Ⓒ	Ⓓ	161.	Ⓐ	Ⓑ	Ⓒ	Ⓓ	195.	Ⓐ Ⓑ Ⓒ Ⓓ
128.	Ⓐ	Ⓑ	Ⓒ	Ⓓ	162.	Ⓐ	Ⓑ	Ⓒ	Ⓓ	196.	Ⓐ Ⓑ Ⓒ Ⓓ
129.	Ⓐ	Ⓑ	Ⓒ	Ⓓ	163.	Ⓐ	Ⓑ	Ⓒ	Ⓓ	197.	Ⓐ Ⓑ Ⓒ Ⓓ
130.	Ⓐ	Ⓑ	Ⓒ	Ⓓ	164.	Ⓐ	Ⓑ	Ⓒ	Ⓓ	198.	Ⓐ Ⓑ Ⓒ Ⓓ
131.	Ⓐ	Ⓑ	Ⓒ	Ⓓ	165.	Ⓐ	Ⓑ	Ⓒ	Ⓓ	199.	Ⓐ Ⓑ Ⓒ Ⓓ
132.	Ⓐ	Ⓑ	Ⓒ	Ⓓ	166.	Ⓐ	Ⓑ	Ⓒ	Ⓓ	200.	Ⓐ Ⓑ Ⓒ Ⓓ
133.	Ⓐ	Ⓑ	Ⓒ	Ⓓ	167.	Ⓐ	Ⓑ	Ⓒ	Ⓓ		
134.	Ⓐ	Ⓑ	Ⓒ	Ⓓ	168.	Ⓐ	Ⓑ	Ⓒ	Ⓓ		

TEST THREE — ANSWER SHEET

Listening Comprehension

1. Ⓐ Ⓑ Ⓒ Ⓓ
2. Ⓐ Ⓑ Ⓒ Ⓓ
3. Ⓐ Ⓑ Ⓒ Ⓓ
4. Ⓐ Ⓑ Ⓒ Ⓓ
5. Ⓐ Ⓑ Ⓒ Ⓓ
6. Ⓐ Ⓑ Ⓒ Ⓓ
7. Ⓐ Ⓑ Ⓒ Ⓓ
8. Ⓐ Ⓑ Ⓒ Ⓓ
9. Ⓐ Ⓑ Ⓒ Ⓓ
10. Ⓐ Ⓑ Ⓒ Ⓓ
11. Ⓐ Ⓑ Ⓒ Ⓓ
12. Ⓐ Ⓑ Ⓒ Ⓓ
13. Ⓐ Ⓑ Ⓒ Ⓓ
14. Ⓐ Ⓑ Ⓒ Ⓓ
15. Ⓐ Ⓑ Ⓒ Ⓓ
16. Ⓐ Ⓑ Ⓒ Ⓓ
17. Ⓐ Ⓑ Ⓒ Ⓓ
18. Ⓐ Ⓑ Ⓒ Ⓓ
19. Ⓐ Ⓑ Ⓒ Ⓓ
20. Ⓐ Ⓑ Ⓒ Ⓓ
21. Ⓐ Ⓑ Ⓒ Ⓓ
22. Ⓐ Ⓑ Ⓒ Ⓓ
23. Ⓐ Ⓑ Ⓒ Ⓓ
24. Ⓐ Ⓑ Ⓒ Ⓓ
25. Ⓐ Ⓑ Ⓒ Ⓓ
26. Ⓐ Ⓑ Ⓒ Ⓓ
27. Ⓐ Ⓑ Ⓒ Ⓓ
28. Ⓐ Ⓑ Ⓒ Ⓓ
29. Ⓐ Ⓑ Ⓒ Ⓓ
30. Ⓐ Ⓑ Ⓒ Ⓓ
31. Ⓐ Ⓑ Ⓒ Ⓓ
32. Ⓐ Ⓑ Ⓒ Ⓓ
33. Ⓐ Ⓑ Ⓒ Ⓓ
34. Ⓐ Ⓑ Ⓒ Ⓓ
35. Ⓐ Ⓑ Ⓒ Ⓓ
36. Ⓐ Ⓑ Ⓒ Ⓓ
37. Ⓐ Ⓑ Ⓒ Ⓓ
38. Ⓐ Ⓑ Ⓒ Ⓓ
39. Ⓐ Ⓑ Ⓒ Ⓓ
40. Ⓐ Ⓑ Ⓒ Ⓓ
41. Ⓐ Ⓑ Ⓒ Ⓓ
42. Ⓐ Ⓑ Ⓒ Ⓓ
43. Ⓐ Ⓑ Ⓒ Ⓓ
44. Ⓐ Ⓑ Ⓒ Ⓓ
45. Ⓐ Ⓑ Ⓒ Ⓓ
46. Ⓐ Ⓑ Ⓒ Ⓓ
47. Ⓐ Ⓑ Ⓒ Ⓓ
48. Ⓐ Ⓑ Ⓒ Ⓓ
49. Ⓐ Ⓑ Ⓒ Ⓓ
50. Ⓐ Ⓑ Ⓒ Ⓓ
51. Ⓐ Ⓑ Ⓒ Ⓓ
52. Ⓐ Ⓑ Ⓒ Ⓓ
53. Ⓐ Ⓑ Ⓒ Ⓓ
54. Ⓐ Ⓑ Ⓒ Ⓓ
55. Ⓐ Ⓑ Ⓒ Ⓓ
56. Ⓐ Ⓑ Ⓒ Ⓓ
57. Ⓐ Ⓑ Ⓒ Ⓓ
58. Ⓐ Ⓑ Ⓒ Ⓓ
59. Ⓐ Ⓑ Ⓒ Ⓓ
60. Ⓐ Ⓑ Ⓒ Ⓓ
61. Ⓐ Ⓑ Ⓒ Ⓓ
62. Ⓐ Ⓑ Ⓒ Ⓓ
63. Ⓐ Ⓑ Ⓒ Ⓓ
64. Ⓐ Ⓑ Ⓒ Ⓓ
65. Ⓐ Ⓑ Ⓒ Ⓓ
66. Ⓐ Ⓑ Ⓒ Ⓓ
67. Ⓐ Ⓑ Ⓒ Ⓓ
68. Ⓐ Ⓑ Ⓒ Ⓓ
69. Ⓐ Ⓑ Ⓒ Ⓓ
70. Ⓐ Ⓑ Ⓒ Ⓓ
71. Ⓐ Ⓑ Ⓒ Ⓓ
72. Ⓐ Ⓑ Ⓒ Ⓓ
73. Ⓐ Ⓑ Ⓒ Ⓓ
74. Ⓐ Ⓑ Ⓒ Ⓓ
75. Ⓐ Ⓑ Ⓒ Ⓓ
76. Ⓐ Ⓑ Ⓒ Ⓓ
77. Ⓐ Ⓑ Ⓒ Ⓓ
78. Ⓐ Ⓑ Ⓒ Ⓓ
79. Ⓐ Ⓑ Ⓒ Ⓓ
80. Ⓐ Ⓑ Ⓒ Ⓓ
81. Ⓐ Ⓑ Ⓒ Ⓓ
82. Ⓐ Ⓑ Ⓒ Ⓓ
83. Ⓐ Ⓑ Ⓒ Ⓓ
84. Ⓐ Ⓑ Ⓒ Ⓓ
85. Ⓐ Ⓑ Ⓒ Ⓓ
86. Ⓐ Ⓑ Ⓒ Ⓓ
87. Ⓐ Ⓑ Ⓒ Ⓓ
88. Ⓐ Ⓑ Ⓒ Ⓓ
89. Ⓐ Ⓑ Ⓒ Ⓓ
90. Ⓐ Ⓑ Ⓒ Ⓓ
91. Ⓐ Ⓑ Ⓒ Ⓓ
92. Ⓐ Ⓑ Ⓒ Ⓓ
93. Ⓐ Ⓑ Ⓒ Ⓓ
94. Ⓐ Ⓑ Ⓒ Ⓓ
95. Ⓐ Ⓑ Ⓒ Ⓓ
96. Ⓐ Ⓑ Ⓒ Ⓓ
97. Ⓐ Ⓑ Ⓒ Ⓓ
98. Ⓐ Ⓑ Ⓒ Ⓓ
99. Ⓐ Ⓑ Ⓒ Ⓓ
100. Ⓐ Ⓑ Ⓒ Ⓓ

Reading Comprehension

101. Ⓐ Ⓑ Ⓒ Ⓓ
102. Ⓐ Ⓑ Ⓒ Ⓓ
103. Ⓐ Ⓑ Ⓒ Ⓓ
104. Ⓐ Ⓑ Ⓒ Ⓓ
105. Ⓐ Ⓑ Ⓒ Ⓓ
106. Ⓐ Ⓑ Ⓒ Ⓓ
107. Ⓐ Ⓑ Ⓒ Ⓓ
108. Ⓐ Ⓑ Ⓒ Ⓓ
109. Ⓐ Ⓑ Ⓒ Ⓓ
110. Ⓐ Ⓑ Ⓒ Ⓓ
111. Ⓐ Ⓑ Ⓒ Ⓓ
112. Ⓐ Ⓑ Ⓒ Ⓓ
113. Ⓐ Ⓑ Ⓒ Ⓓ
114. Ⓐ Ⓑ Ⓒ Ⓓ
115. Ⓐ Ⓑ Ⓒ Ⓓ
116. Ⓐ Ⓑ Ⓒ Ⓓ
117. Ⓐ Ⓑ Ⓒ Ⓓ
118. Ⓐ Ⓑ Ⓒ Ⓓ
119. Ⓐ Ⓑ Ⓒ Ⓓ
120. Ⓐ Ⓑ Ⓒ Ⓓ
121. Ⓐ Ⓑ Ⓒ Ⓓ
122. Ⓐ Ⓑ Ⓒ Ⓓ
123. Ⓐ Ⓑ Ⓒ Ⓓ
124. Ⓐ Ⓑ Ⓒ Ⓓ
125. Ⓐ Ⓑ Ⓒ Ⓓ
126. Ⓐ Ⓑ Ⓒ Ⓓ
127. Ⓐ Ⓑ Ⓒ Ⓓ
128. Ⓐ Ⓑ Ⓒ Ⓓ
129. Ⓐ Ⓑ Ⓒ Ⓓ
130. Ⓐ Ⓑ Ⓒ Ⓓ
131. Ⓐ Ⓑ Ⓒ Ⓓ
132. Ⓐ Ⓑ Ⓒ Ⓓ
133. Ⓐ Ⓑ Ⓒ Ⓓ
134. Ⓐ Ⓑ Ⓒ Ⓓ
135. Ⓐ Ⓑ Ⓒ Ⓓ
136. Ⓐ Ⓑ Ⓒ Ⓓ
137. Ⓐ Ⓑ Ⓒ Ⓓ
138. Ⓐ Ⓑ Ⓒ Ⓓ
139. Ⓐ Ⓑ Ⓒ Ⓓ
140. Ⓐ Ⓑ Ⓒ Ⓓ
141. Ⓐ Ⓑ Ⓒ Ⓓ
142. Ⓐ Ⓑ Ⓒ Ⓓ
143. Ⓐ Ⓑ Ⓒ Ⓓ
144. Ⓐ Ⓑ Ⓒ Ⓓ
145. Ⓐ Ⓑ Ⓒ Ⓓ
146. Ⓐ Ⓑ Ⓒ Ⓓ
147. Ⓐ Ⓑ Ⓒ Ⓓ
148. Ⓐ Ⓑ Ⓒ Ⓓ
149. Ⓐ Ⓑ Ⓒ Ⓓ
150. Ⓐ Ⓑ Ⓒ Ⓓ
151. Ⓐ Ⓑ Ⓒ Ⓓ
152. Ⓐ Ⓑ Ⓒ Ⓓ
153. Ⓐ Ⓑ Ⓒ Ⓓ
154. Ⓐ Ⓑ Ⓒ Ⓓ
155. Ⓐ Ⓑ Ⓒ Ⓓ
156. Ⓐ Ⓑ Ⓒ Ⓓ
157. Ⓐ Ⓑ Ⓒ Ⓓ
158. Ⓐ Ⓑ Ⓒ Ⓓ
159. Ⓐ Ⓑ Ⓒ Ⓓ
160. Ⓐ Ⓑ Ⓒ Ⓓ
161. Ⓐ Ⓑ Ⓒ Ⓓ
162. Ⓐ Ⓑ Ⓒ Ⓓ
163. Ⓐ Ⓑ Ⓒ Ⓓ
164. Ⓐ Ⓑ Ⓒ Ⓓ
165. Ⓐ Ⓑ Ⓒ Ⓓ
166. Ⓐ Ⓑ Ⓒ Ⓓ
167. Ⓐ Ⓑ Ⓒ Ⓓ
168. Ⓐ Ⓑ Ⓒ Ⓓ
169. Ⓐ Ⓑ Ⓒ Ⓓ
170. Ⓐ Ⓑ Ⓒ Ⓓ
171. Ⓐ Ⓑ Ⓒ Ⓓ
172. Ⓐ Ⓑ Ⓒ Ⓓ
173. Ⓐ Ⓑ Ⓒ Ⓓ
174. Ⓐ Ⓑ Ⓒ Ⓓ
175. Ⓐ Ⓑ Ⓒ Ⓓ
176. Ⓐ Ⓑ Ⓒ Ⓓ
177. Ⓐ Ⓑ Ⓒ Ⓓ
178. Ⓐ Ⓑ Ⓒ Ⓓ
179. Ⓐ Ⓑ Ⓒ Ⓓ
180. Ⓐ Ⓑ Ⓒ Ⓓ
181. Ⓐ Ⓑ Ⓒ Ⓓ
182. Ⓐ Ⓑ Ⓒ Ⓓ
183. Ⓐ Ⓑ Ⓒ Ⓓ
184. Ⓐ Ⓑ Ⓒ Ⓓ
185. Ⓐ Ⓑ Ⓒ Ⓓ
186. Ⓐ Ⓑ Ⓒ Ⓓ
187. Ⓐ Ⓑ Ⓒ Ⓓ
188. Ⓐ Ⓑ Ⓒ Ⓓ
189. Ⓐ Ⓑ Ⓒ Ⓓ
190. Ⓐ Ⓑ Ⓒ Ⓓ
191. Ⓐ Ⓑ Ⓒ Ⓓ
192. Ⓐ Ⓑ Ⓒ Ⓓ
193. Ⓐ Ⓑ Ⓒ Ⓓ
194. Ⓐ Ⓑ Ⓒ Ⓓ
195. Ⓐ Ⓑ Ⓒ Ⓓ
196. Ⓐ Ⓑ Ⓒ Ⓓ
197. Ⓐ Ⓑ Ⓒ Ⓓ
198. Ⓐ Ⓑ Ⓒ Ⓓ
199. Ⓐ Ⓑ Ⓒ Ⓓ
200. Ⓐ Ⓑ Ⓒ Ⓓ

ANSWER SHEET